Return on or before the
last date stamped below.

Learning Resources
Centre

Kingston College
Kingston Hall Road
Kingston upon Thames
KT1 2AQ

Sultans of Spin

By the same author

STRIKES AND THE MEDIA (1986)
ELECTION '92 (1992)
SOUNDBITES AND SPIN DOCTORS (1995)
CAMPAIGN 1997 (1997)

Sultans of Spin

Nicholas Jones

VICTOR GOLLANCZ
LONDON

First published in Great Britain in 1999
by Victor Gollancz
An imprint of Orion Books Ltd
Orion House, 5 Upper St Martin's Lane, London WC2H 9EA

A CIP catalogue record for this book
is available from the British Library.

ISBN 0 575 06732 2

Typeset by Selwood Systems, Midsomer Norton
Printed and bound in Great Britain by
Butler & Tanner Ltd, Frome and London

Contents

Preface
'A completely unexceptional activity'?

After well over a decade of broadcasting and writing about the highly manipulative world of political journalism, I know only too well that my explorations are rarely welcomed. Intense competition within the news media has added to the stresses and strains bearing on the news gatherers – pressures which the political parties and their publicists have become increasingly adept at exploiting. Few relationships are harder to penetrate than the elusive, off-the-record encounters and liaisons which can prove so mutually beneficial to the aspiring journalist and the up-and-coming politician.

My own attempts to investigate the often hidden connections between the promoters and the reporters of politics are widely regarded by both sides as a nuisance; indeed, many of the participants consider my preoccupation with their activities to be nothing short of a time-wasting obsession. The argument advanced by the spin doctors is that ordinary people are not particularly bothered about the minutiae of the processes through which they receive political news; what the public are really concerned with are the reasons for government action and the precise details of what it is that a politician has said or done. Voters (they say) want an assessment of the likely impact of policy changes and an indication of the degree to which their lives might or might not be affected by them. Therefore, say the publicists and the spin doctors, the danger of becoming too engrossed in the mechanics of political communication is that insufficient attention is paid to the political considerations which shape important government decisions, resulting not only in a failure to take full account of the political implications of any decision but also in a tendency to overlook the impact and likely repercussions of the policy announcement itself.

I take the protestations of party political propagandists in my stride. Coming as I do from a family with strong journalistic connections, I have witnessed both at work and at home the consequences of the rapid changes which have taken place in the lives of reporters and politicians alike over recent years. Newspaper production techniques have been revolutionised; broadcasting services have been expanded out of all recognition; editorial standards have undergone a sea change – for example, to countenance a much greater degree of intrusion; and there has been a transformation too in the presentational techniques deployed by the political parties. The days have long gone when parliamentary candidates were left to their own devices, with carte blanche from the party leadership to give their own personal interpretation of party policy. Elections – by-elections as well as general elections – are now tightly controlled from the centre; and the spin doctors' airy dismissals of observations about their work, and their denigration of any investigation into the leverage they seek to exercise behind the scenes, belies their own fear and fascination in the face of the power wielded by newspapers, television and radio.

Many of the changes which have taken place within the media have worked to the advantage of those who seek to manipulate the news agenda. The growth of rolling news services on radio and television, and the emergence of seven-day newspapers, have whetted the appetite for a constant diet of fresh stories to feed the relentless demands of the twenty-four-hour news cycle. A fast-moving news agenda, and the speedier turnover of stories, suited the Labour Party well in the run-up to the 1997 general election. As the Conservatives discovered to their cost, every chance was taken by Tony Blair's burgeoning band of spin doctors to exploit the disarray of John Major's administration and the failings of his party. Once in government, Blair and his colleagues reached new heights in their ability to command favourable news coverage and to dominate the newspapers and the airwaves. Through the skilful orchestration of events and the sometimes all too eager support of willing accomplices in the news media, one day's damaging headlines can be obliterated the next. While the party propagandists miss no opportunity to condemn the newspapers for having all but abandoned the straight reporting of political debate, the politicians themselves take every advantage of the growth in personality-led news coverage and, although they frequently seek to deny it, they are prepared to go to almost any lengths to satisfy the constant demand for agenda-setting stories.

Alastair Campbell and Peter Mandelson have frequently berated me about my fixation with what they both assert are the trifling technicalities of their trade (though their contention that my books are simply a pointless manifestation of the news media's obsession with itself seems to fly in the face of their equally forceful assertion that more should be done to raise media standards). To this charge, I have to plead guilty. My interest in the potential impact of a journalist's work, and the often unseen influence of those who seek to guide and direct the way news is reported, has deep roots. My father, Clement Jones, was the editor of one of the biggest evening newspapers in the provinces, the Wolverhampton *Express and Star*, and my late mother, Marjorie Jones, was a local justice of the peace and the author of *Justice and Journalism*, a study of the influence of newspaper reporting upon the administration of justice by magistrates' courts. During my own career as a newspaper reporter and broadcaster, I too have tried, on occasion, to stand back and reflect upon the consequences of the way news is reported. I acknowledge immediately the limitations of my own attempts to understand and expose the powerful and sometimes covert forces which influence political reporting. Nevertheless I continue to believe that in today's media-driven environment there should be a wider understanding of the methods deployed by politicians and their parties in their never-ending quest for favourable publicity. Although the techniques at their disposal have had to adapt to meet the changing requirements of the media, the bottom line remains the same: their one and only consideration is to find ways of securing the most beneficial exposure possible, whether in terms of factual reporting or comment. The stakes are high; for while positive coverage can pay dividends, the latent dangers in courting publicity are immense. One false step can spell disaster and result in political ruin. In the months that I have spent thinking about the prospective contents of this book, I have found that I have needed to look no further than my own family to appreciate the calamitous consequences which can sometimes ensue when a politician seeking to manipulate the news media takes a step too far.

My introduction to the avid desire of politicians to acquire the latest know-how on the tricks of the journalist's trade dates back to the 1950s and my schooldays in Wolverhampton. My father, who had joined the *Express and Star* as a reporter in 1943, struck up an immediate friendship with the late Enoch Powell when the latter was chosen as the prospective Conservative candidate for Wolverhampton South West. Both men were on the fast track for promotion: my father became news editor and then editor of his paper, while Powell was appointed a junior housing minister within five years of being elected a Member of Parliament in the 1950 general election, and joined the cabinet in 1960 as minister of health. We lived only a short walk from Powell's constituency home, and he quite frequently dropped in to see my father. On these occasions they would talk animatedly for hours, and soon there was a strong bond of family friendship. My father particularly admired Powell's diligence as a constituency MP. During parliamentary recesses Powell would get out the electoral roll and walk the streets: he aimed to knock on the door of every constituent each year.

Powell was fascinated by the processes involved in news management and, although the detail of his conversations with my parents was way above my head, I sensed that he was taking considerable interest in the way that he was being reported. By the late 1950s, when I was training to be a journalist, I became more aware of what was in effect a two-way trade: my father was getting an unprecedented insight into the thinking of a government minister and Powell was picking up tips on how to use the media to promote his political career. By the time the Conservatives lost the 1964 general election I had left home and was working as a reporter on the Portsmouth *Evening News*, so I missed out on all the excitement in Wolverhampton the following year when Powell fought unsuccessfully for the Tory leadership. With his party in opposition, he was more determined than ever to get maximum exposure and my father told me how Powell asked him to help devise a strategy to maximise his coverage in the newspapers.

As is so often the case with MPs who find themselves at odds with the party leadership, Powell was dissatisfied with the way his speeches were being handled by the party machine and my father instructed him on how best to short-circuit Conservative Central Office. His advice was that a Saturday afternoon was perhaps the most opportune moment to deliver a hard-hitting political speech. Inevitably there had to be a degree of subterfuge and manipulation. The trick was to deliver an embargoed copy of the speech the previous Thursday or Friday to a hand-picked group of political editors and leader writers on the Sunday newspapers: they would be only too keen to preserve the embargo and would be most likely to give the speech a good show as they would be getting a fresh story for their Sunday editions which would not have been trailed in advance by the daily papers, and if all went as planned, Powell would end up getting sustained exposure throughout the weekend. The aim of my father's strategy was to stretch the coverage for one of Powell's speeches over three days: first it would get reported by the Saturday teatime and evening news bulletins on radio and television; then there would be the Sunday papers – and as the journalists had been given plenty of advance warning, there was no danger of their being caught out by a late-breaking speech, so if it was newsworthy it would be included; and then, if the pump priming had worked, and the speech was sufficiently controversial, the coverage in the Sunday papers would be picked up again by radio and television programmes that day and carried through to Monday's papers, which usually have little alternative but to feed off the comment and reaction sparked off by the Sundays. Needless to say, Powell was meticulous in following my father's advice, both on the overall strategy and on points of detail, such as the need to highlight on the front page of the press release the two or three most important sentences from the speech. My father used to remark that he had 'a good pupil' in the local MP who, he said, had a 'wonderful turn of phrase' when it came to spotting a potential headline.

During my visits home in the late 1960s, when I was local government reporter on the *Oxford Mail*, I began to detect signs of a slight uneasiness in the relationship between Powell and my father. Wolverhampton had absorbed a large influx of immigrants, mainly West Indians and Kenyan Asians, and there were increasing fears of racial tension in the town. Powell's first public reference to these local anxieties was in a speech in Walsall in March 1968 in which he described the concern of one of his constituents who had complained that his daughter was the only white child in her class at primary school. This speech was reported locally, by the *Express and Star* and the Birmingham *Evening Mail*. After journalists from his paper had failed to track down either the child or the class, my father challenged

Powell about the story and explained to him that as editor of the local paper he had been receiving similar anonymous complaints but that they had all proved to be false and could be traced back to members of the National Front. Powell would not accept it. He told my father that as a result of the Walsall speech he had received bags of supportive mail. Three weeks later, during a subsequent visit to my parents' home, he told them he was planning another speech at three o'clock that coming Saturday afternoon. He would not say what it was about but, according to my father, he promised him an advance copy and then made the following tantalising comment: 'Look, Clem, I'm not telling you what is in the speech. But you know how a rocket goes up into the air, explodes into lots of stars and then falls down to the ground. Well, this speech is going to go up like a rocket, and when it gets up to the top, the stars are going to stay up.'

For his speech in Birmingham that Saturday afternoon in April 1968 Powell had followed faithfully my father's instructions on distributing advance copies and, as he had predicted, the fallout from the rocket fired off by a former health minister succeeded in lighting up the political firmament as never before in his career as an MP. The shock waves from what came to be known as the infamous 'rivers of blood' speech reverberated for months. Powell had quoted a prophecy of doom from Virgil to reinforce his argument that Britain must be 'mad, literally mad, as a nation to be permitting the annual inflow of some fifty thousand dependants... As I look ahead, I am filled with foreboding. Like the Roman, I seem to see the river Tiber foaming with much blood.' Powell was immediately sacked from the shadow cabinet by Ted Heath for exacerbating racial tensions; London dockers marched in his support; and journalists from the *Express and Star* began a fruitless search of the Wolverhampton South West constituency for the old age pensioner who, Powell had said, had had excrement pushed through her letter box and who found that when she went outside her home she was followed by 'charming, wide-grinning piccaninnies' chanting the word 'racialist' at her.

Inevitably a price had to be paid for the political mayhem which Powell had unleashed, and part of it was his friendship with my father and mother. On the Saturday afternoon that he delivered the speech my parents had been looking after Enoch and Pam Powell's two daughters, Susan and Jennifer. The events that followed are imprinted on family memory: my mother was so shocked by the racist tone of the speech, and the cold and calculated way in which it had been planned and executed, that she told my father that she did not want to see Powell ever again. My father was equally appalled by the speech but said that he 'funked it' that afternoon. He could not bring himself to greet Powell on his return from Birmingham or tell him exactly what he thought of the speech, so my mother was left the task of taking the two girls to the front door when Powell called to collect them.

My father said the look on my mother's face and her demeanour as she answered the door must have forewarned him. 'She was strong willed and she said to Enoch, "I don't think we shall be seeing each other again for a very long time." Powell said to her, "Well, I suppose it's the end of a good friendship now, isn't it?" And she said, "Yes, it is." She handed over the two girls and that was it.'

The events of the next week, as editor of the local paper, were almost too horrible to recall. Even at the time I knew that my parents went through a searing experience, but my father always retained a degree of loyalty to his old friend and it was only in the weeks after Powell's death in February 1998 that I finally heard his full account of the events that occurred that unhappy Saturday afternoon and the trauma of the days that followed.

'Ted Heath had made a martyr out of Enoch, but as far as the *Express and Star*'s circulation area was concerned, virtually the whole area was determined to make a saint out of him. From the Tuesday through to the end of the week, I had ten, fifteen or twenty bags full of readers' letters every day. I suppose ninety to ninety-five per cent were pro-Enoch. In each edition we gave over a couple of pages to them but we had to scrape, every day, to try to find a few balancing letters. Some were pretty abusive about me, containing excrement and that sort of thing, half a dozen sheets of used toilet paper. I had people ringing me at home, all sorts of hours, saying, "Oh, is that the bloody nigger lover?" Just like that. I had a couple of windows broken at home. I suffered, I think, as much as anybody.'

In fact, my father's anguish was to continue for months. Letters of support for the 'rivers of blood' speech had also been arriving by the sackful at the Powells' family home in Belgravia. When interviewed in 1995 for *Odd Man Out*, a BBC profile of her father, Susan Powell said she had noted in her diary how in the week after the speech a Royal Mail van had turned up outside their home each morning packed with sacks of mail. Emboldened by the support he received, Powell started libel proceedings against the *Sunday Times*, which had questioned the accuracy of his account of the elderly widow having excrement pushed through her letter box. In a leading article, the paper accused Powell of spouting 'the fantasies of racial purity'. The suggestion that he had indulged in Goebbels-like propaganda was repeated on posters at anti-Powell demonstrations in London. A report of one protest march, which was sent out on the wire service of the Press Association news agency, contained a reference to a demonstrator carrying a placard accusing Powell of Nazi-like tactics. When the Press Association story was published by the *Express and Star*, Powell extended his libel proceedings to include my father's paper. It was, in effect, a 'gagging writ', intended to prevent newspapers from repeating the allegation about Nazi-style propaganda.

After months of legal correspondence, Powell was forced to settle his action in April 1970. He received an apology in court from the *Sunday Times* but no damages or costs, and obtained no more than a retraction from the *Express and Star*, which maintained throughout that it had printed the Press Association report in good faith. This limited outcome, said my father, was attributable to Powell's refusal to reveal the identity of either the pensioner who was said to have suffered at the hands of the 'charming, wide-grinning piccaninnies' or the constituent who had written the letter describing her plight, arguing that all correspondence between MPs and their constituents enjoyed parliamentary privilege and therefore could not be disclosed without permission.

My father's recollections have only served to reinforce my belief that the mechanics of political communication can provide valuable insights into politicians' motivation and behaviour. Their significance is all the more pertinent in the light of the tributes and obituaries which have followed Powell's death. Some political commentators and biographers have asserted that Powell had no prior inkling of the outcry and racial tension that would be provoked by his 'rivers of blood' speech. If my parents are to be believed, the truth is that Powell knew his speech would create a furore and that it was my father who had instructed him on how best to exploit the opportunity. He had advised Powell to highlight key sentences of his speeches on the press releases that accompanied the advance copies; and, as he recalled, the reference to 'the river Tiber foaming with much blood' was one of the sentences thus picked out for special emphasis. The dark forces which Powell's speech had marshalled were only too easy to awaken; careful preparation and the spark of publicity were all it took to set off a con-flagration. Getting caught in the slipstream of a media maelstrom can be a chastening experience for anyone; for a journalist it is a salutary reminder of the impact of our work.

During the years that followed, as I discussed the repercussions of Powell's speech with my parents, I detected a growing divergence between the approaches they were each taking to the power exercised by the media. My father is a newspaperman through and through. He will defend to the hilt a journalist's right to decide what is news. My mother was far more questioning. In her work as a magistrate she had found that the penalty of publicity in the local newspaper was often far greater, and potentially far more damaging, than any punishment which the courts could impose. She would ask us how we three jour-nalists – that is, my father, myself and my brother (George Jones, now political editor of the *Daily Telegraph*) – could defend a situation in which two women who were fined on the same day by the magistrates for shoplifting could end up being treated so differently by their local paper. Both women were in a mid-life crisis, both had stolen a piffling amount of groceries from one of the supermarkets; but because one was the wife of a local vicar or headmaster it was her name which was splashed across the front page of the evening newspaper while the other woman, who had no newsworthy connections, did not merit even the smallest paragraph. Because of the publicity and the shame, one woman was probably on the brink of suicide, while the other, with her anonymity preserved, probably had every chance of putting the court appearance behind her. My mother knew the score: it might have been a sharp-eyed journalist, perusing the day's court list, who had spotted a name that rang a bell locally; or perhaps it was a police officer or court official who was friendly with the court reporters who had tipped them off as to the right court to go to. As journalists we never succeeded in convincing my mother that press freedom had to remain paramount, even though, as we acknowledged, it can some-times exact a terrible price in personal terms.

My mother's book *Justice and Journalism*, published in 1974, remains a testament to her conviction that the task of communicating the decisions of magistrates' courts to the public should rest primarily with those who administer justice, because publicity for summary charges was 'now incurred by a random selection of accused persons, for reasons which have to do with news value, not with justice'. Her strictures about the unfairness of court reporting were a constant reminder to me that every now and again journalists should pause for a moment, step back and think through their place in society and their relationship with the public; but I little thought that a decade later her questioning attitude would prove an inspiration for my first book, *Strikes and the Media*.

As a labour affairs correspondent for BBC Radio during the big industrial disputes of the late 1970s and early 1980s I had become increasingly aware that the employers and the government were far more successful than the trade unions in putting their case across to the workforce, through the effective use of newspapers, radio and television. I came to the conclusion that expertise in manipulating the news media had become a vital weapon in the armoury of management in any attempt to defeat industrial action. The specific event which prompted the book was the 1984–5 miners' strike. As the dispute dragged on for month after month, and as the nation witnessed a violent trial of strength between Arthur Scargill and Margaret Thatcher, most of the popular newspapers were in no doubt as to where they stood. They had taken the side of those who wanted to break the strike. However hard we as radio and television journalists tried to remain impartial, we found we were being dragged inexorably towards giving at least tacit support to the push for a return to work.

Each weekend there would be a flurry of stories emanating from the National Coal Board and the government aimed at influencing those miners who it was thought might be on the point of abandoning the strike or accepting redundancy payments. In the early hours of each Monday morning television crews, photographers and reporters would gather outside the gates of the biggest pits to count and record the number of what were dubbed the 'new faces' reporting for work. Every Monday, the news bulletins were dominated by the latest figures for those who were returning. By late February 1985 half the men were working normally: 93,000 according to the NCB's calculations, representing 50.2 per cent of employees who belonged to the National Union of Mineworkers. Margaret Thatcher was able to declare that the strike was over. The day after this announcement, the NUM's national executive agreed to call another delegate conference which, despite Scargill's opposition, approved a South Wales resolution recommending a return to work without an agreement.

I felt I had experienced at first hand the power of the news media and had seen the ease with which it could be exploited. Although the national newspapers were, by and large, on the government's side from the very start of the dispute, the way in which the coverage was orchestrated against Scargill in the final months of the strike had to be seen, in retrospect, as a textbook example of media manipulation. Once the management had contrived to turn the Monday morning return to work into a weekly trial of strength with the NUM, and once the forces of law and order were sure they could guarantee the safety of the men wishing to abandon the strike, the presence of the television cameras to publicise what was happening was all it took to ensure that the nation would see the 'new faces' as the heroes. The government had realised that it would take time to defeat the NUM, but the calculation must have been that eventually Margaret Thatcher's tactic of standing firm in the face of Scargill's demands would prevail.

My conclusion in *Strikes and the Media*, that a coordinated media strategy had played a part in the NUM's defeat, was roundly rejected by Sir Ian MacGregor, the Coal Board chairman at the time of the strike. In his autobiography, *The Enemies Within*, he said that the country was indebted to a BBC correspondent for 'making us privy to his beliefs and theories', but 'Jones is clearly a believer in the conspiracy theory of history and sees sinister motives behind the most innocuous of events'.

And yet some events were far from innocuous, as I was subsequently to confirm. On returning to political journalism in 1988, and rejoining the BBC's political staff at Westminster, I gained access for the first time to the lobby briefings given by the Prime Minister's press secretary, Sir Bernard Ingham. In the final months of the miners' strike industrial journalists like myself, who had spent countless hours waiting outside in the street for the conclusion of management and union meetings, had known that Ingham was giving the political correspondents a faster and far fuller account of the latest developments than we were getting. For instance, in January 1985 lobby correspondents were told about the failure of the National Coal Board's final initiative to get a negotiated settlement some hours before the management had intended to give their response to the NUM or make a public statement. The Board's spokesman, Michael Eaton, asked me personally to discover the precise time of Ingham's lobby briefing because he blamed Mrs Thatcher for blocking progress in the talks. In her autobiography, *The Downing Street Years*, Mrs Thatcher said she was 'enormously relieved' when the negotiations collapsed (because she wanted visibly to deny Scargill a victory). When writing *Strikes and the Media* I enquired about Ingham's role but he told me he had no intention of breaking the silence which he maintained about the nature of his work. Once I was back at Westminster and able to see for myself how Ingham operated, and to observe at first hand the transformation which had taken place in political reporting in the twenty years that had elapsed since I had joined *The Times* as a parliamentary correspondent in 1968, I found it hard not to take an interest in the black arts of political communication.

My fascination with Ingham's techniques, reinforced by my realisation that rapid expansion in radio and television had in many ways strengthened the position of the Prime Minister's press secretary, was the stimulus for my first attempt to examine the workings of the Downing Street media machine: *The Most Important Man*, a forty-minute profile of Margaret Thatcher's press secretary broadcast by BBC Radio Four in April 1989 as one of the programmes marking the Prime Minister's first decade in power. I had taken the title from one of the many interventions in the House of Commons by the Labour MP Tam Dalyell, who described Ingham as 'the most important man in the government and the real Deputy Prime Minister'. Needless to say, at the time I recorded the programme Ingham was not prepared to be interviewed by me, nor would he answer any of my questions about the various controversies in which he had become embroiled — a refusal which has been consistently repeated whenever I have made similar approaches to his successors. In the final section of the programme I looked at the case for opening up the lobby system, for holding lobby briefings on an attributable basis so that they could be recorded and televised. I concluded by saying that there should be greater opportunity – in public – for political correspondents to 'test the validity and accuracy of government statements'. In the decade that has elapsed since that programme went out, there has been some pressure for the Downing Street briefings to be televised, as happens with presidential briefings at the White House in Washington, but most correspondents, working for television and radio as well as for the newspapers, are reluctant to change the system. They contend that although opening up lobby briefings would have some attractions these would be largely superficial: a televised system would tend to produce only bland statements from the government of the day, whereas the chance to probe the thinking of the Prime Minister's press secretary in the privacy of a lobby briefing will always be more productive and informative.

Having served for over four years as Tony Blair's press secretary, nearly two of them as the Prime Minister's official spokesman, Alastair Campbell remains resolutely opposed to televised briefings. He argues that for the government to go so far as allowing the Prime Minister's press secretary to appear on camera, answering journalists' questions each morning about the business of the day, would be regarded by the House of Commons as a further attack on parliamentary privilege and the accountability of ministers to parliament. Campbell and his colleagues in Downing Street have already been reprimanded by the Speaker, Betty Boothroyd, for the way policy announcements are trailed in the news media and for allowing details of government statements to be given to journalists before being announced to MPs. Nevertheless Campbell has made no secret of his determination to force the Whitehall publicity machine to 'raise its game' and do more to set the agenda for the policy initiatives which are being announced by the government.

The effectiveness of the new government's media strategy could not be ignored. As the new administration settled into office, Tony Blair's popularity ratings rose rather than fell. Campbell's determination to control and coordinate the presentation of policy announcements paid handsome dividends, and the weeks when the government failed to set the news agenda were few and far between. But notwithstanding his success there are issues which should be addressed, and which I explore in this book, such as the repercussions of the changes which have taken place and the ease with which it has been possible for the government to manipulate the lobby system.

Campbell's efforts to galvanise civil service information officers, to get them to be proactive and to go on the offensive when putting the case of their departments, have prompted complaints from both Conservative and Liberal Democrat MPs. They believe the government information and communication service has been politicised, an accusation which was investigated in June 1998 by the House of Commons Select Committee on Public Administration.

In giving his evidence to the select committee, Campbell had no hesitation in throwing down the gauntlet to anyone who might seek to examine his record as press secretary. He was categorical in asserting that he was playing it by the book: that he and the government had no favourites when it came to dealing with the newspapers, television and radio; that he and his staff in Downing Street had not crossed the line into promoting the affairs of the Labour Party; that the work of civil service information officers had not been politicised; and that the many additional ministerial special advisers appointed by the Labour Party were not spending all day briefing journalists. He had, he said, 'never seen a substantive convincing piece of evidence about politicisation' of the Information and Communication Service. That assurance was accepted by the committee in its majority report, although it did take note of the undertaking given by the Cabinet Secretary, Sir Richard Wilson, to ensure the 'policing of the difficult boundary between effective presentation and party political advocacy'.

Campbell's checklist for his own impartiality was not, however, accepted by Conservative and Liberal Democrat MPs on the select committee. They published their own minority report claiming that the changes approved by Tony Blair had given an 'undue advantage' to the government; that through the introduction of 'pre-briefings' for selected journalists, information was being given to the media before it was presented to parliament; and that the government should consider the introduction of a new code of conduct to govern contact between special advisers and journalists.

For once, the importance of political communication, and the argument over whether there should be tighter restraints on the government of the day, is out in the open and being debated in parliament; and an administration which has invested so much in presentation cannot complain if its techniques are scrutinised and its leading players held to account. There is no doubt that Alastair Campbell played a leading role in Labour's 1997 general election victory. His contribution to the campaign is singled out for praise by Philip Gould, one of Labour's leading modernisers, who advises Blair on political tactics and how to interpret the findings of focus groups and opinion polls. In his book, *The Unfinished Revolution*, published in October 1998, Gould says Campbell is 'more than just a media spokesperson... he is an outstanding strategist'. Nevertheless, he sticks firmly to the New Labour creed in ridiculing journalists like myself who write about 'spin doctors' and the 'black arts' of campaigning. Gould says this is just media nonsense; if spin doctors exist at all, they are the media spokespeople for the political parties, 'a long standing and completely unexceptional activity'. In *Sultans of Spin* I shall examine whether the black arts of Labour's spin doctors are as unexceptional as Gould suggests.

1 The morning after

Labour's high command were unprepared for and overwhelmed by the sheer scale of Tony Blair's historic victory in May 1997. Blair's campaign strategists had been so single-minded for so long in their pursuit of power that they seemed to have difficulty absorbing the full implications of their stunning achievement.

During the interminable wait for John Major to go to the country, Labour's vast campaign team had been on perpetual alert. Blair's tactic of keeping his party on a constant election footing had proved a phenomenal success. But so much effort had gone into promoting the party, and in trying to pursue a news agenda which favoured Labour's policy programme while disadvantaging the Conservatives, that even after Blair had gained an unprecedented mandate – his majority of 179 far exceeding Clement Attlee's of 146 after Labour's 1945 triumph – his propagandists could not ease up. They seemed unwilling or unable to forgo the buzz which they had derived from their ability to influence the news media and to manipulate political journalists, who had often been only too eager to comply with expectations in return for exclusive access and information. Endless years in opposition had so conditioned Labour thinking that the party leadership still felt a compulsion to try to turn each day's headlines to their advantage. Instead of asking ministers in his newly formed cabinet to step back from the media spotlight, at least to begin with, so as to think through in greater detail the implementation of their manifesto commitments, Blair immediately set them a new target: they had to think ahead to winning the next general election and to the goal of what for Labour would be another historic achievement, the completion of a second successive full parliamentary term in government.

Presentation was to remain paramount. Even if detailed policy formulation had not been completed and all that could be promised was a strategic review, an announcement could not be delayed: there had to be action by the government, so great was the desire to maintain the momentum which Labour had achieved in opposition. Alastair Campbell, the Prime Minister's trusted companion and confidant, who had accompanied Blair into Downing Street and had been appointed his press secretary, immediately set in train changes which would transform the Whitehall publicity machine. Many of the Labour Party press officers who had worked for members of the shadow cabinet in opposition were smartly found jobs inside government departments where they were appointed special advisers to ministers. When it came to generating publicity, the New Labour publicists-turned-advisers had their feet firmly on the accelerator and were expected to continue working at the same fever pitch that they had maintained in the hectic months up to polling day.

Amid all the frenetic activity which followed the change of government, Blair's closest counsellors seemed to be in danger of misunderstanding what people had voted for. So great had been the general contempt for John Major's administration that the new Prime Minister had in effect been given a blank sheet of paper and told to get on with the job. There was no public appetite for renewed political point-scoring. The electorate appeared to have faith in their own judgement, and moreover to have had quite enough of electioneering and political opportunism. Blair would be given ample time and opportunity to prove himself. As the opinion polls were to demonstrate month after month, voters remained remarkably settled in their thinking. Irrespective of whatever contortions might be taking place within his own party, or the supposedly calamitous events reported by the news media, all the surveys indicated that the Prime Minister continued to enjoy a virtually uninterrupted political honeymoon. Yet despite these signs of continued voter satisfaction, Blair's strategists remained so consumed by an over-riding obsession to control and dictate the way the new government's affairs were being presented and reported that they gave the impression they feared their election victory might suddenly be snatched away if the headlines went against them for longer than a week.

As the months went by, and events crowded in on the new government, their expertise in massaging the news agenda was to prove no substitute for effective decision-making and substantive action. The new administration had no real need to be fearful of their lack of experience. Senior civil servants had expected and prepared for a change of power. Whatever private doubts cabinet ministers might have had about their own individual capabilities, the virtual annihilation of the Conservatives had demonstrated the power of the incoming administration's collective strength and determination. Nevertheless, the focus seemed to remain firmly on presentation rather than action; and here Labour's self-evident competence while in opposition, and their success in communicating policy announcements to the public, did tend to encourage a sense of superiority. Blair's inner circle remained supremely confident in the infallibility of their news judgement and, when it came to constructing and promulgating a news-driven agenda, it was clear that it would be the civil service which would have to be taking lessons from the Labour Party.

Blair continued to be feted by the news media for far longer than party members could have dared to hope, and there was no doubt that the success of New Labour in catching and holding the imagination and attention of journalists on its ideals and objectives continued after it took up the reins of government, in stark contrast to the Conservatives' failure to construct a coherent message, let alone communicate it. But Labour miscalculated in thinking that the flair they had shown when fighting the election, in ruthlessly pressing forward their news-driven agenda, was necessarily the one and only tactic which they could or should pursue once in power.

Ministers do not need to be constantly tempting the appetite of the news media. If their policies are proving successful and they have established a reputation for effective government, political journalists will soon seek them out. Indeed, there are positive dangers for the government of the day if it tries to perpetuate the kind of hectic feeding frenzy which is not only to be expected but is essential during an election campaign. For a well-run government, a well-planned, well-thought-out ministerial announcement, delivered competently and with style, should look after itself when it comes to setting the agenda and gaining publicity. The far harder task is to devise strategies to minimise damaging speculation or to cope with unexpected events, premature disclosures or embarrassing revelations. The most important lesson to be learned by media managers is to know when, and how, to wind down journalistic expectations. Successful exploitation of the media can take many forms. Blair's spin doctors had built their reputations on being proactive, on courting the attention of journalists, an approach which in some ways was to prove not just unproductive but a distinct liability when press sentiment turned against them. Many senior figures within the government were equally to blame for ill-advised attempts to stimulate high-profile news coverage about themselves rather than about their work as ministers; they too, having been driven for so long by a never-ending courtship of the media, failed – like their advisers – to see the dangers ahead and remained dangerously in awe of the potential power of personal publicity.

In the run-up to the general election, when Blair was seeking to establish and promote the concept of New Labour, he had been able to take full advantage of the considerable media expertise which existed within his party. Many Labour MPs and many of their advisers had a close affinity with journalism or some other facet of the publishing or entertainment industries. Even those who had not been employed by newspapers or broadcasting organisations – as a significant number of them had – were more than likely at some stage in their careers to have tried their hand at journalism or to have made regular radio and television appearances. Acquiring an understanding of the mechanics of the media was regarded as an essential part of the political learning curve. In today's media-driven age, every aspiring politician has to be able to write a press release or provide a comment column for the local newspaper. During their eighteen years out of government, high-flyers within the Parliamentary Labour Party could not afford to ignore the need for self-promotion because it was those with the highest media profiles and the greatest degree of public recognition who had always tended to do best when it came to the annual elections for a place in the shadow cabinet or a seat on the party's ruling national executive committee.

Every summer and autumn, as these annual beauty contests gathered pace, Labour's frontbench team had little alternative but to put themselves about and seek out the company of political journalists in the hope of being interviewed on radio and television or gaining favourable mentions in the newspapers. Each shadow cabinet member tended to build up a coterie of MPs and parliamentary assistants whose job it was to find ways to promote their candidate at the expense of his or her rivals. These groups were usually self-contained and indeed somewhat self-serving. If one of the key contests was in the offing, and if through misfortune or an inopportune speech a prominent frontbencher had got into trouble, colleagues rarely rallied to his or her defence, as they needed to attract all the votes they could muster for themselves. Those who participated in the political manoeuvrings which surrounded the shadow cabinet and NEC elections were usually only too happy to cooperate with enterprising journalists. In return for publicising a speech or a new political pamphlet by one of the candidates, a reporter might be given the lowdown on the latest internal policy dispute or offered a juicy morsel designed to discredit another contender.

After so long in opposition, these habits had become deeply ingrained, and for many in the party, at all levels, treading the byways of media manipulation had become a way of life. In some MPs' offices even junior assistants took delight in tipping off journalists or leaking information. Seeing their handiwork in print — whether as a front-page news story or a mere diary paragraph — was an experience to savour. However small or insignificant their achievements, the ability to engage or even to excite journalists with the information which they could offer provided even these lowly figures with an opportunity to taste real political influence, and the satisfaction was all the greater if their efforts boosted the boss or did down an opponent. And the obsessive fascination with the techniques for influencing the media went right to the very top of New Labour. Tony Blair's two most influential advisers were steeped in the traditions of party infighting and the devious exploitation of political journalism. Alastair Campbell, a committed Labour supporter, was formerly political editor of the *Daily Mirror* and a gifted tabloid journalist; and Peter Mandelson, despite having worked only briefly as a television producer on the ground-breaking political programme *Weekend World*, had built up unrivalled connections in the broadcasting and the entertainment industries.

Most of the major players in Blair's frontbench team were acutely alive to the opportunities to promote the party — and themselves — through the media. As they dug in for the long haul to the general election, they would jump at any opportunity to write articles for national newspapers, and had nothing to fear from high-profile interviews. If offered the chance to take part in a fly-on-the-wall television documentary they would be only too happy to oblige, their sole concern being to ensure that the programme was broadcast at the most beneficial moment for their own personal advancement. While a high proportion of Conservative MPs had, over the years, developed equally strong connections with the world of newspapers, television and radio, far fewer had been practising journalists or broadcasters. Many had closer ties with marketing, advertising and corporate publicity, and as a result the Conservative Party's relationship with media folk was nothing like as close or as fruitful as the links forged by the Labour Party when Neil Kinnock was party leader and expanded and consolidated under Blair. Nevertheless, when it came to the task of achieving successful media management while in government, rather than in opposition, the Conservatives' knowledge and experience of the tactics deployed by big business had at times proved a distinct advantage. Most profitable companies are keen to keep their internal affairs out of the public eye. While they are only too ready to seek favourable publicity for their products and services, they realise that, by and large, their corporate interests are usually best served by maintaining the lowest possible profile; and that requires releasing as little information to the public as possible. Ministers frequently face the same dilemmas as big companies, but do not always understand the benefits of a corporate culture which frowns on the hectic, proactive news management which was second nature to Alastair Campbell and Peter Mandelson.

If news reports keep focusing on an awkward political issue, governments tend to counter the problem by providing facts and figures to justify the stance or decision under scrutiny. But relying on a strategy of rebuttal raises the danger that, as fresh material is released, journalists might discover further damaging revelations hidden away in the small print of the documentation. There are moments in the political cycle when it can become counterproductive to strive too hard to dominate the agenda and a more astute course of action would be to find ways to minimise media interest. Advisers on corporate communications are well aware of the balance which has to be struck and the need to have defensive strategies in place. Promotional work has to be carefully targeted, because a high public profile at the wrong moment, with all the attendant publicity, can become a liability if there is an unexpected commercial mishap and trading conditions take a sudden turn for the worse. Conservative administrations have on occasion proved quite adept at following commercial practice and, by damping down interest at times of actual or potential vulnerability, seeking to avoid damaging political repercussions. A similar ethos has thrived within the civil service: if left to their own devices, government departments would rarely seek publicity for its own sake. Whitehall mandarins are far happier if they can keep out of the public eye, and by nature are far more cautious than ministers when asked to advise on how far the government should go in cooperating with the news media. However, in the after-glow of New Labour's election victory there was no inkling that the party's fabled prowess in news management might one day go awry, and the credo remained unchallenged: the best form of defence is rebuttal, followed by attack.

Tony Blair's carefully staged arrival in Downing Street, complete with a well-deserved and much-admired family photo-call on the steps of No. 10, heralded the start of an action-packed performance of the full New Labour repertoire. In what transpired to be a series of well-rehearsed routines, ministers spent day after day unveiling a dazzling display of policy declarations and initiatives. The new government was intent, said the spin doctors, on 'hitting the ground running' and it fulfilled that prediction at breathtaking speed with a cascade of announcements and news conferences. All the events seemed to have been planned in the belief that Labour's hold on power was secured by fingertips, that this flurry of activity was a necessary provision in case party managers were confronted with the nightmare scenario of having to face another general election within months.

Day after day in May 1997 the newspaper front pages reflected the frantic pace which the government had set itself. The sheer momentum which had been generated by the New Labour news machine was awesome to behold, as was its ability to command the news media's attention. The favourable, upbeat tone which was struck by this publicity could not be faulted; but there was also a strong current of aggression, as though the Tories deserved to have their noses rubbed in the mess they had left behind. The underlying message which journalists picked up was that Blair and his ministers were only too anxious to have their record contrasted on a day-to-day basis with that of the Conservatives. The government had effectively thrown down the gauntlet, challenging journalists to apply to New Labour the very same tests of competence and morality which had done so much to undermine John Major's administration. No thought appeared to have been given to the likelihood that such tactics might rebound to Blair's disadvantage; so, once the heady euphoria had subsided and the party's relationship with the news media had begun to cool off, there were anguished howls of protest and lurid accusations to the effect that political journalists were trying to pin on New Labour the same deadly sins which had brought down the Tories.

The event which best illustrated New Labour's cavalier disregard of the inherent dangers in inviting the media to bite back was organised by Peter Mandelson, the newly installed minister without portfolio. Although charged in this position with responsibility for coordinating government presentation, he was anxious to put his days as a spin doctor behind him and to shake off what he considered was his unwarranted reputation for deviousness and unpleasant behind-the-scenes manipulation. He had been Labour's head of election planning for the 1997 campaign; now, having at last achieved his ambition of holding government office, he was determined to show his capability as a minister.

Mandelson had been forced to wait until the summer recess for his first real opportunity to make his mark. August is usually the quietest period in the political calendar, but the middle of the month marked the completion of Tony Blair's first hundred days in office and, as the Prime Minister was on holiday, the news conference to celebrate the occasion was chaired jointly by Mandelson and the Deputy Prime Minister, John Prescott. Reporters were supplied with a checklist of the government's achievements. No journalist could fail to be impressed by the list of momentous decisions which had been announced so expeditiously. Within a week of taking office the Chancellor of the Exchequer, Gordon Brown, had passed to the Bank of England responsibility for controlling interest rates. After the first cabinet meeting had agreed the government's legislative programme, a committee of ministers set to work implementing Labour's New Deal, which aimed to take 250,000 unemployed youngsters off the dole. And, as Blair had promised throughout the election campaign, the Queen's Speech opening the new parliament made education the government's number one priority. Class sizes would be cut and the assisted places scheme phased out. In honouring another election pledge, bills were introduced to hold referendums in Scotland and Wales on the establishment of a Scottish parliament and a Welsh assembly. In his first budget, Gordon Brown imposed the windfall levy on the privatised utilities and announced a 5 per cent cut in the rate of value added tax on domestic fuel.

There could be no reasonable doubt, then, that the new Prime Minister had demonstrated that he had taken a grip on the affairs of government. The staccato recital at the news conference of key commitments from the manifesto was intended to provide a sharp reminder of the indecision of John Major's administration. Nevertheless, the small print in the list of New Labour's '100 achievements in 100 days' revealed that many of the announcements were, to put it mildly, a triumph of presentation over substance and simply a recycling of what had been said before: 'a campaign of zero tolerance of underperformance in education'...'tough action to tackle crime and the causes of crime'...'a tough package of anti-stalking measures'...'an efficiency task force to cut back NHS bureaucracy'...'the launch of a national debate about economic and monetary union'. David McKie, writing in the *Guardian*, took the government to task for compiling what was inevitably a partisan checklist. He suggested, tongue in cheek, that as Peter Mandelson was the minister responsible for coordinating the presentation of government policy, he should have seen to it that New Labour had first established an independent authority, called perhaps 'Ofgov', which could have compiled an objective scoreboard. McKie was convinced that an independent regulator would have noted how often the word 'tough', which was irredeemably unquantifiable, recurred throughout the list of one hundred achievements. The *New Statesman* had pre-empted Mandelson's news conference the week before with an even more pertinent set of statistics. Its columnist Caroline Daniel revealed that in the government's first hundred days ministers had set up more than fifty task forces, advisory groups and reviews. She said they were regarded as 'emblems of Labour's desire to be seen to be implementing manifesto pledges briskly and in a spirit of trust'.

Nor was the elusive nature of the achievements so proudly listed the only vulnerable point in Mandelson's *coup de théâtre*. Although he tried to portray New Labour as having proceeded at a pace unmatched by any previous government, the list of '100 achievements in 100 days' inevitably drew attention to the promises whose fulfilment was having to be postponed, and provided an untimely reminder of the 'hard choices' which Blair had pledged his government would make but had not yet got round to tackling.

The news conference was an unhappy augury for the unlikely summer partnership of Messrs Prescott and Mandelson, to whom the Prime Minister had entrusted the task of minding the shop during his August holiday. In his first three months in Downing Street, Blair had maintained a punishing personal schedule, so determined was he to ensure that the new government made a noticeable impact on the nation's affairs. Despite all the risks inherent in this approach he had put hardly a foot wrong, and on his departure for a family holiday in Tuscany and the Ariège region of France there seemed to be no end in sight to the praise he was attracting in the popular press. However, once the Prime Minister and his press secretary had left for their holidays, bumps started to appear in the smooth presentation which had become the hallmark of the new government, and Labour were beset by what the newspapers were to claim was a series of gaffes and scandals. It was Mandelson's misfortune that he had chosen to leave the shadowy world of spin doctoring and to launch his career as an all-purpose, upfront government spokesman in the middle of the summer silly season, when the establishment goes on holiday and news-hungry journalists tend to be starved of their usual fare.

Even though many people are away on holiday throughout August, the pages of the newspapers still have to be filled, as do the news bulletins on radio and television. This state of affairs is fraught with danger for the unwary, and the wisest course of action for government departments and political parties is to lower their profile and to seek publicity only if they are totally confident about the validity and accuracy of what they want to say. Ill-judged political events can backfire spectacularly when there is so little hard news around. As the same storylines have to be reworked and, where possible, freshened up on what might seem to be the slimmest of pretexts, embarrassing allegations and political own goals can be repeated continuously, even *ad nauseam*, whereas in less fallow times they would be replaced quite quickly by fresh news stories arising from a succession of other events. The great drawback for a publicity-seeking politician who is tripped up during the silly season is that this extended exposure does tend to get noticed, albeit by fewer people. The holidaymaker who decides to buy a newspaper probably has the time to read it with a greater degree of thoroughness than usual, just as many of those who rarely watch news bulletins or listen to the radio do like to tune in when they are no longer under constant pressure from thoughts of work or family duties. Therefore, although fewer newspapers are being sold and radio and television audiences are smaller, the repetition of unwelcome summer storylines can have a cumulative and damaging effect. Some of the reporting in August 1997 probably was exaggerated and the coverage excessive; but the risk of this happening should have been perfectly apparent to Labour's experienced campaigners.

'Labour's awful August' was the headline given by the London *Evening Standard* to a catalogue of blunders which it said had blighted the government once Blair had left the country's destiny in the hands of Prescott and Mandelson. Even before they took charge, the *News of the World*'s disclosures at the very beginning of the month about an affair between the Foreign Secretary, Robin Cook, and his secretary, Gaynor Regan, had provided a sensational curtain-raiser to a sequence of unconnected events which, over the weeks which followed, exposed New Labour's raw edges. The long road from opposition to government had finally taken its toll. Inner tensions which had been masked for months, if not years, out of loyalty and self-discipline, could not be tolerated or hidden any longer. Margaret Cook lost not only her annual holiday that summer but also her husband. Her wrath at the Foreign Secretary's behaviour was intense. Needless to say, the acrimony in the Cook household was hardly the kind of backdrop which the party had planned for its celebration a week later of New Labour's first hundred days in government. Another week on and there were further unwelcome revelations, this time about the sudden death the previous month of the Paisley MP, Gordon McMaster. A suicide note revealed McMaster's fear that allegations about him had been made by a parliamentary neighbour, Tommy Graham, Labour MP for Renfrewshire West – who was promptly suspended (and subsequently expelled) by the party when he made outspoken comments about the affair. The party infighting within Scotland over McMaster's death provoked another suspended Labour member, Bob Wareing, MP for Liverpool West Derby, to reveal that he had informed the chief whip that he too felt 'suicidal' because of the 'scurrilous allegations' concerning covert links with a front organisation for the Bosnian Serbs which had been made against him.

Amid this mayhem the Deputy Prime Minister selected the weirdest possible photo-opportunity to promote the prospects of Peter Mandelson, who had chosen Blair's absence to announce his intention to seek election to Labour's national executive committee. Such was Prescott's sense of fun that a photo-call with the Deputy Prime Minister was nearly always newsworthy. Unlike Tony Blair, who rarely if ever deviated from what had been agreed in advance with Alastair Campbell, Prescott was renowned for his sheer unpredictability. On this occasion, having inspected plans for new flood defences to protect the site of the Millennium Dome at Greenwich, and having observed how this might help improve the shoreline of the Thames, Prescott picked up a specimen jar containing one of the Chinese mitten crabs which can be found in the mud at low tide. Much to the amusement of the attendant photographers and television crews, Prescott held it in front of his face and, trying hard to control a fit of the giggles, declared that the crab was named Peter. He then proceeded to converse with it: 'Me and my mate Peter. Do you think you will get on the executive, Peter?'

Seeing how much interest he had created, Prescott immediately tried to play down his conversation with the crab, as did Mandelson when he was asked for his reaction. To the cameras and microphones the two men insisted it was a joke, while behind the scenes they were trying frantically to limit any adverse publicity. Mandelson complained bitterly about a report on the *Six o'Clock News* by one of the BBC's political correspondents, David Walter, who had said that Mandelson was 'never, according to rumour, one of Prescott's closest soulmates'. Mandelson said that although they might have been regarded as political enemies in the past they were 'very close now' and Prescott's calling the crab Peter was a 'friendly reference'. As was only to be expected, the Deputy Prime Minister's 'joke' became front-page news the next day. 'Prescott mocks Mandelson' was the splash headline in the *Daily Telegraph*, over an article which claimed that Prescott had revealed his 'growing frustration' with Mandelson as the two ministers clashed over the construction of the Millennium Dome.

Mandelson had taken charge of this already controversial project in June, since when it had proved to be a constant source of contention. At one point Prescott had described the decision to award the contract for the PVC-coated roofing fabric for the Dome to the German firm Koch Hightex as a 'sad reflection on the competency' of the British construction industry. (The decision was later reversed in favour of glass fibre-coated cladding supplied by the American company Birdair.) As soon as he realised that naming the crab Peter had both drawn attention to problems over the Dome and fuelled newspaper reports suggesting that the two ministers had an acrimonious relationship, Prescott issued a statement to clear up any misunderstanding: 'I wish Peter all the best in his attempt to claw his way on to the NEC. I hope that his pincer movement goes well.' He had little alternative but to proffer his support because Mandelson had already told journalists that he had Blair's backing to stand for the NEC; but the words he chose were ambiguous in tone if not in content.

Prescott's tongue-in-cheek endorsement of his colleague only heightened the news media's interest in the relations among the absent Prime Minister's lieutenants, helping to sustain further analysis of the presentational blunders which had occurred that summer. Much of the coverage focused on the way Mandelson was fulfilling his role as minister without portfolio, moving on to explore the implications of his decision to use the Prime Minister's holiday as an opportunity to campaign for a seat on the party's executive. He told the *New Statesman* that he had decided to stand for election at the 'last minute', and in an interview for the *Observer*, which the paper's political editor, Patrick Wintour, said was part of a 'media blitz' being generated to promote his candidacy, explained why he wanted to rid himself of the tag of chief courtier to Blair. 'I do not want to be seen constantly as a placeman, or someone who has been put in as a result of someone else's decision. I want to be my own man much more, I want to be seen to be independent... An election would make me accountable to the party as a whole.'

As for Prescott, although most newspapers dutifully relayed his repeated assertion that journalists had misconstrued a joke about Mandelson, his attempts to play down his musings to the crab did not convince his many admirers in the trade union movement. Andrew Murray, head of communications for the Transport and General Workers Union, told me that Prescott had made it clear to his union contacts what had annoyed him most of all about the episode: namely, that after his photo-call with the crab he had heard that journalists had been led to believe that Mandelson's bid for a seat on the NEC had his backing as well as Blair's, whereas Prescott had hitherto always made a point of refusing to take sides in elections to the executive.

The Millennium Dome and the NEC aside, Blair's very decision to put Prescott and Mandelson jointly in charge while he was on holiday had proved to be a constant source of friction. The Prime Minister's instructions were said to have been vague and open to misinterpretation, leaving it uncertain precisely where authority rested on some issues. On the face of it the division was clear: Prescott was responsible for policy but Mandelson had control of publicity, in line with his ministerial responsibility for coordinating presentation of the government's activities. In the event conflict had been inevitable as the two men ended up vying with each other for the headlines whenever they sought to promote the government's achievements.

By so blatantly exploiting the high-profile role which he had acquired as a result of Blair's absence, and by using his ministerial engagements as a means of promoting his campaign for a seat on the NEC, Mandelson had left himself vulnerable to criticism. When the attacks came, he met them with his trademark aggression. Challenged about his wide-ranging duties at the news conference held on 9 August to mark Labour's first hundred days, he publicly rebuked one of the BBC's political correspondents, Nick Robinson, saying he had 'never heard such a stream of vainglorious, self-indulgent questions from members of the media about how they are allegedly managed by me'. During an interview the previous day on *The World at One*, in response to being asked why a minister outside the cabinet should have been given such an exalted position by the Prime Minister he turned on the programme's presenter, Martha Kearney. The reason, he claimed, why Ms Kearney kept asking about news management and questioning him as to why he had become the 'face of the government' was because media people preferred talking about themselves and their 'lives in the media, rather than talking about things that interest the bulk of the population'. This tirade was a godsend for political journalists who might otherwise have had little alternative but to rework yet again Labour's press releases listing the achievements of the government's first hundred days. 'Mandelson outburst at BBC overshadows poll landmark' was the headline in the next day's *Times*. Francis Maude, the Conservatives' cultural affairs spokesman, was quoted as saying that Mandelson seemed to be 'suffering from midsummer madness verging on megalomania'.

Mandelson himself remained apparently unperturbed by the lurid coverage he was attracting. Clearly his aim was to put himself about as much as possible so as to raise his profile with party members; and he had his own ideas about the nature of much of the resulting comment. He told the *Independent*'s Donald Macintyre that it was no accident that he had become the main political news story that summer. Mandelson was convinced that the media and the opposition were mounting a concerted attempt to make him the whipping boy for the government. 'First the Tories say it. The BBC run with it and then the newspapers run with it and report it as fact. Whatever it is. Mandelson's taking over; Mandelson's a megalomaniac. Mandelson's doing this; Mandelson's doing that. It's all a way of diverting attention from what the Tories really fear, which is the government's record, its effectiveness and its enduring popularity.' When Macintyre asked why Mandelson had thrust himself into the limelight, he defended his role as chief ministerial spokesman. 'Instead of being behind the scenes, off the record, an "in the dark" briefer, I'm a spokesman. What is surprising or unusual about that? It becomes particularly exposed in August when so many other ministers are away ...But in August things which go completely unremarked for the rest of the year suddenly become stories. That is the definition of an August story.'

By no stretch of the imagination could it be said that Messrs Prescott and Mandelson had failed to do their bit that summer to provide gainful employment for otherwise underutilised political correspondents. In view of his reputation for finding ways to combat damaging headlines, Mandelson should have needed no reminding of the potential pitfalls of the silly season; but his craving for a popular mandate, and his desire for some recognition within the party of the contribution which he had made to the success of New Labour, seemed to have blinded him to the inherent dangers of taking on the news media in August. In yet another highly revealing interview, this time in the *Guardian*, Mandelson again threw caution to the winds as he gaily set about the task of defining his role as the coordinator of government presentation. Under the headline 'The Ministry of Truth', Katharine Viner gave a blow-by-blow account of what appeared by the end of her conversation to have turned into a pretty frosty encounter with the minister without portfolio at his room in the Cabinet Office in Whitehall.

When she asked him why he was invariably portrayed in the newspapers as 'slimy and calculating', Mandelson said it was not his job to 'worry and fuss about every nuance of press coverage'. Dissatisfied with this answer, Ms Viner persisted: 'Of course it is, that is exactly what you do.' 'No, it's not. My job is to serve the party and to serve the government. The success of the government will in time reflect on me." Come on, I say, you are one of the most ruthless practitioners of news management of our age. "Well, it depends what you mean by news management," he says. "If you're accusing me of getting the truth across about what the government has decided to do, that I'm putting the very best face or gloss on the government's policies, that I'm trying to avoid gaffes or setbacks and that I'm trying to create the truth – if that's news management, I plead guilty." ...What a chilling phrase that is: "To create the truth." ... He turns to me and says, "So many of these interviews with the *Guardian* are all about my image, rather than what I think and do." Well, I say, this time we've talked about thinking and doing, haven't we? "We have," he says, "and it's probably the first time ever." ... And then he is gone, without a goodbye, without a handshake, leaving me alone in that office until an aide scuttles in to remove me.'

As Ms Viner had every justification in observing, the minister without portfolio had rarely been so forthcoming about his objectives and the lengths to which he goes to secure them. By being so forthright about his mission to 'create the truth' Mandelson had certainly given yet another unexpected twist to the definition of a spin doctor's duties.

After nearly a month of such high-profile exposure Mandelson's much-vaunted 'media blitz' began attracting the ire of both left and right. Hugh Macpherson, political columnist for the Labour weekly *Tribune*, acknowledged that the minister without portfolio had made an 'indelible public impression'; but, he went on, when exposed to the light of public examination, his 'vulpine demeanour, his belligerent arrogance incongruously expressed in epicene tones, speaks volumes'. An equally vehement tone was adopted in a *Sun* editorial which accused the 'king of spin' of putting up a 'smokescreen with a decidedly dodgy hint' to obscure a succession of U-turns and bungles which in Blair's absence had turned New Labour into an 'Old Shambles'. Mandelson had 'been on TV more times than the Teletubbies', but all he had managed to do was to emphasise that the government was a one-man band. 'Take away the captain and the ship veers off course . . . Come home, Tony. Your country needs you.'

But it would be wrong to give the impression that Labour's summer misfortunes were entirely down to Blair's chosen pair of minders. If John Prescott had imagined that his encounter with Peter the crab would allow him to walk away with the top prize for doing most to contribute to the gaiety of the silly season, he had clearly for-gotten about the unerring ability of Clare Short, the Secretary of State for International Development, to find bizarre ways of hitting the headlines. When asked by the *Observer* about the attitude of the inhabitants of the island of Montserrat, who had been driven from their homes by volcanic eruptions and whose representatives had rejected Britain's offer of £2,500 per head for resettlement, she attacked their greed and 'sheer irresponsibility'. She added: 'They will be wanting golden elephants next.' Single-handedly Ms Short had succeeded in livening up what had hitherto given every indication of being a politics-free August bank holiday weekend. Not surprisingly, her antagonistic approach, and her accusation that the island's gov-ernment was playing 'silly political games', provoked widespread criticism. Alastair Goodlad, the Conservatives' spokesman on interna-tional development, called on her to apologise for her 'insensitive and insulting' remarks. Although Ms Short immediately thought better of her interview, and conceded that the reference to 'golden elephants' had been extremely unfortunate, her handling of the crisis had annoyed her colleagues in government and had done further harm to her reputation. She would not escape unscathed. After weeks of drift, the *Sun*'s appeal for Tony Blair to take command again appeared to have been answered, because suddenly the Prime Minister's office was back in action with a vengeance.

Although Blair himself was still away, Alastair Campbell had just returned. In the middle of the bank holiday Monday afternoon, the Press Association news agency sent out a newsflash quoting a Downing Street announcement to the effect that officials from five government departments would meet the following morning to coordinate help for the people of Montserrat. The statement was under a strict embargo and could not be broadcast or published until after ten o'clock that evening. In response to an enquiry whether there was any way the information could be used in the main teatime news bulletin that Monday, the duty press officer said that was not possible as the announcement was intended for Tuesday morning's newspapers. 'We have done a ring round of the political editors to tell them about the setting up of this action group of officials. We have made the announcement this way in order to be helpful to the news-papers. It is not about No. 10 taking control.' In reporting the Downing Street announcement for the breakfast news programmes next morning, I said it was obvious that by calling the meeting and announcing it publicly the government intended to get a grip on what had become a rather fractious dispute with the Montserrat gov-ernment and, as befitted the return from holiday of the Prime Minister's official spokesman, we had clearly seen the 'smack of firm news management'. Later that Tuesday morning political correspon-dents gathered in Downing Street for Campbell's first lobby briefing since the end of his summer break. As he entered the room he gave me a withering look and enquired aloud why it was that after having been back in the country for only twenty minutes, it had been his misfortune to have to listen to one of my reports on the car radio – about the change of tack on the cladding for the Millennium Dome. My complimentary references that morning to Downing Street's swift response over Montserrat had obviously done nothing to improve my standing with Blair's official spokesman.

None the less, the contrast with the final years of John Major's administration could not have been sharper. Instead of allowing the newspapers to whip up the row over the 'golden elephants' gaffe into a full-scale diplomatic incident, the government had used the simple device of announcing a meeting of the relevant Whitehall officials to sideline and bypass the embattled Ms Short. As is so often the case in successful news management, the timing provided the *coup de grâce*. The Downing Street statement was released under embargo in the middle of the afternoon, giving the newsrooms of the morning papers plenty of time to think through their coverage, safe in the knowledge that if they made the story their front-page splash it would not have been pre-empted by the main news bulletins the evening before. The headline writers had required no further prompting: 'Short eased aside over volcano aid' (*The Times*); 'Cook snubs Short over Montserrat' (*Daily Telegraph*); 'The humbling of Clare Short' (*Daily Mail*); 'Clare is blown out by Cook for her volcano gaffe' (*Sun*). As Campbell sat back and took the first questions at the lobby briefing that Tuesday morning, he confirmed that his office had briefed journalists on the significance of the meeting of Foreign Office officials. He made no attempt to challenge or even question the unanimous verdict of the news media in interpreting the Downing Street statement as a snub to Ms Short. He said that the Prime Minister's office was alerted in advance about the *Observer*'s intention to interview Short, but that No. 10 had received no prior notification of her reference to golden elephants. For once, Campbell was happy to expound the guidelines which he expected ministers to follow in their dealings with the news media. 'What I do know is that Clare did not break the rules on giving advance notice about her interview . . . and therefore I can confidently say No. 10 exists happily whether I am in or out of the country.' Although Campbell said nothing to suggest that the minister had effectively been silenced, that certainly seemed to be the implication of his briefing.

Clare Short herself was deeply hurt by the way in which the story about her being 'sidelined' had been reproduced so faithfully by all the morning newspapers, and she retaliated the following weekend by giving an interview to the *Independent on Sunday* in which she castigated the 'dishonesty' of Labour's spin doctors. 'Heavy briefing suggested that the Foreign Office was taking up a new duty to coordinate. That was simply untrue . . . It's not to do with the truth. It's to do with finding a scapegoat, but I'm shocked that complete misinformation can go so far . . . This "snub to me" briefing must have been spin-doctored because it was in every single outlet. Lots of fairly vitriolic stuff.' Short said she had accepted a personal assurance from

Alastair Campbell that he was not responsible. Her exoneration of the Prime Minister's press secretary mystified the *Daily Mail*'s political correspondent, Paul Eastham, who said in a follow-up story that while the news of the Foreign Office meeting had been 'passed to journalists by a relatively junior member' of Campbell's team of press officers, it was 'inconceivable such an important statement would have been put out without top level approval'. I agreed with Eastham's assessment, because I had taken the trouble that bank holiday Monday to check on Campbell's whereabouts before making my comment about the 'smack of firm news management'. I was told by the Downing Street duty press officer that Campbell had returned from his holiday the previous Friday – as he had confirmed himself at the Tuesday morning lobby briefing, when he had bemoaned having had to endure my reports on Radio Four that day about the Millennium Dome. The only conclusion one could draw was that Campbell must have been aware of the statement which Downing Street had released, not least because on the morning it was reported he made no complaint about the way it had been interpreted by political correspondents, nor about the tough tone taken in news-paper headlines.

On this occasion Campbell was perhaps correct in assuming there would be little sympathy for Short. In an explosive interview the year before, she had told the *New Statesman*'s political editor, Steve Richards, of her profound misgivings about the activities of Blair's spin doctors, whom she described as the 'people who live in the dark'. Richards considered that in view of the seriousness of her own gaffe about the Montserrat crisis, her renewed attack on the Downing Street spin doctors was 'widely judged to be petty and ill-timed'. Moreover, in his determination at that Tuesday's briefing to make light of the put-down to Short and to distance himself from the saga of the golden elephants, Campbell had his sights on matters beyond the immediate episode and beyond the wayward minister herself: he wanted political correspondents to concentrate on looking ahead to Blair's return from holiday that evening. He listed the Prime Minister's engagements for the rest of the week and said they would demonstrate that the government remained focused on the 'big picture' of delivering Labour's election promises on schools and hospitals. Blair would not be diverted by 'all that stuff' which had so preoccupied the news media while he had been away on holiday. The Downing Street publicity machine would soon be slipping effortlessly back into top gear. Campbell could be relied upon to deliver.

2 Premier on parade

Years of continuous expansion in broadcasting and the printed media, and the ever tighter news deadlines imposed by technological advance and heightened competition, have generated a growing intensity in what, of necessity, has become one of the closest bonds in British politics: the pivotal relationship between the Prime Minister and the Downing Street press secretary. Three premiers of recent decades – Harold Wilson, Margaret Thatcher and Tony Blair – have each demonstrated in their own particular way the power and influence which can be exercised when the Prime Minister of the day manages to harness, however briefly, the full, supportive force of much of the news media; and all three did so largely through the offices of a key individual in that crucial post.

Blair's extended honeymoon in the tabloid papers had many parallels with the press excitement which greeted the early years of the Wilson government, following the Conservatives' defeat in 1964, while Thatcher secured the unshakeable support of most newspaper proprietors after her victory in the 1982 Falklands War and her defeat of the trades unions, above all in the 1984–5 miners' strike. All three Prime Ministers succeeded in winning over to their cause a streetwise journalist who then gave unstinting service and whose loyalty as press secretary could not be questioned. For seven years Joe Haines, a former political reporter, was Wilson's daily companion. During the 1980s, Sir Bernard Ingham's devotion to Lady Thatcher became legendary. Yet both have been surpassed by Alastair Campbell, in the sure touch of his tabloid wizardry and the depth of his personal commitment to Blair and to the Labour Party. No one other than the two men themselves, and their closest aides, is in a position to assess the relationship between the Prime Minister and his official spokesman as individuals; my analysis of its political significance is based on my experience as an observer of those highly visible moments when Blair makes a public appearance, conducts a news conference or is being harried in the street by reporters, photographers and television crews.

Whenever they are out and about together in the presence of the news media, the two men slip, almost imperceptibly, into a highly polished and ruthlessly efficient routine. No chances are taken when the premier is on parade. Campbell's role is to help orchestrate the best possible publicity for the Prime Minister, and he knows only too well the dangers which can lurk in what might appear to be a harmless photo-opportunity. In the cut and thrust of the televised doorstep encounters which now form part of everyday political life, a cool head is essential. The coordination which the two men display is almost subliminal. A fleeting glance or a nod of acknowledgement is all that is needed by way of communication. Of even greater significance in terms of news management is their uncanny ability to synchronise the delivery of a political message. So seamless is their joint operation that political journalists frequently cannot remember precisely from whose lips it was that they first heard mention of a particular phrase or idea. Did it come from the Prime Minister himself, perhaps in a speech or an interview, or from one of the innumerable newspaper articles which have appeared under Blair's by-line? Alternatively, should it be sourced to one of Campbell's often abrasive briefings for lobby correspondents, or simply a throwaway remark from the press secretary to the journalistic pack? Whatever the origin, there is rarely any doubt about the impact. Within a trice, it seems, the same punchy line is appearing everywhere, in headlines, in newspaper reports and as a soundbite in radio and television news bulletins. As the months went by, and the new government bedded itself deeper and deeper into the fabric of Whitehall, some of the concepts which Blair had espoused were put firmly on the backburner; a few disappeared from view altogether. But political reporters would be hard pressed to cite examples of where this was the result of poor communication on Campbell's part or sloppy handiwork at his lobby briefings.

There has on occasion been some dispute as to the total accuracy of the information which has been offered, but, as was the case with his two high-profile predecessors, who had also spent much of their earlier working lives as journalists, there would be few grounds on which political correspondents could question either the force or the authority of the guidance which Campbell has given on the Prime Minister's behalf. I can attest from my own experience that the same assertion could certainly be made about Bernard Ingham's stint in Downing Street. In his day, few journalists doubted that when he briefed the lobby he mirrored faithfully the views of Margaret Thatcher. Even if it emerged subsequently, as was sometimes the case, that he had actually been unaware of her precise opinion, his gut reaction was invariably in tune with hers and could quite safely be regarded as an accurate indication of her likely response. Ingham's writings and broadcasts in later years have confirmed this – and also the fact that he subscribed to both the political creed and the tone of true Thatcherism. Even so, after the change of government in May 1997, just as previously when Labour were in opposition, there seemed to be a far closer partnership, and a far greater degree of cooperation and coordination, between Prime Minister and press secretary than had been the case with any previous incumbent in the No. 10 press office.

No doubt we shall have to await publication of Campbell's reflections on his days as Blair's official spokesman before we can assess what impact the relentless pressure of being at the very heart of government had on his judgement and whether, over the years, it affected the strength of his attachment to what became known in New Labour circles as 'the project'. With the Blair government still in its early years, there are inevitably few reliable accounts of the political interplay which takes place in the privacy of Downing Street, the Cabinet Office or other secure premises such as Chequers, the Prime Minister's country residence. Nevertheless, on most significant issues Campbell has seemed to be entirely at one with Blair; and even in the few instances where there have subsequently been suggestions of a difference of opinion, few journalists can honestly claim to have detected this at the time through anything the press secretary said or from his demeanour. Even when it came to some of Blair's self-evident blind spots, like his distrust of the trade union movement, Campbell clearly shared the Prime Minister's feelings and, if the occasion required it, could be just as dogmatic and unforgiving as his boss about the failings of Old Labour – although sometimes, when the occasion demanded that Campbell give journalists a full-hearted rendition from the New Labour song sheet, he could clearly see the funny side of what he was saying and found it hard to wipe away a smile.

Thus far, then, there are clear similarities between the Blair–Campbell axis and its 1980s predecessor. In one fundamental respect, however, the current regime is significantly different. While Thatcher relied on Ingham's expertise when it came to news management, and while she would have given full weight to his tactical advice when framing and timing what she wanted to say, there was never any suggestion that her press secretary was regularly feeding her the kind of populist lines and ideas which Blair has succeeded in delivering with such ease and authority. The full extent of Campbell's contribution in this area will have to remain a matter of conjecture, at least for the moment; but it is beyond doubt that his input has been prodigious and that the help he has given in devising and writing the Prime Minister's speeches, and in steering his interviews and newspaper articles towards embracing the kind of concepts and language which have resonated so well in the popular press, has been indispensable.

Successful press secretaries know the rules: even small talk about the advice given to a Prime Minister is strictly taboo, as is gossip about the inner workings of Downing Street. Nevertheless, the depth and strength of the accord between the two men are readily enough apparent to those like myself who have observed them on a daily basis, and it is surely attributable to this relationship that Blair is more closely attuned than any previous Prime Minister to the daily news agenda, more willing to meet the media's never-ending demands and constantly changing requirements. Campbell has been Blair's steadfast companion since agreeing to become his personal press officer in the summer of 1994, after the Labour leadership election which followed the death of John Smith. When the Prime Minister is in the public eye, his press secretary is usually at his side. They sit together on the back seat of the car travelling to and from engagements, and when Blair is being filmed getting in or out of one of the rear doors, Campbell can often be spotted somewhere in the vicinity. His close attendance reflects the dictates of the media. The rapid growth in continuous news services on television and radio has heightened the pressures on a media-conscious Prime Minister, anxious not to ignore the waiting cameras and microphones. Blair has always sought to make a virtue of his ability to give an instant response, be it to a fresh development in the government's affairs, the death of a famous celebrity or even the prospects for the latest sporting fixture. Delivering soundbites to order, on the doorstep, day after day, is no easy task, and he has become increasingly dependent on Campbell's nimble footwork and populist touch. The speeding up of deadlines has added enormously to the burdens placed on the press secretary's shoulders, and the pressures imposed by today's twenty-four-hour news services are far more demanding than those bearing on Joe Haines in the late 1960s, when his paramount objective was to meet the late afternoon and early evening edition times of the national newspapers.

Campbell's involvement in the Prime Minister's daily life is far closer than that of his counterpart in the Thatcher era. Crucially, his status as a special adviser allows him far greater access and freedom than Ingham ever had. Campbell accompanies Blair to Labour Party functions as well as government events, while Margaret Thatcher's press secretary, though always at her side on high-profile public engagements, and frequently during official visits abroad, remained a civil servant and did not get involved in the affairs of the Conservative Party. The friendship, moreover, is strengthened by family intimacy. Both men have young children. Campbell's partner Fiona Millar served as Cherie Blair's press officer during the general election and was subsequently appointed her special adviser on media appearances.

Despite his protestations to the contrary Campbell courts personal publicity, and he likes to be flattered. In the early 1990s he had established himself as a regular and pugnacious broadcaster. He took great delight in his frequent television appearances reviewing the morning papers on BBC *Breakfast News* – exposure which he reluctantly forsook on becoming Blair's press officer. He clearly enjoys his well-earned reputation as one of the slickest tabloid journalists of his generation, and he does nothing to undermine the widely held assumption that Blair must be mightily indebted to his press secretary for all the astute advice and support which he has received. As perhaps is only to be expected, whenever I ask Campbell questions on points of detail, about either the nature of his work or his advice to Blair, he becomes thoroughly evasive. Only through patient observation does one detect signs of the totally disciplined approach which the two men adopt when they come face to face with reporters and photographers. Their unfailing ability to make the most of such encounters – a fusion of Blair's sure-footed political presence with Campbell's knack of first anticipating what will excite the news media and then delivering it – sometimes verges on sheer artistry.

Invariably the ground has been well prepared. A neatly timed tip off to a handful of favoured political journalists ensures that the event is well trailed in advance by those newspaper correspondents who are trusted by Downing Street. The theme of the Prime Minister's speech or interview is then likely to be expanded upon at the morning or afternoon lobby briefings when broadcasters get their first official confirmation of the line which he will take. Rare indeed are the occasions when Blair is found wanting or his words fall short of what has been promised by his press secretary. The next day sees articles in the newspapers over the by-line of the Prime Minister or one of his cabinet colleagues, designed to attract follow-through publicity and ram home the message of the moment.

The build-up to Blair's return from holiday at the end of August 1997 followed the usual pattern. Campbell's first objective was to generate some positive headlines, and on the day after Bank Holiday Monday he told the lobby that the Prime Minister would not be deflected by the 'summer froth' on which journalists had gorged themselves during his absence. All the silly season stories about Clare Short's 'golden elephants' and the tales of infighting between John Prescott and Peter Mandelson would not deter Blair from focusing on the 'big picture' of delivering Labour's manifesto commitments on health and education. His first public engagement would be a visit the following Thursday morning to an East London comprehensive school; this, Campbell promised, would highlight education as the government's number one priority.

Morpeth School in Tower Hamlets had been taking part in a summer literacy programme of the kind which Labour had promised during the election campaign, providing extra lessons in the holidays for children who needed help with their reading and writing. Here the two men, clearly refreshed from their holidays, laid on a virtuoso performance of their seemingly effortless but highly synchronised double act. On reaching the school, well ahead of Blair's scheduled arrival, I was struck by the care which had gone into the preparations. Siobhan Kenny, a Downing Street press officer, was already in attendance and seemed rather on edge. She said Blair planned to use the visit to announce a significant expansion in the literacy programme, and it was evident No. 10 was anxious the occasion should pass off without a hitch. Ms Kenny looked rather troubled when I asked somewhat mischievously what she thought of the speculation in some newspapers that, as there had been so many gaffes and scandals during August, Campbell might have to be told that in future he could not go away at the same time as the Blairs were on holiday. She muttered something to the effect that her boss did not think much of the idea, but she did acknowledge that it had been a difficult summer for the government and especially the Downing Street press office. 'Yes, it was a bit steamy for us... The trouble is that when there is so little news around, some stories do get far more exposure than they are really worth and that can be very annoying.'

The drive to haul the news agenda back on to the government's preferred ground had begun even before the Prime Minister disembarked from the plane bringing him back to Britain. On the evening of his family's return flight from France, Blair had gone to great lengths to avoid the end of his holiday adding to the unfavourable news coverage by inadvertently provoking yet more embarrassing photographs or headlines. The experience of the former Labour premier James Callaghan during the so-called winter of discontent has rendered subsequent Prime Ministers especially fearful of possible attempts by the news media to use their arrival back in the country from trips to sunnier climes as an excuse to generate a flurry of damaging publicity. On returning from the Guadeloupe economic summit at the height of the industrial disputes during the winter of 1978–9, Callaghan told reporters at Heathrow that he did not think that other people in the world would share the view that there was 'mounting chaos' in Britain. Next day the *Sun* printed its famous headline: 'Crisis, what crisis?' It was a salutary reminder that one word out of place was all it took to provoke the headline writers on the tabloids.

Throughout August 1997 there had been a succession of

photo-spreads in the popular press illustrating the various stages of the Blairs' twenty-five-day holiday. The family were shown in casual clothes, walking hand in hand outside their villa in Tuscany and then sightseeing in Bologna. During the second leg of their holiday, at a chateau in south-west France, a suntanned Tony and Cherie were pictured smiling beside a Pyrenees pony which had been presented as a gift to their children. There had been much discussion in the newspapers about the length of the Blairs' holiday. By going away for a three-week continental break he had, according to *The Times*, chalked up another record and had taken 'the longest foreign holiday of any Prime Minister... since an ailing Winston Churchill spent three weeks working on his war memoirs in Jamaica in 1953'. By and large, though, Blair's resolve to enjoy a proper family holiday had attracted favourable press comment; most leader writers judged it to be a well-deserved break after the success of Labour's first hundred days in office. Campbell must have been anxious to ensure these positive sentiments were not dissipated at the last moment through any slip-up at the airport.

When the plane touched down at RAF Northolt, Blair descended by himself, leaving the rest of the family on board. His holiday attire was nowhere to be seen. Instead he was wearing a grey suit, a spotted tie and brown shoes. To add a touch of real authority he was carrying his prime ministerial red box. There was no opportunity for reporters to ask questions; the photo-opportunity was designed to say it all. Blair was trying to underline the fact that he had remained in charge of events throughout his holiday and had assumed total control again from the moment he stepped off the aircraft. The care which he had taken to appear businesslike was commented upon by Charles Reiss, political editor of the London *Evening Standard*, who revealed that Cherie and the children had been told to hang back until the cameras had gone. He said in his report that it was obvious that for the 'true professional, every detail counts'.

The careful stage managing of events at RAF Northolt was repeated two days later at Morpeth School, where it soon became evident that Campbell had taken every possible precaution to ensure that the Prime Minister would not be bounced into answering awkward questions about the difficulties which the government had faced during his absence. The first real opportunity for the media pack to get close to Blair was inside one of the classrooms, where he chatted away with eleven pupils who had been taking part in the summer literacy programme and who were full of praise for the opportunities which the scheme had given them. At the end of an impromptu question-and-answer session, the press photographers asked the Prime Minister to stand with the pupils for a group picture. One cameraman suggested Blair should pick up the red felt pen on the table in front of him, turn round and write 'Literacy the No. 1 priority' on a white board on the classroom wall. For an instant, before responding, Blair stopped. He immediately looked across the room, trying anxiously to pick out the face of his official spokesman from among the melee of photographers and reporters who were penned up together in a roped-off section of the classroom.

Campbell was a few feet away from me and, as Blair silently mouthed the word 'literacy', I saw his spokesman shake his head, ever so slightly. Blair tried again, this time suggesting 'education' as an alternative. Campbell signalled his approval with a quick nod. Blair set to work immediately, smiling away as he wrote 'Education No. 1 priority', repeating on the classroom wall one of Labour's enduring pledges from the 1997 general election. After underlining the words with a broad sweep of his felt pen, he kept the tip of it firmly in place at the end of the line, turned his face to the cameras and punctuated his own photo-opportunity with a big grin, giving the photographers just what they wanted.

The preliminary eye contact between Blair and Campbell, and their brief, silent communication with each other, had lasted for no more than a matter of seconds. Few of those in the classroom would be likely to have noticed it amid the excitement and general hubbub of the occasion. Campbell had, in effect, provided not only an extra pair of eyes and ears for the Prime Minister but an extra brain, instantly reflecting on the probable repercussions and implications of the choice of a single word, and we had witnessed another faultless display from two masters of presentation. Throughout the visit Campbell had taken great care to mingle with the photographers and reporters, so that he could observe what they were up to and could, if necessary, have taken evasive action or warned Blair of any skulduggery afoot. Sometimes Campbell intervenes during school tours if he thinks the pictures are likely to be unflattering. When politicians visit primary schools they should always get down to the same level as the children, especially if the pupils are seated, otherwise the eyeline will not be right and the television or newspaper pictures will show them in a potentially unfriendly pose, peering down at the class. In the event, the request that Blair write 'literacy' on the classroom board was a harmless, run-of-the-mill suggestion, reflecting no more than the desire of the photographers to set up a picture which had some action in it. But Blair had been so well trained, and was so self-disciplined, that he stopped for a moment and automatically sought the nod from Campbell before complying.

Waiting for a few moments before agreeing to the demands of photographers and camera crews is a vital precaution. Many a politician has rued the day that they failed to pause for a second or two or forgot to check with their minder. Being photographed in unseemly circumstances, or getting caught in an ill-judged pose, can, in political terms, be a matter of life or death for an ambitious minister or aspiring MP. Campbell knows every trick of the trade when it comes to the kind of stunts which tickle the fancy of tabloid editors. He realises the need to station himself, in effect, behind the lens, so that he can monitor the images which the photographers are attempting to capture – sometimes, to create. As he is well over six feet tall, he towers above the crowd and takes no hostages if he spots a photographer or reporter trying to pull a fast one on the Prime Minister. As I observed the pair at work that morning I could not help thinking that in another life Campbell would have made a marvellous lookout for a sharp-shooting gangster. If a mafia boss had been holed up in that classroom he would have known that he had the best minder in town, and he would have waited for a flick of the head from Campbell to indicate the all clear before walking out through the door.

Blair's self-discipline in always checking with his support staff before responding to media demands earned him the admiration of the team of press officers drafted in to assist Labour during the 1997 general election. Dee Sullivan, at the time senior media officer for the Trades Union Congress, spent the campaign ministering to the needs of a coachful of impatient journalists who toured the country following the Labour leader's election battle bus. 'What made Blair so impressive as a political campaigner was that whenever the news media were around him, he never did anything which was unplanned or unexpected. As he was so self-disciplined himself, he expected Labour MPs and candidates to be just as careful.'

Once the classroom photo-call had been completed, Blair and Campbell were just as effective in batting away some barbed enquiries about the government's difficulties that summer. Blair had agreed to take reporters' questions on his departure and there were six attempts to get him to address the problems which had arisen while he had been on holiday. Each time he insisted that whatever else might be happening, he intended to concentrate on delivering Labour's election pledges. In a final attempt to provoke a 'Crisis, what crisis?' response, ITN's political editor, Michael Brunson, asked if Blair had by any chance found time since returning from holiday to knock a few ministers' heads together, but the question proved no more productive than its predecessors. Campbell, who had again positioned himself with the pack, chirruped 'Nice try, Michael' as Blair made for his car. Yet despite all their sharp political footwork at Morpeth School, the Prime Minister and his press secretary realised that the government could not remain impervious to the concern which had built up among the party's rank and file over the damage inflicted that summer to the good name of New Labour. Rather than be forced to acknowledge this unease in a doorstep interview, under pressure from the news media, Blair was determined to respond on his own terms and, as he intended to spend the weekend in his Sedgefield constituency, he decided to use a speech at a rally of party activists in Darlington to defend the government's record and to look ahead to the party reforms which he hoped would be approved at Labour's annual conference that autumn.

The setbacks of the summer had provided a timely opportunity to warn party members of the dangers of complacency and, as his speech progressed, it hit all the bull points, and delivered all the key phrases, which Campbell had taken the trouble to outline at his briefing for political correspondents the previous Tuesday morning, well before Blair's plane had touched down at Northolt. When it came, there was no mistaking the carefully crafted soundbite which Campbell had been trying out on journalists all week: 'As ever, August has brought its share of problems for the Labour Party. Much of it has little to do with the big picture. A lot of it is summer froth. But froth or not, we've had a timely reminder, you take nothing for granted . . . But let us take our mild kicking with humility and carry on with that big picture.' John Sweeney, who reported the Darlington rally for the *Observer,* said that although the Prime Minister looked 'as the cliché has it, relaxed and tanned after his holiday', he had shown that he was ready to depart from the general rule applied by those in power of never admitting they were wrong. Indeed, for the first time in his premiership, Blair was in effect apologising to the public – a tactic which, as the months went by, would be turned into an art form by the government once New Labour's spin doctors realised that the simple act of saying 'I'm sorry' was an invaluable presentational device: a sure-fire way of both generating interest in the news media and helping to draw a line under a troublesome news story, especially if the over-riding objective was to find a way of appeasing tabloid newspapers and neutralising hostile coverage.

Blair's humility in facing up to the savaging which his government had endured that summer was greeted sympathetically by most of the Sunday newspapers; but, well before they had even been delivered the next morning, Blair and Campbell were already hard at work on the telephone preparing the Prime Minister's response to the tragedy which was unfolding in Paris. News of the car crash involving Diana, Princess of Wales, and her friend Dodi Fayed broke just before midnight on Saturday 30 August; at 2 a.m., when the seriousness of the accident emerged, Blair was woken. The Prime Minister and his press secretary were about to face their toughest public relations test since the general election. They were to demonstrate early that morning not only that they were in tune with the mood of the country but that they were in fact a step ahead of public opinion, capable of both influencing and shaping it. Over the days that were to follow the country would become gripped by a mass eruption of public grief over Diana's death. While the royal family was seen to flounder and find that its responses were considered to be inept, Blair, guided by Campbell's tabloid instincts, was able from the start to turn the tragedy to the government's advantage. Far from being caught out by the unexpected, Campbell showed that even in a crisis, his belief in the need for ministers never to lose sight of the likely headlines in next day's newspapers was an essential part of effective government.

Blair had been spending the night at his constituency home and he was kept promptly informed of developments. At 5 a.m., after Diana's death had been confirmed publicly, a statement was put out on the Prime Minister's behalf by the Press Association news agency. It expressed his devastation at the news: 'Diana was a wonderful, warm, compassionate person who people, not just in Britain, but throughout the world loved, and she will be mourned as a friend.' BBC Radio Four had begun a live transmission in the early hours of the morning and as I was the duty political correspondent I had been called into Broadcasting House to gather political reaction. On receiving Blair's statement through the Press Association, I rang Downing Street and was put through to the deputy press secretary, Alan Percival. He said that No. 10 had been in touch with Buckingham Palace and the Prime Minister was anxious to do all he could to assist the royal family in the arrangements that would have to be made. Percival was not sure of Blair's precise movements, as the Prime Minister had been due to spend the day with his family in his constituency, so he could not comment one way or the other as to whether the Prime Minister might pay a public tribute to Diana later that morning.

As the enormity of the story became apparent, and with the main radio and television services switching to live coverage, the pressure was increasing for a fuller and more formal response from the government. Politicians rarely pass up the opportunity to broadcast a tribute on the death of a celebrated friend or foe. Obituaries on radio and television are generally even-handed in tone, and they are a powerful form of communication. In the daily ebb and flow of what might be considered newsworthy or topical, reports about the death of well-known and well-loved or even notorious public figures do tend to engage the attention of most viewers and listeners. There is usually no shortage of interview material, as even hard-bitten political opponents of the deceased are generally only too ready to pay their respects, or to supply an amusing anecdote, hoping no doubt that in the process they might get the chance to show a sympathetic side to their own character. Alastair Campbell would have realised instantly that the reporting of Diana's death would be in a league of its own: that it would dominate the British press for days, if not weeks, and would attract televised tributes from politicians and celebrities around the world. Therefore, although speed was of the essence, Blair would have to take great care in thinking through what he wanted to say and would have to ensure that his remarks were delivered in an appropriate setting.

Events were to move very quickly that Sunday morning once newsrooms were informed by Downing Street that the Prime Minister intended to pay his tribute to Diana on his way into Trimdon parish church. There then followed a mad scramble to get reporters, television crews and their outside broadcast equipment into place outside the church of St Mary Magdalene in time for the start of morning service. The shock of Diana's death made for gripping radio and television, and the audience for the live coverage had grown rapidly during the morning. The broadcasters were having to contend with a dearth of hard information about precisely what had happened to the princess and her companion, and, amid the conflicting reports and wild speculation surrounding the appalling circumstances of the crash, there was an urgent need for some calm, statesmanlike reflection. Shortly after 10 a.m., almost in unison, the rival television stations switched to their outside broadcast cameras at the church in the Prime Minister's constituency to show his arrival with Cherie and the children. As the American news channels started joining the coverage from Sedgefield, Blair began picking up a live television audience around the world for what, in retrospect, would be seen as a defining moment of his premiership.

He was wearing a sombre suit and a black tie. His voice broke with emotion when he said that the thoughts of everyone in the country were with Princess Diana's family and especially her two sons. 'She was a wonderful and a warm human being, although her own life was often sadly touched by tragedy. She touched the lives of so many others in Britain and throughout the world with joy and with comfort. How many times shall we remember her in how many different ways, with the sick, the dying, with children, with the needy? With just a look or a gesture that spoke so much more than words, she would reveal to all of us the depth of her compassion and her humanity. We know how difficult things were for her from time to time. I am sure we can only guess at that. But people everywhere, not just here in Britain, kept faith with Princess Diana. They liked her, they loved her, they regarded her as one of the people. She was the People's Princess and that is how she will stay, how she will remain in our hearts and our memories for ever.'

Blair's poise and delivery on reaching the climax of his eulogy were not just moving but mesmerising. Journalists in the newsroom where

I was working had stopped what they were doing, as if transfixed. Until then many of the tributes had seemed almost mechanical, even (dare one say) pedestrian, but the Prime Minister, by comparison, had managed to express himself in a way which seemed entirely in tune with the emotions of the morning, with the shock and disbelief of those for whom Princess Diana had become a real and vibrant part of their daily lives. The words which Blair used came across as startlingly fresh and different from the stock phrases about 'shock' and 'grief' which are so commonplace in tributes of that kind. His reference to Princess Diana's sons seemed heartfelt; with children of his own, he knew how terrible the impact of her death would be on two impressionable young boys.

Although journalists would subsequently question the true spontaneity of what he had said, no one could deny that he had spoken for Britain in a way which commanded support throughout the country; and, bearing in mind the limited time he had to prepare for his hurriedly arranged appearance before the cameras, he had remained in total control throughout and had carried it off superbly. The depth of feeling that he had succeeded in conveying had an impact far greater than anything either he or Alastair Campbell could have imagined. His tribute heralded a public outpouring of grief the like of which the country has rarely witnessed. Although Campbell has never publicly claimed the authorship of the Prime Minister's oration to the 'People's Princess', the unashamed sentimentality of Blair's remarks and the skilful way in which he approached the princess's horrific death from the standpoint of the people rather than the establishment reflected the tabloid flair and ingenuity of his press secretary. Campbell, who was in London that weekend, spent much of the early morning talking to Blair on the telephone, and he insisted subsequently that the Prime Minister's short speech was very much a joint effort.

One of the few journalists to have succeeded in getting Campbell to talk about what went on that morning was the author Kevin Toolis, who wrote a profile of him for the *Guardian Weekend* in April 1998 to mark the Labour regime's approach to its first anniversary. Campbell told Toolis about the hectic build-up to Blair's televised tribute. 'The phone was ringing off the hook and Tony was working out how to say what he was going to say. It was both of us going back and forth. A dialogue. You have to remember that we both knew and liked her very much. It was shocking. We'd both break off: "How could this have happened?" It was an important moment. Tony had to say something that united and settled the country and articulated what people were feeling. It was Tony who said it.'

Some days after his interview Toolis asked me what I made of Campbell's answer. He wanted to know why journalists like myself were so insistent in saying that the 'People's Princess' tribute was Campbell's finest moment when he had not gone so far as claiming credit for it in his *Guardian* interview. I explained that press secretaries and political speech writers usually tried to be self-effacing, as Campbell had indeed been, but that he had nevertheless given the game away with his remark: 'It was Tony who said it.' In my view that implied that Blair had taken the responsibility for choosing to utter a line suggested to him by his official spokesman; but in a situation like that, involving something as highly personal as the reference to the 'People's Princess', no press secretary or speech writer would ever suggest that Blair's words were anything other than his own. What had clinched it as far as I was concerned was that later that Sunday, Campbell began briefing political correspondents about the Prime Minister's wish for the princess to have a 'people's funeral'; this to my mind confirmed that Blair's reference to the 'People's Princess' was not a chance remark but had been carefully thought through in advance as part of a calculated strategy.

Toolis referred to my observation about the link to the 'people's funeral' in his profile, which paid fulsome tribute to what he acknowledged was Campbell's triumph. 'It was the ultimate in spin – a simple phrase that directed the entire nation into a government defined channel of national mourning. Even in those difficult hours, Campbell had a clear vision of how it was going to play... No one believes Campbell's denials because the lachrymose "People's Princess" phrase is too brilliant in its tabloid compression to have ever been dreamed up by Tony Blair. It takes years of tabloid hackery to achieve such an edge – it was repeated ad nauseam but never bettered by the collective mass of British sub-editors.'

Toolis's account of Campbell's first year in Downing Street was not alone in recalling the significance of Blair's highly emotional response to the death of the princess and Campbell's role in it; indeed, it featured in most of the newspaper and magazine articles marking Labour's anniversary. Among those in politics and the media who monitor the work of the party spin doctors there is no doubt about the authorship of the tribute. Joy Johnson, a former BBC political news editor who was Labour's communications director for a brief period before the 1997 election, was sure that Campbell was behind it. She said she was always struck during internal party briefings by the way Campbell insisted that, if ever it became necessary to take a stance, Labour should always take the side of Diana, rather than the palace, during discussions about the break-up of her marriage. Another insider equally confident about what happened was Paul Richards, who stood unsuccessfully for Labour at Billericay at the general election. Richards, who has frequently argued the case of the New Labour modernisers on radio and television, said in his book *Be Your Own Spin Doctor* that it was definitely Campbell who put the words into Tony Blair's mouth. Some journalists have given the novelist Julie Burchill credit for having been the first to baptise Diana the 'People's Princess'; but there was universal praise for the way the phrase had been woven into the Prime Minister's tribute. Philip Norman, writing in the *Sunday Times* magazine, considered that the death of the Princess of Wales was as much the making of Tony Blair as invading the Falklands was the making of Margaret Thatcher. 'Who can forget the figure he cut on that shell-shocked morning-after with his just-loose-enough black suit and tie, arriving to face the media not in a cold-hearted official limousine, but in a homely (and, maybe, inspirational) People Carrier? Who can forget the boyish face firmly wiped of its usual grin, the subdued voice that so perfectly delivered that one-line epitaph: "She was (half-a-beat pause) the People's Princess."?'

Needless to say, the day after her death the newspapers devoted page after page to the glamour and heartache of Princess Diana's short life. Most of the tabloids gave prominent coverage to Blair's tribute. Under the headline 'Princess of the People', the *Sun's* political editor, Trevor Kavanagh, said the Prime Minister was 'close to tears' and his 'voice shook' as he described how the country would remember her with the deepest love. Among a page full of political tributes reported by the *Sun* there was no mention of any word from the former Prime Minister, John Major. He did, however, merit a few lines in some newspapers, including *The Times, Daily Telegraph* and *Mirror*, which quoted him as saying he always found the princess to be 'warm-hearted and vulnerable'. Major added: 'She was one of the icons of our age and she will leave an imperishable memory in the minds of millions. Everyone's heart will go out to Prince William and Prince Harry and the Princess's family and friends.' Extracting that short tribute from the former premier, which was put out on his behalf by the Press Association, had proved a delicate and time-consuming task for Sheila Gunn, who had continued to serve as Major's personal press officer after the Conservatives' election defeat. Ms Gunn's dogged attempt to persuade him to express publicly his shock and sorrow at Diana's death provides a telling illustration of Major's innate reluctance to exploit the news media for personal publicity. The alacrity with which the Blair machine had seized on the tragedy, and the sheer superiority of its communication techniques, came as no surprise to Ms Gunn as she struggled to get Major to respond to the calls bombarding her from radio and television stations. As Major had been intimately involved, as Prime Minister, with the repercussions of the breakdown in Diana's marriage and the subsequent arrangements for her divorce and the welfare of her two sons, his reflections on her untimely death were inevitably in great demand that morning and eagerly awaited by the broadcasters.

Ms Gunn woke Major with the news at 4.30 a.m. that Sunday morning. 'I could hear Norma in the background, expressing her concern, wanting to know if it was someone in their family who had been killed. I told him to prepare to do radio and television interviews but he refused. He said he wasn't going to do any shroud waving. When I said that whatever else he did, he would have to put out a press statement, he told me he would have to think about it and I should ring back in an hour.' Despite the rebuff, Ms Gunn began preparing some words for him. 'It wasn't until after 9 a.m. that he finally agreed to put out a statement. He still wouldn't do interviews, but it was obvious he was deeply involved in what was going on because he told me he had already spoken twice to Prince Charles. He insisted this information was "private" and was not "spinnable". He said he knew that when it came to the tragic death of Diana the "Blair lot would spin anything". All I could do was give out a short statement on his behalf to the Press Association.' Ms Gunn, who had spent the final twenty months of the Conservative government working as a press officer for Central Office, liaising with lobby journalists, told me that since losing the general election Major had come to realise how comprehensively he had been outgunned in public relations terms by Labour's spin doctors. 'He accepts that he was upstaged by Blair in the run-up to the election and that he didn't spend enough time promoting himself. That's why I keep telling him that unless he's careful he'll become the forgotten Prime Minister. The media always seem to be jumping straight from Thatcher to Blair and he's in danger of being ignored.'

Ms Gunn's difficulties in seeking to generate favourable news coverage for Major during his final months in power were compounded by the fact that, in her role as a party press officer, she could only get involved in publicising political events and those activities which had been organised by the Conservatives or were being held in support of them. Arrangements for publicity involving the Prime Minister's duties in government were outside her sphere of activity and were handled by the then Downing Street press secretary, Jonathan Haslam, with whom Ms Gunn had a close working relationship. Haslam had wide experience within the Government Information Service but, like his two predecessors during the earlier years of the Major administration, Gus O'Donnell and Christopher Meyer, he was a civil servant and was therefore bound by strict rules on political neutrality. In view of the split in responsibilities between the Downing Street press secretary and Conservative Central Office, and because, in her dealings with journalists, she lacked the clout of a larger-than-life figure like Sir Bernard Ingham, Ms Gunn was no match for the bombastic Alastair Campbell, who was unencumbered by any such constraints and whose relationship with Blair could hardly have been closer or more productive.

Major had played safe in choosing press secretaries steeped in the traditions of the civil service rather than journalism. At times of crisis during his premiership – the Gulf War, the withdrawal from the exchange rate mechanism and his many confrontations with the European Union – Major benefited from having press secretaries who had a deep understanding of the complexities of the Whitehall machine; but for his last two years in government, when the Conservatives were in effect on a perpetual election footing, Major was at a severe disadvantage in competing with Blair, who was getting the undivided attention of two renowned political streetfighters, Alastair Campbell and Peter Mandelson.

One of the crosses Ms Gunn had to bear was Major's reluctance to take part in photo-opportunities. Ever since the 1995 Labour conference, when Blair had gone head-to-head with the Newcastle United manager, Kevin Keegan, keeping a football in the air for twenty-seven consecutive headers, Ms Gunn had tried to persuade Major to take more advantage of his interest in cricket – to no avail. 'Once, when photographers asked him to throw a cricket ball, he refused point blank and he told me to tell them that he couldn't run because he hadn't got a left knee cap, which was true, but really it was because he didn't like taking part in stunts.' Major's aversion to photo-opportunities was pretty comprehensive, and even when his staff went to great lengths to arrange events in such a way as to keep his participation to a minimum, he would still decline to take part, telling them crisply: 'That's not for me.'

Ms Gunn said that if ever groups of children toured Downing Street, Major refused to let the photographers accompany them inside No. 10. 'Norma couldn't abide having the cameras there during visits by handicapped children but now, under the Blairs, anything goes, and whenever parties of families and children go inside No. 10, the cameras always seem to be there. It's the same with party political stunts. The civil servants refused to let Major do television interviews around the cabinet table if they were on party issues, but Blair's lot play by a completely different set of rules.' While Ms Gunn thought Major could have done more to promote himself, she believed his decency shone through when contrasted with Blair's opportunism. She advised Major not to allow the Blairs to go with him to Dunblane after the shootings at the town's primary school in March 1996, fearing that Blair would make capital out of the Prime Minister's gesture. She considered her warning vindicated when Blair recalled the visit in his speech to the 1996 Labour conference and described in emotional terms how he went to the school gym and talked to the parents sitting on the 'tiny chairs where once their children sat'. Having seen Blair's speech on television, Ms Gunn prepared a statement on Major's behalf. 'I was very cross about it and felt we should protest at the way Blair had broken the political neutrality of the Dunblane visit, but Major refused. He didn't want to exploit Dunblane for political purposes, so my statement never went out.'

As events unfolded that Sunday morning after the Paris car crash, Tony Blair's readiness to speak so swiftly and so movingly about Princess Diana had seemed entirely appropriate, given the tragic circumstances of her death. The Prime Minister and his press secretary had sensed, quite correctly, that despite the recriminations which surrounded the break-up of her marriage, the public's sympathy would be with the princess and her two sons. However, by having spoken on behalf of the nation in such an emotional way about the 'People's Princess' and the contribution she had made towards creating a caring society, the Prime Minister only drew attention to the lack of an immediate public response from either the Queen or Prince Charles – neither of whom had been mentioned directly by Blair in his tribute outside Trimdon parish church. In those first days after the crash, as people flocked in their thousands to lay flowers outside Buckingham Palace and Kensington Palace, the failure of the royals to speak publicly of the anguish they might have been experiencing as a family, and their apparent inability to find ways of sharing the public's grief or of acknowledging Diana's work for good causes, became a focus for press criticism. Even before her body had arrived at RAF Northolt, there had been speculation as to whether the princess would be afforded a full state funeral. The consensus among the commentators was that because of her divorce from Prince Charles, and as she had lost the title of Her Royal Highness, this would be frowned upon by the palace authorities. Nevertheless, Blair had swiftly turned his thoughts to the arrangements which would have to be made and, shortly after nine o'clock that Sunday evening, Alastair Campbell told the BBC's newsroom that Blair was keen that the funeral should be an occasion which allowed 'the people to show the nation's gratitude to Princess Diana'.

As the week wore on, and as the Queen and Prince Charles struggled to come to terms with the flood of emotion which engulfed the country, Blair and Campbell continued to demonstrate their intuitive grasp of the likely fallout from the sensational circumstances surrounding Diana's death and their understanding of the need to satisfy the public's demand for an event which would serve as a unifying occasion for the country as well as the royal family and the Princess's relatives. As details began to emerge of the arrangements that were being made for the funeral service at Westminster Abbey the following Saturday, it soon became evident that behind the scenes the guiding hand of the Prime Minister was having a profound effect. By siding so openly with Diana's grief-stricken admirers, the Downing Street machine could have ended up at odds with the royals, but the palace authorities were known to be in awe of the presentational successes notched up by the Blair government and the Prime Minister's advice and assistance must have been invaluable. Within a matter of days, it seemed, the modernising influences of New Labour had begun to have a discreet but significant impact on royal protocol. Some newspapers were particularly blunt in their assessment of the part played by Messrs Blair, Campbell and Mandelson, judging the strategy they had adopted all too reminiscent of the campaign techniques which had been perfected at the Labour Party's headquarters in Millbank during the election. The day after the funeral service the headline over the *Observer*'s two-page investigation into what it described as the 'frantic Blairisation of a beleaguered House of Windsor' left no room for doubt: 'How Blair gave the monarchy a Millbank makeover'. That morning the Prime Minister was the main interviewee on *Breakfast with Frost*, and after the most momentous few days of his premiership was only too happy to reflect publicly on the drama which had so engrossed the nation.

Political life had been at a standstill for days, but there were significant undercurrents for those attuned to them. Blair's readiness to speak publicly about his evident satisfaction at the palace's willingness to respond to the modernising influences which had been at work the previous week provided a pertinent reminder to trade union leaders of their own beleaguered position under New Labour. The day after the funeral, delegates had begun assembling in Brighton for the next day's opening of the annual conference of the Trades Union Congress. In view of Blair's repeated strictures about the need for the unions to be outward-looking and to strike up a new relationship with the government, the TUC general secretary, John Monks, told me that he had inevitably thought long and hard that week about the way the royal family had been forced to abandon protocol and respond to the pressure for a 'people's funeral'. On the Sunday morning of Diana's death, Monks said, he was on his way to

Cheltenham, where there was to be a celebration to mark the ending of the ban on trade unions at the GCHQ intelligence-gathering centre, and he heard the Prime Minister's tribute to the 'People's Princess' on his car radio. 'Initially I thought Blair had gone over the top, but as the day went on I realised what he was doing. He was positioning himself to move against the royal family, just as he had done to move against the trade union movement. What happens? Well, Blair calls for change, then Campbell and Mandelson brief against you and say you're out of step. So Blair managed to outmanoeuvre the royals, just as he did the unions.' John Edmonds, general secretary of the GMB union, told me the Prime Minister could not be faulted for the speed with which he had seized his opportunity after the princess's death. 'I am positive Blair used the same tactics against us as he used against the royals. He told us that if the unions wanted to be part of his vision, we had to change. That's what it would have been like for the palace. If they wanted to be part of his vision for a new Britain they had to modernise.'

If the TUC leadership had few illusions about the effectiveness of Downing Street's manipulative techniques, they were also wary of the potential pitfalls which loomed as a result of the raw emotions aroused by Diana's death, and they were sensible enough during the week of their annual conference not to air their views in public – a trap which the newly elected Conservative leader, William Hague, failed to observe and avoid. The praise which Blair had attracted over his handling of the funeral arrangements had proved particularly irksome to one of Hague's closest confidants, the Conservative MP Alan Duncan, who had been his campaign manager during the 1997 Tory leadership contest and had subsequently been appointed the leader's parliamentary political secretary. A week after the Westminster Abbey service, Duncan took it upon himself to push the boat out on Hague's behalf with a story which became the front-page splash in the Sunday edition of the *Express*. Duncan told the paper's political editor, Simon Walters, that Hague would use an interview on *Breakfast with Frost* to accuse the Prime Minister of trying to 'hijack the royal family'. Duncan was quoted as saying that Hague believed Downing Street had 'embarrassed' the Queen by 'giving the impression that they had to tell her how to react to Diana's death'. Far from ensuring that the aftermath of the tragedy remained non-political, the accusation ran, the Labour Party had behaved as though it owned the royal family. Worse was to follow. Instead of simply acknowledging these misgivings, and limiting himself to making critical noises about the political capital which Labour and the government seemed to have made out of the tragedy, Hague opened up a new and far more dangerous line of attack, targeting directly the activities of the Downing Street press office: although he did not name names, the clear implication was that he had Alastair Campbell in his sights.

Sir David Frost could hardly have expected the Tory leader to be so specific, but Hague was adamant that press briefings given on Blair's behalf had abused royal confidences for political advantage. 'What has annoyed me most of all, and it has to be said at some stage, is the leaking of confidential advice given to the royal family, the apparent briefings to the press, that advice was given to the royal family that puts the government in a good light and the royal family in a bad light. That's shabby politics and it's bad government.' Hague insisted that discussions between Downing Street and the palace should always remain confidential, as had happened under the Conservatives.

At no point in the interview did Hague seek to substantiate his allegations, and the Conservatives' failure subsequently to give chapter and verse on precisely what confidential advice they claimed had been leaked opened the way for some rapid rebuttal by Campbell. Downing Street said it was 'totally untrue' that the government had briefed journalists on conversations between the Prime Minister and the Queen: information which had been supplied to the news media about the funeral arrangements had been issued with the 'full backing and agreement' of the palace. Most political journalists sided with Campbell, because they had no recollection of having heard him step out of line during his briefings and give even a hint as to what might have been said in Blair's conversations with the Queen and Prince Charles. Hague, aided and abetted by Duncan, had made the mistake of assuming there was a degree of certainty about precisely what was said during lobby briefings, and he had ended up believing that New Labour's spin could somehow be sourced to official guidance.

Under the headline 'Hague attack over funeral backfires', Anthony Bevins, then the *Independent*'s political editor, described the two briefings which Campbell had given lobby journalists in the week before the funeral. At the first he had explained that the palace had decided to break with tradition by excluding some of the 'great and the good' from the guest list; later, at the second – after the royal family had been attacked in the press for being out of touch – Campbell had outlined some of the 'common-touch ideas' for the funeral which had been initiated by the palace. By failing to sustain Hague's attack, and by enabling Downing Street to issue a categorical denial on the narrow point of the alleged breach of confidentiality, the Prime Minister's office had no difficulty in deflecting attention from the Conservatives' wider charge about Blair having sought political advantage from the death of the princess.

I had tried myself without success the week before, during Tony Blair's visit to the TUC conference in Brighton, to tempt Alastair Campbell to give me an inkling of what it had been like being the Prime Minister's press secretary on a story which had gripped the world's news media. 'It was nothing to do with me,' he said brusquely. 'It was all the responsibility of the palace.' I realised there was nothing to be gained by pursuing the point: Campbell had nothing but contempt for my interest in the machinations of the Downing Street press office and his tactic was always to feign indifference and brush aside my questions. None the less my continued persistence in seeking to explore the activities of Labour's spin doctors did rankle with him.

This undercurrent of irritation was apparently exacerbated by the BBC's decision to nominate me for inclusion in the press party to accompany Blair on a two-day trip to Moscow in early October. Because the visit coincided with the start of the Conservatives' 1997 annual conference the BBC's political editor, Robin Oakley, and other senior correspondents were unable to go and, quite unexpectedly, I found I had been designated to represent the Corporation on my first ever foreign trip with the Prime Minister. As Campbell realised only too well from his days as the *Daily Mirror's* political editor, when he had relished his role as chief mischief-maker on John Major's foreign tours, there was always something of a risk in allowing a correspondent considered to be a member of the awkward squad to take a seat on the Prime Minister's plane. Having now risen from lobby poacher to gamekeeper he regarded my reluctance to observe all the proprieties of lobby etiquette, and my attempts to lift the veil on the darker side of his endeavours, if not as a threat, then at least as a nuisance. Campbell's assistant in the press office, Tim Allan, rather foolishly let the cat out of the bag when discussing Blair's trip to Moscow with my brother George in the *Daily Telegraph*'s room in the House of Commons press gallery. George had deputed one of his correspondents, Rachel Sylvester, to represent the paper and the rest of the team were amused to hear Allan's entreaties to my brother: 'Alastair is still hoping that you'll come to Moscow, George. We want someone on the plane to keep Nick Jones in order and stop Alastair punching him on the nose.'

In the event the trip passed off without incident. (On both the outward and return flights Blair remained out of view in a section of the plane which had been curtained off, so there was no opportunity for any of the correspondents on the flight to pull off anything resembling Campbell's infamous exploit on a return trip from Washington, when he claimed to have noticed that John Major wore his shirt tucked inside his underpants – an observation that lived on for years in the work of the *Guardian*'s cartoonist, Steve Bell, who regularly depicted Major wearing his Y-fronts outside his trousers.) The visit to Moscow itself was all too brief. Blair arrived in time for a dinner appointment with two of the leading Russian reformers, first deputies Anatoly Chubais and Boris Nemtsov; the following day, after a morning meeting with President Yeltsin and an afternoon of promotional activities at the British Embassy, it was back to the airport. Even in this short space of time the Prime Minister and his press secretary, on top form, had the Moscow press corps eating out of their hands. Blair's landslide victory in the general election, and his consummate skill in presenting himself as a people's Prime Minister, had generated considerable interest in Russia, especially among the local politicians. The chance to bask in the glow of some reciprocal publicity had certainly not been overlooked by either President Yeltsin or another prominent self-publicist, the Mayor of Moscow Yuri Luzhkov, who commandeered the Prime Minister during a visit to the Manezh Square shopping centre and promptly took him on an unscheduled walkabout to see the sights. For the photographers, however, there was only one picture which really mattered: Yeltsin embracing Blair at the Kremlin, an encounter which the *Express* headlined as 'A Blairhug for that clever young Tony'. Yeltsin had not required any tutoring by Labour's spin doctors. He hugged Blair, slapped him on the back and welcomed him as 'a young, energetic and thrusting politician' whom he recognised as having won enormous support in the United Kingdom. Campbell, looking on with pleasure and mingling as usual with the media pack, took it all in his stride, not letting on that he had his own ideas as to which of the day's photo-opportunities might get most exposure in the newspapers back home.

A highlight of the visit was to be a trip on the Moscow metro. We were told it was the first time a visiting Prime Minister or head of state had asked to travel by underground. On being escorted out of Manezh Square by Mayor Luzhkov, Blair's entourage headed straight for the Ploschad Revolutsii station. By now the Prime Minister had attracted such a large crowd that we were all swept along together through the station concourse, down the escalator and on to the platform. There seemed to have been a fair degree of orchestration behind what happened next. The first train to arrive was empty, and the carriage we entered was decorated with British Council posters illustrating the work of Russian and British poets. Blair ended up beside a tube card featuring Roger McGough's poem 'I wanna be the leader', and there to chat to him was an English-speaking Russian student, Irina Silina, who was quick to point out that she had never seen any Russian statesmen on the metro. Reporters, photographers and television crews were corralled together in the middle of the carriage. Through the noise I could hear Judith Dawson, a political correspondent for *Sky News*, trying to attract Blair's attention, urging him to turn round to face the cameras. Finally, when Blair looked towards the photographers, I could see that Campbell, who was a few paces away from me, kept signalling to him, jerking his hand up in the air towards the handrail above our heads. It took a second or two for this to register with Blair, but he quickly got the message: straphanging was an everyday experience for most tube passengers and that was what the picture had to say. Within an instant Blair had regained his composure. He gripped the rail above his head with his right hand and then turned nonchalantly towards the television crews and photographers with the thumb of his left hand tucked casually into the top of his trousers, looking for all the world as if he travelled by tube every day of his life.

Blair's final engagement was a cameo appearance in a radio soap opera entitled *Dom Syem, Podjezd Chetirie*, which was produced by the BBC Marshall Plan of the Mind – an educational charity set up by the BBC World Service – and was billed as a Russian version of *The Archers*. After a rather shaky rehearsal in the compound of the British embassy, and an instruction from Campbell to 'give it some welly', Blair played himself, pretending to stop his prime ministerial motorcade to help a widow who had dropped her shopping in the street.

Later, at a farewell reception, I had a chance to compliment Campbell on his success in providing us with such an imaginative range of pictures and stories, given the short duration of the visit. He studiously ignored my compliment but did reveal that what he and Blair had found of great interest was that the leading Russian reformers did not attach great significance to the importance of news management as a means of pushing forward political change. At the dinner with Chubais and Nemtsov, Blair had described how the projection of the ideals of New Labour had been a central part of the modernising project. Campbell was struck by the fact that their hosts seemed suspicious of the role that could be played by the news media and doubted whether it made much difference. In a country where politicians had such long memories of state-controlled news coverage, and where figures such as President Yeltsin and Mayor Luzhkov were hardly likely to feel that they needed to seek a personal consultation with a spin doctor, there was nothing like the same fascination with the arts of media manipulation that prevailed at home.

While Campbell could not read the minds of the picture editors on Russian newspapers, he certainly had no reason to doubt his own flair in orchestrating Blair's photo-opportunities in Moscow and in gaining favourable publicity for the government back home. Blair had been surrounded by photographers at every stage of his visit, and next morning the British newspapers were spoiled for choice. *The Times, Guardian, Daily Mail* and *Express* went for 'Boris's Blair hug'; the *Daily Telegraph* and *Independent* chose the photograph of Blair strap-hanging on the Moscow metro. New Labour's modernising Prime Minister, the picture assured us, knew just what it was like for passengers struggling to find a seat on the crowded trains of the London Underground.

3 **Raising the game**

Alastair Campbell's edict to the one thousand civil service information officers who are employed to publicise the government's activities was simple and to the point. In a letter circulated to all Whitehall departments in September 1997, the Prime Minister's press secretary said the election of a new administration had provided a 'real opportunity for the government information service to raise its game and be right at the heart of government'. Campbell's intervention was prompted by his concern that, despite all the favourable media coverage which heralded Labour's first few months in power, the policy initiatives which were being announced by Tony Blair's ministers were still not getting sufficient publicity. He also considered that the civil servants whose task it was to disseminate information were not responding robustly enough on behalf of their departments when news stories went wrong. Campbell was determined to ensure that the government machine remained in fighting form throughout the parliament, ready for the next general election. There was ample justification for his apprehension. His acerbic assessment of the inadequacies of the public relations and publicity services being provided on behalf of the government in the final years of John Major's administration had not gone unnoticed. During the long downward spiral to their crushing defeat in May 1997, the Tories had been outgunned on every flank by the superiority of Labour's propaganda machine, and they were only too well aware that not all the blame could be laid at the door of their own staff at Conservative Central Office. As one presentational disaster followed another, and as the Major administration began imploding amid Tory infighting over the party's split on European monetary policy, government information officers frequently gave journalists the impression that they were marking time:

they recognised that the country wanted a change of government and, as if in sympathy, some were in effect virtually sitting on their hands, just waiting for the general election.

When the expected election result materialised, however, the information service found itself falling short of the demands of its new masters. After having served the same political masters for eighteen years, there was a fair degree of complacency within its upper echelons; and the enthusiasm and efficiency which incoming ministers might have expected to find on taking office were too often remarkable by their absence. Many of the directors and heads of information had only themselves to blame for the denouement that awaited them: they had known all along that New Labour's leading modernisers were preoccupied with presentation, yet they had failed to anticipate the upheaval this change of tempo would involve. Staff deployment and shift patterns within government information departments had not kept pace with the rapid expansion in media outlets, nor had sufficient attention been paid to the added burdens imposed by the introduction of rolling news services on radio and television. Shadow ministers had grown accustomed before the general election to receiving a round-the-clock service from the Labour Party's media centre at Millbank Tower. They had been able to get an instant digest of the top new stories of the day, obtain advance warning of the issues which were most likely to cause embarrass-ment and were best avoided, and get briefed on those subjects where decisions were imminent and where it was essential they followed the party line. Now some of the newly installed ministers had a rude awakening when they were asked at short notice to appear on breakfast-time television and radio programmes, finding that the advice and assistance forthcoming from their own departments were not a patch on the back-up which had been provided by the party.

In the first few months of the new government, information officers assigned to accompany ministers on their early-morning rounds of interviews rarely had a full rundown of what was being said by that day's newspapers, let alone an indication of the likely running order for news stories on the various radio and television pro-grammes. As a result potential pitfalls had not always been identified and, unsure what to expect, ministers felt ill at ease and unnecessarily exposed as they toured the studios. Accustomed before the election to hearing horror stories about Conservative ministers feeling let down by the failure of their departments to rebut exaggerated or inaccurate news stories, some members of the Blair government soon felt similarly aggrieved, especially at weekends when the evening news bulletins often had their biggest audiences of the week and the Sunday morning airwaves were dominated by political talk shows.

Outwardly, Campbell's instruction to the Government Information Service to 'raise its game' gave every appearance of being concerned solely with an overhaul of professional standards and the need to modernise the government's communication services. His letter set out the steps which he believed should be taken to establish a 'media plan' for 'big positive announcements' and to ensure that the government succeeded in laying down 'big messages' around every event. Looked at in isolation, the Downing Street directive was the kind of pep talk which might have been expected from any new incumbent in the Prime Minister's press office; but when viewed alongside other changes in the way the government sought to handle relations with the news media, it should have been seen for what it was, a harbinger of an unprecedented shake-up which within a year would culminate in accusations that New Labour had politicised the information service. By wrapping up the whole exercise in the language of modernisation and efficiency, Campbell had created a smokescreen which would allow the Blair administration to drive a coach and horses through long-established traditions of civil service neutrality. As the months went by a series of far-reaching changes began to have an impact. The new government doubled the number of special advisers who were appointed by ministers from within the Labour Party but whose salaries were paid by the state. A far higher proportion than ever before were engaged not on policy issues but on media relations work, which encouraged ministers to second-guess or bypass their civil service information officers. In some departments ministers found themselves at odds with their directors and heads of information, prompting a series of unseemly personality clashes which culminated in an exodus of senior staff. Journalists who were sympathetic to the ideals of New Labour were recruited to take their place. In another unprecedented development two prominent pro-Labour newspaper correspondents were appointed to give a hard journalistic edge to a strategic communications unit which was established within the Prime Minister's office and asked to think long-term and plan for the presentation of future policy announcements.

At the root of Campbell's frustration with the arrangements he had inherited was a problem which had bedevilled previous administrations: the requirement for a straightforward demarcation line between the tasks of promoting the affairs of the state and publicising the political activities of the party in power. The civil service had always insisted that there was a clear division between advancing the policies of the government of the day and action which could be seen as providing an unfair political advantage to their current political masters, to the detriment of opposition parties. On a number of occasions information officers had been known to blow the whistle and alert the news media when they believed ministers were trying to get round the rules. Opposition MPs would pounce on any infringement, and the civil service unions always promised to stand by any of their members who felt they had been pressurised into undertaking political work. Nevertheless, for the government of the day the dividing line between government and party publicity can be rather arbitrary and, when under attack, or having to respond to fast-moving political news stories, there is an obvious temptation to break the rules. Blair and Campbell took the view that they had helped to regularise the position by doubling the number of special advisers who would work inside ministers' private offices and who, unlike the departmental information officers, had the freedom to provide guidance to journalists on the political implications of a minister's work. Yet for all the good intentions behind it – or claimed to be behind it – this mass influx of political appointees did represent another significant shift towards the politicisation of the points of contact between the government and the news media.

The biggest transformation of all was presided over by Alastair Campbell himself. As the Prime Minister's press secretary, he was one of six political appointees in the No. 10 press office who, in addition to a team of government information officers drawn from the civil service, were all assigned to deal with the news media on Downing Street's behalf. The significance of this unprecedented expansion cannot be overestimated. During the eighteen preceding years of Conservative rule, John Major and Margaret Thatcher had both refrained from making political appointments in the Downing Street press office, preferring instead to draw on experienced staff from the information service and other government departments. Responsibility for briefings and guidance about party issues rested with Conservative Central Office, and the No. 10 staff were expected to observe the demarcation line. Of all the complaints levelled against Campbell's colourful predecessor, Sir Bernard Ingham, the one that I considered had never been substantiated was the suggestion that he had abused his position in Downing Street to advance Tory party business. Certainly his dogged loyalty to Thatcher knew no bounds; but, while some political correspondents thought his bombastic behaviour unacceptable, he was nevertheless scrupulous in observing civil service proprieties, even to the extent of taking a week's holiday each year during the Conservatives' annual conference so that there could be no hint or suspicion that he might somehow have been massaging government announcements for the benefit of the Tories. Many were the occasions at Ingham's lobby briefings when journalists were told in the bluntest of terms to direct their questions to Central Office rather than the Downing Street press office.

The radical changes introduced by the Blair government – changes which have now opened the door for a further push towards a media-driven, presidential style of government – built on ground laid much earlier: by Harold Wilson. Of all the postwar Prime Ministers, it was Wilson who effectively broke the mould with the appointment in 1969 of the Labour-supporting political reporter, Joe Haines, as his press secretary. Haines was one of three political appointees in Downing Street who had regular dealings with journalists. As the Downing Street press secretary, he was responsible for briefing lobby correspondents and for helping the Prime Minister write speeches and prepare for interviews. Alongside Haines worked Wilson's political and parliamentary press officer, Gerald Kaufman, another former political reporter who was elected Labour MP for Manchester Ardwick in 1970; and his long-standing political secretary, the formidable Marcia Williams, later Lady Falkender, who always took a close interest in the way the Prime Minister was portrayed in the press.

Although it could be argued that Blair has done no more than follow Wilson's example in taking his key party advisers with him into No. 10, and in recruiting politically committed journalists for his press office, there are fundamental differences in the ground rules for the Downing Street press secretary today. In contrast to Joe Haines, Campbell has an unparalleled degree of latitude and he is able to go back and forth at will across the dividing line between government and party political work. Like Haines, his salary is paid for by the state, and he has also in effect had to become a civil servant; but while Wilson's press secretary was constrained by civil service rules on political neutrality, Campbell is allowed far greater freedom in his operations – a freedom conferred by the advantage of a unique civil service contract which was specially drawn up for the purpose and which expressly allows him to present the government's affairs 'in a political context'. As a result Campbell has free rein to accompany Blair wherever the Prime Minister chooses to take him, be it on government or party business. Nor, like Haines and Ingham, is he confined to barracks during the annual party conference or at election time. Whether Blair is delivering a speech as Prime Minister or as Labour Party leader, Campbell will be just as busy cajoling the news media to portray his boss in the best possible light. Haines wrote ruefully in his autobiography, *The Politics of Power*, about his inability to follow Wilson on the party political trail or to be seen openly campaigning with him. During the 1970 general election campaign he remained in Downing Street, 'writing the odd speech and radio broadcast'. However, in one foretaste of the Campbell era, Haines helped compose about thirty articles for the press, which were issued under Wilson's by-line.

The unprecedented freedom of manoeuvre which Campbell enjoys, reflecting as it does the rewriting of the press secretary's job description, has proved to be invaluable to him in helping to achieve his key objective, trying to ensure that the government does all it can to influence and if possible to dictate the news agenda of the day. If his strategy is to succeed, he needs to ensure coordination between departments, so that ministerial announcements do not clash with each other. Once that cooperation is established, there has to be a concerted attempt to promote important statements and initiatives in advance, so that when the announcement is actually made the news media are primed and ready to give it maximum publicity. Campbell set out succinctly in his letter of September 1997 the fundamentals of his media plan: 'I often get the impression that events happen and the mentality surrounding them is one of damage limitation. Big positive announcements are not getting as good a show as they should. The government must lay down big messages around every event. There are three parts to any story – the build-up, the event and the follow through.' His concern was that government information officers were paying 'all their attention' to the event itself and putting insufficient effort into the task of securing either advance or follow-up publicity, which, he said, required editors, feature writers and other journalists to be briefed both before the occasion and afterwards. 'We should always know how big stories will be playing in next day's papers. If a story is going wrong, or if a policy must be defended, we must respond quickly, confidently and robustly.' As Campbell knows only too well from his own days as a political reporter, the task of engineering the right 'build-up' to a big political announcement can turn into a shady business, sometimes involving the premature disclosure of the contents of ministerial statements which are due to be made in the House of Commons – a practice which the Speaker, Betty Boothroyd, has complained about repeatedly. There can be distinct advantages for the government of the day in encouraging informed speculation. If there is some bad news on the way, and the worst aspects of it are trailed in advance, this can be a useful softening up exercise, minimising the outcry when the announcement is finally made. When challenged about stories which seek to pre-empt what a minister might say, the standard response of the Whitehall department used to be that it could not comment on speculation. Under the changes introduced by Campbell, rebuffs of that kind are no longer so commonplace, and government information officers caught up in the trailing of announcements are far more frequently having to guide journalists towards accepting the validity of stories which would previously have been dismissed as no more than speculative spin.

Civil servants are also working under another severe constraint. Because Campbell attaches so much importance to trying to dictate the news agenda of the day, by hyping up government initiatives, there is less likelihood that information officers will seek to offer words of caution. After forty years' experience as a journalist, during which I have spoken to countless civil service information officers, I would have no hesitation in saying that I have detected a noticeable change since Campbell moved into Downing Street. Government press officers are not as impartial as they used to be and, when following up exclusive and speculative stories in the newspapers, I have found them far less likely than in the past to give what I have tended to regard as a health warning. Information officers in the civil service should have the self-confidence to put a story into context, especially when a political correspondent like myself is straying into a specialist policy area and is not fully briefed on the detail. If a story is simply a reworking or reheating of a known policy position, and contains no new information, then that should be explained, as should the precise status of what is being proposed. Is there a history to the initiative that is under consideration? Has it been suggested in the past by previous governments and perhaps found to be unsuitable or unworkable? I consider it right and proper for Whitehall press officers to make a point of volunteering such information; and I fear that Campbell's directive to government departments to go big on the 'build-up' has put a check on such openness. When responding at weekends to speculative stories in the Sunday newspapers, the duty information officers tend increasingly to say that they understand that briefings have probably been given by the minister's private office to selected journalists and that the best course of action would be to check with one of the special advisers. I suspect they know full well that a policy announcement is deliberately being trailed in advance; they are probably not fully aware of all the details and have no wish to say a word out of place, for fear of incurring criticism from their superiors.

In urging government information officers to feel at home in the sometimes murky world of political spin, where departments have to be proactive if they are to secure the right 'build-up' to an important government story, Campbell has in effect encouraged civil servants, if not to break free from the strict bonds of political neutrality, then at least to loosen them. All too often the advance trailing of a ministerial statement necessitates its being placed in a party political framework, so that it can be contrasted with what the opposition are proposing or perhaps failed to achieve when they were last in government. Special advisers are ideally suited for much of this shadowy work, inhabiting as they do the ill-defined overlap between party politics and the administration of the affairs of state. In reality a special adviser is a hybrid, bound by civil service rules but still able to put a political gloss on a minister's work, so they have exactly the right credentials to undertake the deft and discreet task of supplying tip-offs and giving exclusive one-to-one briefings to picked journalists. Only a small proportion of the political correspondents at Westminster are considered sufficiently useful to get this favoured treatment, and only those who can boast an established track record for being trustworthy and for not revealing their sources can hope to be so favoured.

The ability of the special adviser to act as go-between, negotiating with journalists in a way that few civil servants would dare contemplate, explains why their numbers have increased so rapidly under the Blair government. Each department now has a minimum of two advisers; some have three or four. By early June 1998 the total had risen to seventy-three. A year earlier, in the final twelve months of John Major's government, there were thirty-eight. The largest increase of all has been at No. 10, which now has a staff of nineteen special advisers. Some of these political appointees, such as Jonathan Powell, the Prime Minister's chief of staff, have no daily contact with the news media, nor do they seek it. Others are strictly confined to policy work, providing advice for ministers, and they too make a point of refusing to speak to journalists. But these are in the minority; for the role of the special adviser has changed out of all recognition in the last thirty years, as Hugo Young has observed in his weekly column in the *Guardian*. In Harold Wilson's day the typical adviser was a professor who knew more about pensions, housing or education than the civil service and whose task was to ensure that the Labour government's objectives 'were not crushed by the orthodoxies of Whitehall'. The political advisers employed by the Blair government have tended to have little interest or expertise in policy issues. 'They're the minister's personal familiars, whose prime talent, if any, lies in explaining what the minister wants to get across: the guardians of access and the messengers of perception.' Young rounded off his withering critique by suggesting that this 'new political class of spinners' personified the least acceptable part of the Blair administration: its 'shallowness'.

Yet while a constitutional purist might belittle the duties performed by this new breed of political functionaries, they themselves believe they are at the cutting edge of the New Labour 'project'. Most of them came into the government machine with their ministers, for whom they had worked in opposition, and had been part of the election-winning team which in their view had revolutionised Labour's campaigning techniques. They were as determined as Campbell to ensure that their own mastery of the news media carried through into government, and the pressure to increase the effectiveness of the information service reflected their overall dissatisfaction with the performance of government press officers. On reaching Whitehall at last, and settling into their private offices next to their ministers, they had every reason to consider themselves the best judges of the most opportune moment to trail a policy statement or of which newspaper correspondents would give the most favourable treatment to the story they wanted to plant. Long-standing directors of information discovered they were not being consulted and that their advice was not heeded even when offered. A degree of friction was inevitable.

In some departments there was turmoil for months as the newcomers sought to establish themselves. Charlie Whelan, the volatile, publicity-seeking press secretary to the Chancellor of the Exchequer, Gordon Brown, saw no need to temper his brash, belligerent behaviour just because he had acquired the status of a special adviser at the Treasury. Others preferred a lower profile and were able to work harmoniously with a team of civil service press officers. Ed Owen, special adviser to the Home Secretary, Jack Straw, appeared to have no difficulty working out clear demarcation lines with Mike Granatt, director of communication at the Home Office. Owen's role in trailing stories about Straw's seemingly endless flow of initiatives on law and order was understood and accepted by the civil service information officers, who told me they appreciated his courtesy and frankness. If they were on weekend duty, and were having to respond to calls from broadcasting organisations and news agencies about highly speculative exclusives in the Sunday newspapers, they were able to pick out, despite the political hype, the stories which were most likely to have some validity because they would have been warned about them in advance by Owen.

During the summer of 1997 hardly a weekend went by without news of yet another 'crackdown' by the Home Secretary. Late one Saturday evening in June, when checking out a *Sunday Times* exclusive about the plan to introduce a statutory offence of misconduct in public office, aimed at combating financial sleaze, I was told by the

duty Home Office press officer that she could not help me and that I
should contact Ed Owen direct. In September I had to follow up
another *Sunday Times* exclusive about Straw's plan for a curfew for
young offenders. Again the duty press officer could not have been
more straightforward. She confirmed that the Home Office was publishing its consultation paper on the Crime and Disorder Bill the following week, but said that she personally could not give me any
guidance as to its contents and suggested I contact the special adviser:
'We know that the story was planted in the *Sunday Times* by Jack
Straw's political adviser and we know it is correct but as press officers
we are not allowed to say anything about it.' From the point of view
of Labour's spin doctors this procedure for trailing stories cannot fail.
By planting their exclusive in a reputable Sunday paper, which they
know is likely to hype it up, they have made sure that a favourable
account of the initiative will be the only information that broadcasting services and news agencies have to go on when their journalists
have to follow it up on Saturday evening, once the first editions are
printed. Therefore, in a well-run government department, the special
adviser needs to be sure that the duty information officer from the
department is in the loop and says nothing to undermine what the
newspaper has been told. An astute spin doctor can rework the same
government initiatives time and time again. All it needs is a new twist
to the story, an exclusive planted in the right newspaper, a quiet
weekend on the news front, and there are the headlines again,
blazoning yet another 'crackdown'.

Hugo Young might find it hard to accept, but one of the political
appointees he sought to deride believes his expertise will help a
Labour government fight the political battles of the twenty-first
century. Joe McCrea, special adviser to the Secretary of State for
Health, Frank Dobson, is a communications technocrat who has
developed electronic systems to provide ministers, MPs and constituency parties with instant access to up-to-the-minute briefings on
the latest facts and figures from the Department of Health. In an
article for *Progress*, the magazine for New Labour activists, he
reported on the battle he had waged during Labour's first seven
months in power to get the government's standard of briefing up to
the level which the party had achieved at Millbank before the election.'I haven't had to battle with all of the Department but with those

who want to carry on as usual, with the old ways of doing things, I've told them you can't fight twenty-first century political battles with techniques and technology from thirty years ago . . . It's all about marrying the best of the Labour Party to the best of the civil service. It will take time. But it's begun.' Among the systems which he has developed is a ministerial information networking technology service which gives ministers 'twenty-four-hour remote laptop access to lines to take' on Department of Health announcements, together with all the latest data on the health service and hospital waiting lists. This is backed up by a constituency briefing and regional analysis which breaks down national announcements for regional news outlets so that MPs can tell their constituents 'what difference the new government is actually making to their lives locally'. McCrea takes the greatest pride in a rebuttal system which he has spent three years 'developing and honing' and which he hopes will allow the Department of Health to stand up to their political opponents and their critics in the news media. 'From now on inaccurate attacks will be challenged and logged. If and when they are repeated they will be instantly shot down.'

McCrea's technological wizardry has certainly rattled the Conservatives. Within a year of the introduction of his non-stop service of 'health line briefings' and 'health rebuttals' there were protests from the shadow Secretary of State for Health, Ann Widdecombe. She complained in June 1998 to the new Cabinet Secretary, Sir Richard Wilson, about the way 'large-scale partisan briefings' were being produced and photocopied at taxpayers' expense prior to a House of Commons debate on the fiftieth anniversary of the health service. Frank Dobson took delight in standing by McCrea and putting Ms Widdecombe in her place with a firm rebuttal of his own: 'Every aspect of this activity is entirely consistent with the long-established role of special advisers as set out in the ministerial code.'

Whenever I had spoken to McCrea I had always found him courteous, especially when I had to telephone him at weekends about Sunday newspaper stories. However, he had no hesitation in challenging reporters who he thought were off message – with not always felicitous results. In November 1997 a spat with Jo Revill, health correspondent of the London *Evening Standard*, rebounded when she wrote an exposé of what she considered was his 'bully-boy' behaviour, under the headline 'My shocking treatment from a Labour spin doctor'. Ms Revill had been to a briefing on health spending given by the minister of state, Alan Milburn. When she asked Milburn for more details on the London figures, and then challenged him as to why the allocation was bigger for some regions than others, McCrea intervened on both occasions, insisting that London was getting the national average. On arriving at work next day she found 'the most astonishing' message from McCrea on her answering machine. 'He accused me of writing "the most negative possible write-up of extra health cash for London that it is possible to do" and said that if the *Evening Standard* was "going to kick the s★★★ out of us, then there is no point giving you an advanced briefing".' Ms Revill accepted there was nothing new in the government's desire to manipulate the media but claimed that it was now being done with 'a blatant contempt for the impartial, traditional civil servants who run the press offices. They are losing their jobs or being side-tracked as the spin doctors take over.'

An earlier episode illustrated not only McCrea's success in pushing a story which helped set a favourable agenda for the government, but also the discipline and control which the party had succeeded in imposing on its MPs. In July 1997 the *Sunday Times* had splashed on an exclusive by its political editor, Andrew Grice, saying that the government was about to raise the age at which cigarettes could legally be purchased from sixteen to eighteen. The duty information officer said this was a possibility and was likely to be discussed at a meeting of health experts the following day, but she could not give me any details. When I contacted McCrea, he confirmed the story but insisted that I must not attribute this to an 'official spokesman' and should say instead that it had been confirmed by 'sources close to ministers'. In order to add some weight to my report for the television news that Sunday evening I had secured an interview with Dr Howard Stoate, the new Labour MP for Dartford, who was a member of the House of Commons Select Committee on Health. As he was a general practitioner, I was sure he would support moves to curb teenage smoking. He was forthright in his answer: 'We must do something to curb this epidemic. Lung cancer is becoming the commonest cause of cancer in women. If we don't do something about it, we'll have an even bigger epidemic.' On meeting Dr Stoate next day in the lobby at Westminster I thanked him for his help. He then surprised me by saying that he had felt it necessary, after I had completed the interview, to check with party headquarters at Millbank Tower to see if my approach to him had been in order. He said he had spoken to Labour's duty press officer, Julie Crowley, who had raised no objection. I told him that I had asked him for his opinion because he was a GP as well as an MP, that it had never even crossed my mind that as a family doctor he would have had any hesitation in supporting the need to discourage young people from smoking and that his response to my question was hardly likely to have been of the kind that would have got him into trouble with party headquarters. And yet he had gone to the trouble to check.

Joe McCrea's eager, hands-on approach to the task of gaining favourable publicity for Frank Dobson and the other health ministers was evidently accepted without rancour by the Department of Health's long-standing director of press and publicity, Romola Christopherson; a photograph of McCrea standing by her desk accompanied his article in *Progress*. Ms Christopherson, who was well regarded by political journalists, had in any event probably seen it all before, having earned her spurs in Bernard Ingham's day. But while her laid-back temperament no doubt helped maintain an even keel in the health department, all around her during the summer months of 1997 there were howls of anguish from the embattled corps of Whitehall information directors. By September it was headline news as journalists began compiling lists of the heads of information who had either departed unexpectedly or had been moved sideways during the holidays. Confirmation that Gill Samuel, press secretary and chief of information at the Ministry of Defence, was to be replaced proved to be the trigger for the story. 'Whitehall press officers are purged' was the headline in *The Times* over a story by the paper's Whitehall editor, Valerie Elliott, who said the moving of Ms Samuel to 'other duties' followed the hurried departure of three other directors of information. More casualties were expected, said Ms Elliott, because ministers considered that Whitehall's most senior press officers could not 'match the skills used by the Labour Party's own spin doctors'. Ms Samuel headed a staff of a hundred, many of them serving officers based at military establishments around the country, and her department had been told it had to be 'more innovative, more concerned with shaping the political agenda, and more reactive to events'.

Of the three other heads of department removed that summer, the one with the highest profile was undoubtedly Andy Wood, who had spent ten years in Belfast as director of information at the Northern Ireland Office. Told by the permanent under-secretary, Sir John Chilcot, that his 'style and personal chemistry' were not considered right by the Secretary of State for Northern Ireland, Dr Marjorie Mowlam, he was ordered to clear his desk and sent home on full pay on what civil servants euphemistically call 'gardening leave'. Although Wood acknowledged that Sir John tried to dissuade Dr Mowlam 'from kicking me out', his efforts were in vain. Another of the casualties, Liz Drummond, director of information at the Scottish Office, had been told her department was to be restructured so she had asked for early retirement.

The most intriguing of the four departures was that of Jill Rutter, press secretary and head of communications at the Treasury. A career civil servant, she had asked to leave the press office and return to policy duties. The lack of 'personal chemistry' between Dr Mowlam and Andy Wood was as nothing when compared to the highly charged atmosphere which had faced Ms Rutter and her team of civil servants in the Treasury press office. She found herself having to contend not only with a new Chancellor of the Exchequer, the highly media-conscious Gordon Brown, but also with his personal press officer, the pugnacious Charlie Whelan, who kept in daily contact with lobby correspondents and who organised Brown's radio and television interviews, and thirdly with Ed Balls, the Chancellor's economic adviser, who in addition to working on policy issues, liked to give more detailed advice to political journalists on broadsheet newspapers like *The Times* and *Financial Times*.

Whelan and Balls enjoyed their larger-than-life reputations and were proud to be regarded as Gordon's two bovver boys. Balls had established himself as a formidable number-cruncher; Whelan was the Chancellor's foot-in-the-door fixer, who always seemed to be having arguments with radio and television producers or other errant journalists and was often mightily disappointed if such encounters did not end in a shouting match. The two of them had worked for the Chancellor throughout the long build-up to the general election and there was no doubt that as special advisers they had bonded with their minister. All three were firm friends and defended each other to the hilt. After Labour's election victory there were reports that Tony Blair believed Whelan to be so unreliable that he had asked Brown to sack him, or at least agree to put him under the direct authority of Alastair Campbell. Blair's distrust of Whelan went back some time. At a private party to celebrate his victory in the 1994 Labour leadership election, Blair paid tribute to the help he had received from 'Bobby'. On discovering this was a coded reference to Peter Mandelson, who had asked for his name not to be publicised during the leadership campaign, Whelan leaked the story to the *Daily Telegraph's* Peterborough diary column. Some days later he told me he realised this tip-off would have done little to improve his popularity with either Blair or Mandelson. However, according to John Lloyd's account in the *New Statesman* in October 1997, Blair's demand, issued the day after he became Prime Minister, that Brown curb Whelan's activities received short shrift from the newly installed Chancellor. Nor, said Lloyd, had Brown's refusal to give way wavered since. 'Whelan is a key member of a team around Brown which is closer than any other group of advisers to their minister; they work together, eat together, watch football, play tennis and even holiday together. Whelan has shaped for Brown a media profile which, given the lustre surrounding Blair, is as high as it could be. For the Chancellor, Whelan's future is not negotiable.'

For Jill Rutter, the arrival of Brown's swashbuckling entourage must have been a shock. The outgoing Chancellor, the ebullient Kenneth Clarke, had certainly had some tempestuous moments at the Treasury; but however difficult and testing the final months of the Conservative government might have been, there is nothing to suggest that Clarke ever blamed his civil servants. He had a good working relationship with Ms Rutter, he respected her team of information officers and they appreciated the loyalty which he had shown them. Once Brown took over, Ms Rutter must have realised within days that her position would become untenable; and she was obviously desperate to leave after the humiliation of having her attempts to adjust to the new regime recorded by a television crew for a fly-on-the-wall documentary. Network First had been commissioned to produce two programmes for ITV charting Brown's progress from opposition to government. Publicity for the series coincided with the first news of a 'purge' of Whitehall information directors, so inevitably much of the coverage focused on the tense scenes which were filmed in the Treasury as the new Chancellor pushed through a series of innovations, including the government's decision to give the Bank of England independent control over interest rates. The first programme, *Out of the Shadows*, broadcast on 30 September, showed Brown and his aides on the campaign trail preparing for the general election. Whelan had a starring role. After having been seen threatening a reporter and then being accused of telling journalists half-truths, he remarked: 'You just have to be economical with the truth … you should never lie, but it's very difficult. But they understand: they'll all understand tomorrow and forgive me.' *We Are the Treasury*, the second programme which went out the following week, lived up to its advance billing and revealed the full extent of the discord within the Treasury in the first two months of the new government.

At one point the permanent secretary, Sir Terence Burns, acknowledged diplomatically that Brown's whirlwind approach and reliance on spin was something of a departure and 'not always the same way that we have of doing things'. But far more revealing was the footage of Ms Rutter, showing her frustration at being sidelined by Whelan and Balls. She had been apprehensive from the very first day and said she had feared that the Treasury press office were 'going to be shut out' of the action. To begin with she could be seen making valiant attempts to establish a working relationship with Brown's inner circle. Sensing her annoyance, Whelan reminded her that in opposition Labour were 'driving the news agenda all the time' and that it was all the more important the Chancellor did so in government. But Ms Rutter was excluded from the discussions Brown had with his advisers about news coverage for the surprise announcement, made within a week of the election, that the Bank of England would take over responsibility for setting interest rates. There were to be signed articles by the Chancellor in *The Times* and *Sun*, but Brown was not satisfied and wanted to know more about the line the newspapers were likely to take. He told Whelan to call in the *Sun*'s editor, Stuart Higgins, for a briefing and insisted that the Treasury 'must sell this to the public'. On the morning of the announcement, Ms Rutter was still making arrangements for what she assumed was a standard meeting of the monetary committee when she was told of the announcement at the last minute. Challenged by the programme makers, she did little to hide her disappointment. 'I know I have got Ed and Charlie who we have to consult at every turn...They are clearly the kings of the line and it is quite interesting how they see stories because we see stories in a different context.'

When the camera crew caught up with her again a fortnight later, she looked disconsolate as she fielded calls from journalists impatient to know the date of Brown's first budget. An economics correspondent from the *Daily Telegraph*, exasperated at the lack of information being given out by the press office, had just told her that she had obviously lost all influence in the Treasury. Ms Rutter was approaching breaking point: 'There is a problem with so much being done informally between the Chancellor, Ed Balls and Charlie Whelan, and because so much is filtered through Ed, the most precious commodity in the Treasury at the moment is time with Ed, but Ed spends a lot of time with the Chancellor.' If Ms Rutter had realised she was superfluous, Whelan was on a high. He was shown proudly displaying the front page of the London *Evening Standard*, which bore the front-page headline 'Watchdog with teeth for the City'. As he predicted, the paper had splashed on an announcement about a new regulatory body for securities and investments. Whelan acknowledged that the new regime had not been easy for Ms Rutter. 'The Conservatives have never driven the news agenda from the Treasury. We've wanted to set the news agenda and it has been a culture shock for the Treasury.' The documentary's closing sequence showed Brown delivering his first budget. Tucked in among the credits was a short sentence: 'Jill Rutter has now left the Treasury.'

The programme could scarcely have confirmed more comprehensively what most commentators had suggested: that Brown and his aides were obsessed with news management. Peter Koenig, writing in the *Independent on Sunday*, said that although there was nothing new about governments sending signals to the financial markets, *We Are the Treasury* had revealed a change of direction. 'What is new about Brown & Co. is their recognition that spin is more than just publicity. It is an integral part of economic management.' Koenig noted how the impact of the announcements which Brown had sprung on the financial markets had been judged in presentational terms. 'Image after image flashed up: Brown's team on the phone to reporters, Brown's team chuffed at the way reporters were covering stories, Brown's team talking to Brown about handling the media.'Whelan's role in spinning for the Chancellor was dissected at length. Most columnists and reviewers were amazed by their behaviour. The treatment meted out to Jill Rutter appalled Bruce Anderson. In his *Spectator* column, he said Brown was guilty of not just bad manners but disrespect in refusing to look at, let alone listen to, Ms Rutter while she was trying to 'teach him how to be a grown-up minister and how to handle market sensitive information'. As for Brown and Whelan, it was, he said, as if they were 'competing in an audition for the role of Mr Toad'. John Lloyd, writing in the *New Statesman*, said that Whelan, who had been instrumental in obtaining permission for the fly-on-the-wall television crew to film in the Treasury, had been the star of the two documentaries and it was the government which would have to cope with the consequences of his stardom. 'Brown is not a great television performer. The star was Whelan: hyperactive, frank, profane, funny; and because the cameras found a star to power the fifty hours of footage from which two hours had to be carved, it stuck with him.' In the *Guardian*, Adam Sweeting said Whelan's antics were enough to give even the public relations wizard Max Clifford sleepless nights. Journalists who had been massaged and spoon-fed by Brown's advisers were castigated by Chris Buckland in the *Express*. 'Those newspapers held up with whoops of delight by Charlie & Co because they had fallen for the line should be holding their heads in shame.' However, despite all these reservations there was grudging recognition of the way in which Labour's spin doctors had taken advantage of the competitive forces which drive those who work in the news media. Brown had realised that as the careers of political reporters depended on scoops, he would have greater leverage if Treasury stories were supplied to lobby journalists rather than economic correspondents.

After having had so much exposure Whelan might have been expected to lie low for a while; but just ten days after *We Are the Treasury* went out, on 17 October 1997, it was business as usual in the Red Lion in Whitehall, across the road from the Treasury: Charlie was having a drink with colleagues and doing what comes naturally, haranguing journalists on his mobile phone. Friday nights in the Red

Lion tend to be quite busy; the pub was packed and, as it was a warm autumn evening, customers had spilled outside on to the pavement. Among them were two young press officers working for the Liberal Democrats, Jeremy Browne and Robert Blevin, who kept noticing Whelan leave the bar and start shouting into his phone. 'I just couldn't believe what I was hearing,' said Blevin. 'It was quite crowded outside and at one point Whelan was standing next to me. He didn't know me but I knew who he was. He kept saying: "Yes, Gordon is ruling out British membership of the single currency for the whole of this parliament . . . No, it doesn't say it in the interview, but Gordon is effectively ruling out joining in this parliament." Whelan was speaking so loud, I just couldn't believe it. It shouldn't have taken a great brain to have realised that any of the people outside the pub might have been political press officers or researchers but obviously Whelan didn't think about it.'

Browne and Blevin realised instantly that the line Brown was spinning was something of a sensation. There had been heightened speculation for some weeks about the new government's likely stance on European economic and monetary union, since an authoritative story in the *Financial Times* the previous month had stated that Britain would join the single currency soon after the 1999 start date and well before the next election. Whelan's Red Lion briefing indicated the opposite, so the two Liberal Democrats immediately informed the party's Treasury spokesman, Malcolm Bruce, and alerted their own contacts in the news media. Bruce was lined up straight away to be interviewed later that evening on *Newsnight*, to react to a story which had not even appeared in print. The *Today* programme, phoned by Blevin at 9.30 p.m. from outside the Red Lion, immediately booked Bruce for an interview next morning.

Whelan had been surfing a wave during Labour's first six months in office. The Chancellor seemed to have no difficulty in grabbing the headlines week after week. His team's ability to manipulate the media had begun to appear almost effortless, and his press secretary obviously thought he deserved a drink that Friday evening after what must have seemed like a normal day of agenda-setting at the Treasury preparing, with the help of their two favourite newspapers, for another triumph. Gordon Brown had given his exclusive interview that day to Philip Webster, political editor of *The Times*; the only other journalist briefed in advance was Trevor Kavanagh, political editor of the *Sun*, but Whelan realised that the political correspondents of other newspapers were bound to pick up hints of the story during the evening, well before the first editions of the Saturday papers were published. He had accordingly telephoned selected journalists to warn them of what to expect, and he was ready to brief the other newspapers on what Brown's remarks were intended to convey. What the Chancellor's personal press secretary had not bargained for was that, armed with their own briefing at the Red Lion, the Liberal Democrats had started their own ring-round and were alerting radio and television newsrooms and programmes which might otherwise have been unaware of the story until around 10.30 p.m., when the Press Association usually starts transmitting information about the contents of the next day's newspapers.

Whelan had no inkling that the Liberal Democrats' tip-off about his own conduct in holding an alfresco briefing in Whitehall would become an integral part of the story. The Friday night regulars at the Red Lion were rarely regaled with hot news from the Treasury and the Chancellor's press secretary had effectively held a news conference about one of the most significant announcements of the parliament on the pavement in Whitehall. For all their contempt for what they saw as the obsession of some commentators with the activities of Labour's spin doctors, on this occasion Alastair Campbell and Peter Mandelson could hardly berate the media for taking an interest in Whelan's novel form of presentation and his frenetic attempts to put his own gloss on the Chancellor's interview. Labour could deny all they liked that they relied on spin; here was proof of it, with the Chancellor's words being openly massaged in order to engineer the headlines.

Not unexpectedly, perhaps, both *The Times* and the *Sun* were entirely on message: in return for the privileged access which they had been given, they had accepted without question the interpretation which Brown wanted placed on his interview. He told *The Times* he was anxious to end months of 'frenzied speculation' and expected within weeks to rule out Britain joining the first wave of monetary union on 1 January 1999. 'We said in our manifesto, and it remains true today, that it is highly unlikely that Britain can join in the first wave . . . If we do not join in 1999, our task will be to deliver a period of sustainable growth, tackle the long-term weaknesses of the UK economy and to continue to press for reform in Europe – in other words to make sure the British tests are being met.' For two newspapers which had previously been highly sceptical of British membership of the single currency, and which had been given exclusive access to the Chancellor's thinking, there seemed no ambiguity in his answers. 'Brown rules out single currency for lifetime of this parliament' was the front-page headline in *The Times*, which trumpeted the end to uncertainty with a leading article entitled 'Clarity at last'.

There was even greater certainty among the headline writers at the Thunderer's popular stablemate, who opted for some timely self-congratulation: 'Sun wins first battle in great campaign: Brown says no to the euro'. Yet, as Whelan was perfectly well aware, Brown had not actually given a cast-iron guarantee that Britain would not join during the lifetime of the parliament: that possibility could not be excluded on the basis of what Brown had said. Hence the need for some less than subtle spinning to ensure the desired headlines.

The one great danger for ministers in giving exclusive interviews on significant policy issues, rather than making a statement to the House of Commons or holding a news conference, is that those politicians and journalists who are excluded from the process take greater delight than usual in picking over the entrails of what has been said. George Jones, political editor of the *Daily Telegraph*, believed his paper had been double-crossed by Whelan. It had made an arrangement the previous July to interview the Chancellor in early October; that interview had already been rescheduled once the previous week, and then Whelan had called it off on the morning that Brown spoke to *The Times*. Jones believed there had been a blatant attempt by the government to win over Rupert Murdoch, the proprietor of both *The Times* and the *Sun*. He thought the collusion between the two newspapers must have been extensive. On Friday the deadline for the *Sun*'s first edition was late afternoon, and as Brown's speech was given such extensive coverage by the paper, it must have received its information from *The Times* much earlier in the day. This likelihood only added to the sense of grievance felt by those newspapers wrong-footed by an announcement of such importance. Brown had been caught red-handed taking advantage of two newspapers which were known to be hostile to the euro and which he hoped would be reassured by the spin which he'wanted placed on his interview. Whelan would be the fall guy, but the Chancellor's own reputation had been tarnished.

Inevitably there was a considerable degree of confusion that Friday evening and it was not until 11 p.m., after he had left the Red Lion and was on his way home in a taxi, that Whelan finally confirmed to the BBC that the headline in *The Times* was accurate. Next morning he said that if BBC correspondents had any doubt about the accuracy of his briefing they should check it out with Alastair Campbell, who subsequently verified the interpretation which Whelan had placed on the interview. However, a slightly different line about the background to the announcement was emerging from Downing Street. The headline over a detailed account in the *Sunday Times* was 'How Blair zapped Flash Gordon'. Andrew Grice, its author, said it was Tony Blair who had finally decided that the government had no option but to rule out joining the euro before the next election. Grice claimed that Blair's overriding concern was to prevent arguments over the single currency overshadowing his first term as Prime Minister. Blair had agreed this strategy with Brown the previous Thursday, and it was decided Brown should announce it. Whelan had suggested giving the interview exclusively to *The Times* to reward it for not having tried to exploit alleged differences between Blair and Brown over the single currency, and Campbell had endorsed Whelan's strategy.

Patrick Wintour, the *Observer's* political editor, believed on the contrary that Brown had been the driving force. He was said to have been 'highly agitated' after a report the previous week by the *Independent's* political editor, Anthony Bevins, which claimed 'a damaging rift' had opened up between Prime Minister and Chancellor because of attempts by the Treasury to 'bounce Blair into a decision which could lead to the early death of the pound'. Wintour said Brown pressed his case for giving an interview to *The Times* to demonstrate there was no split between the Treasury and Downing Street. Much of the 'interview' took the form of a statement faxed from the Treasury. For a pro-European newspaper like the *Observer* there were sinister motives in what had happened. Its leading article deplored the way Blair had failed to lead public opinion and had bowed to pressure from media magnates like Rupert Murdoch. 'The adulation of the tabloids and right-wing press is pleasant; but if courting it becomes a governing philosophy, political inertia and disillusion will soon take over.'

Although it was the third week in October, parliament was still in recess and the Conservatives, who had pounced on the uncertainty generated by Brown's interview, demanded that MPs should be recalled so that the Chancellor could make a statement to the Commons. Brown had little alternative but to give an interview for the Sunday evening news bulletins to clarify what he had said. He promised he would announce the government's position in the House of Commons soon after MPs returned to Westminster the following week, but he was determined not to be drawn any further. 'What was new about what I said in my *Times* interview was that we wouldn't make the mistakes of the Conservatives over the ERM where their indecisiveness caused long periods of speculation... Reports will be made to parliament and I will not be bounced into doing it any other way.'

Monday's papers mocked Brown's efforts to restore his authority. Under the headline 'Whelan whispers, Brown stumbles', the *Daily Telegraph*'s leading article declared that the Murdoch press were easily pleased after having been rewarded for not reporting the alleged differences between Blair and Brown over the euro: 'It seems to be part of Mr Brown's commitment to "openness and transparency" to reward people for not reporting things.' Rachel Sylvester, a *Daily Telegraph* political correspondent, who had spoken to Whelan that Friday afternoon, reported how he had boasted of being 'one of the six most important people in the country'. Brown subsequently complained, saying the remark had been meant as a joke. Anne McElvoy, a columnist on the same paper, said that if Brown needed Whelan to interpret what he had told *The Times,* then he had 'fallen prey to the courtly vanity that regards spin doctors as a kind of retinue, reflecting his glory'. It was no wonder, she said, that New Labour were being urged by their own party members to stop spinning. 'The spin-carousel that turned so gaily and productively for Labour in opposition has picked up a frightening speed in office. Flexible Labour spin worked a treat against the rigid Tories. Devoid of this target, the government spins compulsively against itself.' Colin Brown, chief political correspondent for the *Independent,* spared a thought for Jill Rutter. 'Information chiefs, who have been axed for failing to do their jobs effectively, could be forgiven for relishing the spectacle of the ministerial spin doctors getting into a spin.'

The Chancellor's interview in *The Times* was seen by some journalists as a personal setback for Robert Peston, political editor of the *Financial Times*, whose report in September had sparked off speculation about the likelihood of the government adopting a more positive approach to monetary union. But Peston insisted in his report that Monday morning that nothing had really changed: there was still 'a theoretical possibility that sterling will be a member by the important 2002 deadline'. He acknowledged that his original article, based on interviews with senior ministers and officials in the Treasury and Foreign Office, had prompted stories about secret government plans to hold a referendum on joining the single currency in 1999. Eurosceptic newspapers like the *Sun* had as a result stepped up their attack on the government, and that had led one senior Downing Street official to tell Peston that No. 10 had tried to 'kill the FT story but that it had just refused to die'.

The controversy over the Chancellor's intentions had potentially serious implications that went beyond the relationship between members of the government and the news media, and these were not lost on the newspapers outside the magic circle. Peston's front-page report in September had been well received in the City, where London share values had risen by more than £30 billion. How would it react to the government's sudden apparent change of tack over the euro? 'Brown in a spin over Euro policy' was the front-page headline in the *Daily Telegraph*, which predicted turmoil in the Square Mile as a result of the divergence between what a minister had said in public and what his aide had said in private. Most of the national papers predicted mayhem when the markets opened that morning.

The stage had been set with excruciating potential for disaster. The Stock Exchange had chosen the tenth anniversary of what was known as the 'Black Monday' share price crash of 1987 to ask the Chancellor to switch on a new electronic trading system – prompting the *Sun* to forecast another shares collapse which it predicted would become 'Brown Monday'. The Chancellor may have been saved by the long parliamentary recess from being forced to make an immediate statement in the House of Commons, but there was to be no escape from what would undoubtedly be regarded as the worst photo-opportunity of his short career as a cabinet minister. Like most of the New Labour hierarchy, the Chancellor took great care to avoid being filmed or photographed in unflattering or damaging poses; but for once, no amount of bullying by Charlie Whelan could avert catastrophe. As Brown switched on the new trading system on the morning of Monday 20 October, the massive screen behind him went red, indicating that billions of pounds were being wiped off share values. 'The City gives Brown a shock' was the headline in the London *Evening Standard*, which said the 'massive nosedive triggered by the government's muddled stance over Europe' had wiped £20 billion off share values in twenty minutes.

The savaging which Brown had received in Monday's newspapers was repeated the next day. 'Blood on the carpet in Brown Monday shambles' was the *Daily Mail*'s headline over a report which said that Treasury mandarins were incensed and considered that the Chancellor's 'credibility had been shot down in flames'. Almost all the tabloids were able to justify their claim that it had been a 'nail-biting day' for the Chancellor by publishing close-up photographs of Brown's clasped hands, showing fingernails bitten down to the quick. Even the favoured *Sun* was less than complimentary: under a comment column entitled 'Sultans of Spin', the *Sun*'s political editor, Trevor Kavanagh, said the television image of the Chancellor 'framed by a red sea of falling prices' would haunt Brown for the rest of his term at the Treasury. Kavanagh, in fact, was clearly sore at the turn events had taken – as well he might have been, if the previous Friday's collusion had been as extensive as seems likely. Patrick Wintour, the *Observer*'s political editor, claimed that Whelan had suggested to the *Sun*'s editor, Stuart Higgins, that the headline over Kavanagh's story should be 'Brown saves the pound'; and Brown's spokesman, said Kavanagh, had been 'backed by Downing Street' in insisting that the Chancellor's interview the previous Friday had meant that 'the pound was safe until after the next election'. But in subsequent radio and television interviews Brown had refused to 'confirm this interpretation, leaving journalists who fell for the spin looking pretty gullible'. Kavanagh had rarely been so upfront in admitting that he had been led astray by what he considered was 'a pretty disastrous piece of public relations'. He was sure it would lead to 'a careful reappraisal' of the way the government dealt with the media.

Kavanagh seemed convinced that his own soul-searching had been matched in Downing Street, because next day he reported that Blair had 'moved swiftly' to rein in his Chancellor, whose aides had been told to 'shut their traps' so as to 'end the damaging single currency fiasco'. But if Alastair Campbell had thought an edict of that kind could put a stop to the story, he was mistaken: Blair was about to get caught up in the repercussions of the 'Brown Monday' shares crash and have to endure some of the most damaging headlines of his first six months as Prime Minister. 'Blair rocked by City boos' was the *Daily Mail*'s front-page headline, over its report that the Prime Minister had been 'jeered and heckled' by City dealers who had lost millions because of the government's disastrous confusion over the euro. 'Blair feels heat on Europe' was the *Daily Telegraph*'s version. Downing Street was not about to take this slight to the Prime Minister lying down. The occasion that had prompted these headlines was a visit made by Blair on Wednesday 22 October to the trading floor of the London International Financial Futures and Options Exchange, when some traders were heard giving him a hostile reception; most of the newspapers had based their reports on information supplied by the Reuters news agency, and the following day the story filed by its reporter, Lisa Wilson, was challenged by the Downing Street press office.

In a letter to Reuters' editor-in-chief, Mark Wood, which was circulated to national newspapers, Campbell said Ms Wilson's report was 'an absolute travesty of what actually happened': the reception which the Prime Minister had received was 'warm and friendly' and he was not 'loudly booed by traders'. Wood stood by Ms Wilson's version: it was, he said, an eyewitness account from a seasoned Reuters journalist. 'She was the only reporter present when Blair made his appearance. She can recognise a jeer when she hears one, but could also quote to you a few of the catcalls which were made.' I was working late that evening, preparing an overnight report for *Breakfast News*, and I replayed the television footage of Blair's visit several times. There was quite a hubbub when Blair appeared on the trading floor, and some boos and jeers could be heard quite distinctly; there was certainly no applause, nor any of the fawning behaviour that can sometimes be observed on prime ministerial visits. Despite Brown's harrowing experience the previous Monday, when the Stock

Exchange trading screen went red, Campbell had failed to take account of the potential danger in Blair's visit to the financial futures trading floor, and – somewhat inexplicably, in view of the mauling which the government was receiving in the tabloid papers – he did not accompany his boss. As a result, in his letter to Reuters, Campbell had to draw on Blair's own account of what happened; and on his return to Downing Street, it was the Prime Minister himself who had 'commented to colleagues on the warmth of his reception'.

I had rarely known Campbell to be caught out in this way. The shock waves from the confusion caused by the Chancellor's interview had exposed division and disarray in what hitherto had been a largely smooth-running machine. Whelan's folly in allowing himself to be overheard spinning for Gordon Brown was seen as having rebounded not only on the other special advisers but also on the party's press officers.

David Hill, Labour's chief media spokesperson, told me that he had warned Whelan to be more careful in future. 'If Charlie stands outside the Red Lion with a beer in one hand and a mobile phone in the other, and if he can be overheard by Liberal Democrat press officers, then his downfall is his own fault. Obviously Charlie is having to take all the flak, and that is a bit unfair, because it was a joint operation with Alastair. Although he has been saved from being blamed, Alastair would be the first to admit that he was lucky to have escaped. Charlie would probably have been all right if it hadn't been for what happened at the Red Lion.' Hill could not have been more explicit in his account of what happened. He thought Blair and Brown had made a 'terrible mistake' in letting Campbell and Whelan spin a line to *The Times* and *Sun* when it was not substantiated in Brown's interview. While the 'gap between spin and substance' was not always important in opposition, 'it mattered in government'.

There was little sympathy for Messrs Campbell and Whelan among the civil service heads of information. Mike Granatt, director of communication at the Home Office, who was also head of the government information and communication service, said there obviously needed to be a scapegoat and Whelan was in danger of becoming the sacrificial lamb. 'Charlie has lost all credibility. He's just devalued himself. It was obvious he was going to come a cropper once he arranged for that fly-on-the-wall film of Gordon Brown. No press officer should have done that. But Alastair doesn't seem too displeased by Charlie's fall.' Granatt said the heads of information had realised the Blair government would get into a mess over its public relations at some stage. 'We had no idea they were going to go pear-shaped quite so quickly but it was obviously going to be pretty messy when it happened.'

Alastair Campbell was only too well aware that his own credibility was at stake, and he moved swiftly to try to repair his bruised relationship with the lobby. The damage was more than personal: the privileged access granted so obviously to two of the government's favourites, *The Times* and *Sun*, had offended other newspapers, and the reliability of Treasury and Downing Street guidance had been seriously called into question. In view of the confusion over briefings on the euro, Campbell told the Press Association that he wanted to examine whether there were ways of ensuring that important lobby guidance was given on the record, so that there could be less dispute about what had been said. The root of the problem, in his view, was that journalists could exploit the way in which guidance and briefings were given unattributably, which allowed them to embroider what they had been told with impunity. 'What we are thinking about is establishing a clear system of attribution so that it is obvious to the public when someone is speaking with authority ... Hopefully it will breed a culture in which anonymous sources are less trusted and where denials from the centre are believed.' Campbell said that although he wanted guidance to be issued on an on-the-record basis, he had no intention of going so far as having televised briefings in Downing Street, as happened at the White House in Washington. I had discussed that option with him during a break on the Prime Minister's visit to Moscow earlier in the month, well before speculation about a Blair–Brown split over the single currency had got out of hand. At that point Campbell had been considering a dramatic reduction in the number of formal lobby briefings. He told me that he had achieved so much during the summer recess by not having to meet political correspondents twice a day that he was wondering whether to hold no more than two formal lobby briefings a week. His self-confident assertion that he could somehow wind down the lobby system to suit himself was a reflection, I thought, of the easy ride which the government had been enjoying, and I said that if that were to be done, there would be all the more argument for having those two sessions televised; but he insisted he had no intention of letting cameras into his No. 10 briefings.

Campbell's promise to introduce tighter rules of attribution was a recognition that the Blair administration had only itself to blame for allowing a free rein for so long to its burgeoning band of special advisers who, more often than not, were the very 'anonymous sources' he was complaining about. His attempt to curtail the activities of unidentified briefers and spin doctors was welcomed by Labour MP Gerald Kaufman, who had been just as troubled by anonymous sources when he was Harold Wilson's parliamentary press officer in the 1960s. Kaufman told *The World at One* that Downing Street had to take greater control of the way journalists were being briefed. Although he did not blame Whelan personally, there was no doubt that he thought special advisers and their ilk had to be more careful. 'There are people who believe that possession of knowledge gives them such an authoritative status that they must demonstrate that status by briefing somebody...The first rule of Kaufman's law is only brief if you have something that you need to say and if you brief, say what you need to say and nothing more. I'll be even blunter: keep your trap absolutely shut unless you have got something you need to say to help the government.'

However, if Campbell expected his proposals to win him widespread plaudits, he was to be disappointed. The *Sun's* Trevor Kavanagh said Kaufman's rebuke had been inspired by Downing Street and was a warning to the Chancellor to curb Whelan's activities; but Richard Littlejohn, writing in the *Daily Mail*, believed that by wheeling out 'dear old Gerald Kaufman to read the riot act' Campbell had revealed how peeved he was that Whelan was beating him at his own game. Littlejohn said he had known the Prime Minister's press secretary for years, although 'Alastair has stopped talking to me since I set up camp off-message and refused to take part in the deification of his boss', and claimed that many of the unattributable stories which were being complained about had been floated by Campbell in the first place: the first thing he did every day was 'pick up the phone to whichever reporter's turn it is to be thrown a crumb'. No. 10, said Littlejohn, was 'aided and abetted by a bone-idle and corrupt lobby system, littered with journalists who are happy to play the part of spoon-fed stooges'.

Robert Peston, the *Financial Times'* political editor, thought Campbell's enthusiasm for on-the-record conversations with lobby correspondents suggested that in future he wanted to ensure that 'every government leak should be authorised by him, and that all ministerial pronouncements, on or off the record, should pass the test of whether they condition public opinion'. This, said Peston, was no conversion to open government; all Campbell wanted to do was 'bury stories which do not support' the Prime Minister's agenda.

At the end of what had been a traumatic week, the Treasury finally announced – late on Friday afternoon, once the financial markets had closed – that the Chancellor would make a statement to the House of Commons the following Monday, setting out the government's policy on the single currency. This statement, it said, was to be made at the earliest opportunity so as to stop speculation; and 'no official, adviser or minister will speak on behalf of the government beforehand'.

In a bid to pre-empt Brown's statement, the Conservatives had hardened up their opposition to the euro. Hitherto the Tories had said they would oppose monetary union 'for the foreseeable future'; now, after a heated three-hour debate within the shadow cabinet during which pro-Europeans on the party's front bench had put up fierce resistance, William Hague announced the decision to 'rule out joining a single currency during the lifetime of this parliament' and to oppose British membership at the next election 'subject to the agreement of party members nearer the time'.

Hague was right in thinking that the Chancellor's statement would raise the stakes. In his statement to the Commons, Gordon Brown said the government believed that 'in principle, British membership of a successful single currency would be beneficial to Britain'. However, the government would not seek membership of the single currency on 1 January 1999, because Britain could not meet the five economic tests set by the government, such as the need for sustainable convergence; the Treasury's assessment was that in vital areas the economy was not ready for entry and that much remained to be done. 'Therefore, barring some fundamental and unforeseen change in economic circumstances, making a decision, during this parliament, to join is not realistic.' Brown said Britain should begin to prepare to meet the economic tests so that a decision to join a successful single currency could be made early in the next parliament, and steps would be taken with the Bank of England and business to prepare for entry, including the introduction of euro notes and coins.

Next day's newspapers were in little doubt that the Chancellor had paved the way for Britain to join the single currency within a year of the next election. 'Hello euro, bye bye pound' was the headline in the *Mirror*. The *Sun* went for 'I'll trust people to decide'. Both papers published articles signed by the Prime Minister. To *Sun* readers, Tony Blair proclaimed that the political landscape had been clarified. 'I promised that Gordon Brown's statement would be clear, detailed and definitive. It was . . . And let me give you this pledge today. You, the people of Britain, are the people who will make the final decision.' In his article for the *Mirror*, he acknowledged that the government had taken a knock in the past few days. 'But a few bad headlines are a small price to pay for the strength and stability I am determined to build for Britain.'

At a briefing in the press gallery immediately after Brown's statement, Campbell had said the Prime Minister was confident that the government was united and that it was the Conservatives who would be floundering, unable to say whether they supported the principle of British membership. The deepening unease among Tory pro-Europeans was all too apparent when the former Chancellor, Kenneth Clarke, was jeered by his own side for backing Brown and saying it was inevitable that it would be in Britain's interests to join the euro. Campbell took delight in promoting stories which damaged the Conservatives, and the following afternoon, at the 4 p.m. lobby briefing, he was presented with a gift. Amid reports of renewed turmoil in the shadow cabinet, the press secretary proudly held up his pager. He had just been bleeped, and he read out the message: 'BBC speculates that Ian Taylor might resign from front bench.' His press officers at No. 10 had certainly been quick off the mark, because news of Taylor's imminent resignation as a Northern Ireland spokesman had been squeezed into the 3.55 p.m. television news summary at the end of a report by the BBC's political correspondent David Walter.

Charlie Whelan had taken a back seat during the briefing which followed Brown's statement. As journalists crowded round, he stood beside Campbell saying nothing, puffing nervously on a cigarette.

This unwontedly subdued demeanour did not last many days. Late one evening, when I was sitting alone in the BBC's room in the press gallery, he popped his head round the door and came in for a chat. He settled himself into the chair of the BBC's political editor, Robin Oakley, put his feet on the table, and proceeded to tell me what had happened. Soon the air was blue. 'I have been bollocked from here to hell and back again, all for giving out what was factual fucking information. Yes, I said it was likely the Chancellor would rule out of the single currency this parliament, that was fucking accurate. All week you've been shovelling shit over the spin doctors and you've missed what was going on. What we did was force the Conservatives to harden their position on the single currency, which is what the shadow cabinet have done, so they're even more Eurosceptic than they were. We've triggered mayhem in the Tories and we've made sure business will back Labour at the next election but no one in the media has taken any notice of what's really happened, all you've been doing is shovelling shit on the spin doctors.'

There was obvious political logic in what Whelan had said, but securing what might be a short-term advantage for Labour over the Conservatives was hardly a priority six months into the parliament – certainly not at the price of damaging the Prime Minister's reputation for straight dealing. The ineptitude of Whelan's Red Lion briefing had revealed a darker side to New Labour's well-earned reputation for slick presentation, and the news media's interest in the activities of Blair's spin doctors showed no sign of abating in the face of a continuing shake-out among the heads of information in the Whitehall departments. Since the initial exodus, which had been illustrated so graphically by the pained exit of Jill Rutter from the Treasury, another four departmental directors had made a hasty retreat, either at their own request or under pressure, taking the total to eight. By far the most acrimonious in the latest round of departures was that of Steve Reardon, director of information at the Department of Social Security. According to the *Daily Mail* he was 'fired' by Harriet Harman, the Secretary of State for Social Security, as part of the government's 'concerted campaign to install their own spin doctors in key positions'. Reardon said the ostensible reason for his being required to leave his post was the 'need for a change of style, a phrase I constructed myself at the behest of the department to account for my going'. He said that this was a euphemism for a breakdown in his relationship with Ms Harman but also that he had been saddened subsequently to find that he was not even considered worthy of consideration for other vacant posts because – for reasons unstated – he had become *persona non grata* with the government as a whole.

The sudden departure of Jonathan Haslam, director of information at the Department for Education and Employment, was said by *The Times* to have followed his refusal to put out a press release for the minister of state, Stephen Byers, which he considered to be 'too political'. Byers subsequently denied that there had been a disagreement, as did Haslam, who was critical of what he said was a great deal of misinformed comment about his resignation. He had been John Major's press secretary in Downing Street until the Conservatives were defeated, at which point he moved to education. After working in a total of eight government departments, he had been anxious to make a career break and had been offered 'a fantastic job opportunity' as director of corporate affairs at the London Metal Exchange. Haslam said he had 'got on well' with David Blunkett, the Secretary of State for Education. Another of the departing heads of information had also moved to the private sector: Audrey Nelson, head of communication for the Prison Service, was appointed the new director of communications at the Confederation of British Industry. Jean Caines, director of information at the Department of Trade and Industry, had asked for early retirement.

For whatever mixture of reasons, eight heads of department had left in as many weeks. The rapid turnover in these key posts provoked a sharp difference of opinion between two doughty antagonists, Sir Bernard Ingham and his erstwhile tormentor Anthony Bevins, political editor of the *Independent*, who in 1986 had led what was known as the 'Great Lobby Revolt', when journalists on the *Independent* and the *Guardian* boycotted Ingham's briefings in protest at his refusal to allow his guidance to be sourced to the Prime Minister's office. Bevins was not taken in by what he described as the 'whinge from the Whitehall information machine' about 'hapless press officers being purged by Labour storm-troopers'. He made allowance for a few 'honourable exceptions'; but in his personal experience most government information officers were 'a waste of time, space and cash', their service to ministers 'awful' and to the media 'abysmal'. Bevins sided with Alastair Campbell in his attempts to make the service more professional and to get information officers involved in the initial consideration of policy. Sir Bernard, writing in the *Parliamentary Monitor*, said he was not an uncritical admirer of the information service and at its worst it exhibited all the deficiencies of the public sector and was lazy, slow-moving and reactive. 'But the government information service is not there to sell stories. Its job is to present policy. Nor is it there to build ministerial images.' Sir Bernard sympathised with Jill Rutter in her refusal to 'waste her time' at the Treasury trying to compete with Charlie Whelan, 'the hooligan imported into Whitehall by Gordon Brown'.

Peter Kellner was one of the few columnists to see some value in the role performed by Whelan and the other political appointees. In his column in the London *Evening Standard*, Kellner said a sensible solution would be to provide each minister with his or her own personal, political press secretary who could become a partisan advocate for Labour, leaving career press officers in the civil service 'free to perform the impartial function that every department needs'. *The Times*, however, cautioned ministers against thinking they would necessarily be better served by politicised spokesmen, because journalists understood the subtleties of media manipulation and could graduate the degrees of truth in what they were told. 'Chief information officers have at least traditionally been trusted not to lie; and if Downing Street instructs them to deny stories that are true but inconvenient, this will diminish their credibility. Trust is hard earned, and easily lost.'

An equally critical note was struck by the *Daily Telegraph*. In a leading article headed 'The Campbells are coming', it said Labour would purge the 'grey suits' in the Whitehall press offices at their peril. Journalists would fight back against the 'bullyboy tactics' of Tony Blair's 'shiny new spin doctors' and voters would be angry once they realised their taxes had been misappropriated. 'The public will eventually realise that Labour has smuggled in state-funded propaganda through the back door.' The unease was shared by John Lloyd of the *New Statesman*, who contended that Downing Street's efforts to recast the functions of the government's corps of press officers were feared by the directors of information as 'destructive of their neutrality' and went to 'the heart of democratic governance'. Lloyd said Campbell's letter of September 1997 calling on the service to 'raise its game' had told information officers that one of the key messages to be built into their work was that the government was 'providing a new direction for Britain' – a directive that might conflict with their traditional stance of political neutrality.

The argument about the factors that had influenced the departure of so many heads of information refused to go away. It was given further impetus when Mo Mowlam, Secretary of State for Northern Ireland, became the first minister to speak publicly of her dissatisfaction and to explain why she had wanted a new director of information. In an interview with the *New Statesman*'s political editor, Steve Richards, she made it clear that she had asked for her director, Andy Wood, to be replaced because she felt he 'was not up to the job'. Dr Mowlam acknowledged that she was very different from her predecessors. 'I read the papers and come in and ask what are we going to do about this, what are we going to do about that. That's me. I'm a proactive person and that's a very different style to what they have been used to.'

In the week the *New Statesman*'s interview was published, Wood was named the 1997 public relations professional of the year by the magazine *PR Week*, and the mounting unease among government information officers prompted an investigation by their union general secretary, Bill Brett of the Institution of Professionals, Managers and Specialists. Attempts were immediately made to reassure the union. Peter Mandelson, the minister without portfolio who had overall responsibility for the presentation of government policy, told Brett that 'speculative reports about the politicisation' of the information service were 'entirely groundless'. Nevertheless David Luxton, a national officer for the IPMS, told the *Independent* that union members were still worried about a 'blurring at the edges' and uneasy over attempts to get civil servants to act as press officers for individual ministers. The IPMS had decided to intervene after it emerged in early October that Alastair Campbell had written a second letter to the directors of information complaining about the lack of stories in the Sunday newspapers promoting government policies. Dissatisfied with the results from his first letter, urging the government information service to 'raise its game', he wanted still more to be done. 'I have written to you before about the need to co-ordinate Sunday stories more effectively . . . We are still suffering from a dearth of government policy stories, initiatives, re-launches etc. This is damaging in two respects. First, we are losing an opportunity to promote policy and message; second, we are leaving holes in the papers which are being filled with damaging (and usually incorrect) stories, which then have to be corrected on Sunday . . . There is still a feeling among some ministers that if a story previewing an announcement is given to a Sunday paper, the announcement itself will attract no publicity. In my experience this is not true. Giving an outline story to a Sunday paper with off-the-record quotes can serve to highlight an announcement and generate more interest.'

Campbell's letter set out in black and white the tactics which Labour's spin doctors had used so successfully to sustain their media blitz before the 1997 general election. Their sophisticated techniques for manipulating the Sunday newspapers seemed almost foolproof: the same policy proposals were reworked and relaunched time and time again, often with nothing more than a few freshened-up quotes or some other ploy – like the offer of an exclusive interview – to attract the papers' attention. But at that time Labour's success in reheating the same stories reflected a general air of excitement within the news media at the prospect of the Conservatives' defeat and a genuine interest among journalists about the new policies that would follow from a change of power. Campbell seemed confident that Labour's media strategy could be transplanted into government with ease and that every Whitehall department would be able to generate a constant stream of policy stories, whether genuine initiatives or relaunches. He also appeared to have no qualms about asking civil servants to become anonymous sources and engage in the kind of off-the-record conversations with journalists which, according to his public statements, were causing him concern because of the way they sometimes conflicted with what he was saying in Downing Street.

Campbell's defenders, like the *Independent*'s political editor Anthony Bevins, had insisted that the sole objective of the Prime Minister's press secretary was to make the information service 'more professional' and that he had no plan to 'turn these civil servants into lapdog Labour propagandists'. Conservative and Liberal Democrat MPs were not convinced. They feared that the press officers of

Whitehall were being politicised by stealth. The task of adjudication fell to the newly established House of Commons Select Committee on Public Administration, which decided to initiate an inquiry to discover whether the information service had been asked to cross the line and carry out party political work.

At a preliminary hearing in late October 1997, the retiring head of the civil service, the outgoing Cabinet Secretary Sir Robin Butler, was asked by the Liberal Democrat MP Mike Hancock to explain why so many heads of information had jumped ship. Sir Robin said it was 'a disturbing and unsettling matter' for those involved and he did not wish to hide his concern for them. 'I would like to see them staying on when there is a change of government, but I acknowledge the right of a minister to be satisfied and have confidence in someone who holds such an important post.' He supported Alastair Campbell's desire to see information officers 'raise their game' by improving media monitoring, so as to give ministers a round-the-clock service, and by making more use of new technology. He was sure they would remain impartial. 'I do not think "raising the game" means that you cross the boundary into something which is inappropriate or party political . . . I was not consulted about Alastair Campbell's letter but I am perfectly happy with it.' In response to a question from the committee chairman, the Labour MP Rhodri Morgan, about the 'hassling' of journalists, Sir Robin acknowledged that a subtle line had to be drawn. Information officers were expected to present government policy positively and attractively, but if they overstepped the mark, for example by pressing journalists for more coverage, that would be inconsistent with their duties.

Sir Robin's evidence was upstaged by a briefing from Campbell, who told political correspondents that a full evaluation of the future direction of the information service was being conducted inside the Cabinet Office and that the ideas which had been put forward by himself and Peter Mandelson would be considered. This review was being conducted by Robin Mountfield, the permanent secretary for the Office of Public Service, who, in addition to looking at ways of modernising the information service, would examine the problems caused by the increased reliance which political journalists were placing on anonymous sources. He would recommend whether there should be any change in the rules for attributing the guidance which the Prime Minister's press secretary gave at the twice-daily lobby briefings. Campbell said Tony Blair had ordered the review because 'rumours, gossip and tittle-tattle' from unidentified ministerial and Whitehall sources were confusing the government's message. The Prime Minister had also been concerned to find that Downing Street press officers were no longer being believed when they attempted to deny damaging reports. Campbell insisted that the media's fascination with spin doctors was largely to blame for this. 'We have become too much part of the story. The whole spinology nonsense has got to be put in its proper place.'

Asking a top civil servant to undertake what could be presented as an arm's-length review was an astute move by the new Labour administration, in view of the accusations about politicisation. Campbell had made no secret of his frustration at the lack of centralised control and what he thought was the damage-limitation mentality of government press officers and their failure actively to sell the government's policies and achievements. Nor was he in any doubt as to what Mountfield's objective should be when it came to reinforcing the power and authority of the Prime Minister's press office: 'We have got to reach a position where the voice from the centre is clear, trusted and believed.'

4 **The hardest word**

However annoying it must have been for Alastair Campbell, in the autumn of 1997, to have found himself stuck on the defensive amid the confusion surrounding the government's approach to the European single currency, and to have had to endure irritating criticism about his behaviour towards Whitehall's information officers, he could at least take great comfort from the opinion polls. Biting headlines and trenchant editorials were having no discernible effect on the British public. When asked to give their assessment of the new government, voters appeared to be as enthusiastic as they were at the time of the general election: opinion surveys continued to show, month after month, that Labour's massive lead over the Conservatives had not faltered, and Tony Blair's personal popularity rating had hardly been dented since polling day the previous May. Unpleasant though the news coverage might have been for the Downing Street press office and for the government as a whole, little if any of it appeared to have impinged directly on the standing of the Prime Minister. Another bout of bickering in the never-ending political shouting match over European monetary policy, and an arcane dispute about how best to get the civil service to publicise the government's policies, were hardly the stuff of everyday life. Blair knew that he would be judged on his handling of the economy and, although there was the odd prediction here and there of tougher times ahead, the country was enjoying what the Conservatives claimed was the 'golden legacy' which their government had bequeathed to the new administration.

One of the Prime Minister's great strengths was his reputation for personal probity and strong leadership – two features pointedly contrasted with memories of the nightmare endured for so long by John

Major, as the Conservatives sank ever deeper into the financial scandals of the last parliament. Labour MPs were convinced that there was
no danger of the new Prime Minister and his government being
tainted in the same way, and any suggestion that the tag of sleaze
might somehow reappear from nowhere, pin itself to the front door
of No. 10 Downing Street and besmirch the good name of New
Labour would have been dismissed as far-fetched nonsense. Ministers
were doing all they could to keep the spotlight firmly on the
Conservatives' misdemeanours of the past, in accepting secret funds
from business leaders and even shadier donations from foreign bene-
factors, in order to finance the Tories' election campaigns. Labour's
1997 manifesto had promised that the new government would ban
foreign funding; require the identity of those making big donations to
be disclosed; and ask the Committee on Standards in Public Life,
chaired by Lord Nolan, to consider 'how the funding of political
parties should be regulated and reformed'. At the Labour conference
that autumn, in his first speech to party delegates as Prime Minister,
Blair announced that legislation would be introduced compelling
political parties to make public all contributions above £5,000.

There was, however, no mention in his speech of progress towards
honouring another election promise: Labour's manifesto commitment to 'ban tobacco advertising'. In drawing the conference's attention to the appointment of Tessa Jowell as the first ever Minister for
Public Health, Blair linked her task in health education not to the
pledge in the manifesto but to the 'hard choices' that had to be made
in funding healthcare and the need to ensure that the National Health
Service did not 'lose millions every year because of avoidable illnesses
like those from smoking'. Health campaigners, lobbyists for the
tobacco industry and the heads of Formula One motor racing, who
obtained vast sums in sponsorship money from the cigarette manufacturers, might have spotted Blair's omission; as for the vast contin-
gent of political journalists and broadcasters who were reporting the
conference, it appeared to have slipped past them unnoticed.

Alastair Campbell had spent the first two days of the Brighton conference engaged in what he does best, helping to prepare Blair's
annual address and then delivering the best possible reception for it in
next day's newspapers. Blair's key themes were reproduced again and
again in headline form. 'Let's be a beacon to the world', said the front

page of the *Sun*. The *Mirror* cleared its front page for a photograph of Blair at the conference podium, standing with his fists clenched, alongside the Prime Minister's call to 'build a model nation' for the twenty-first century: 'We can never be the biggest. We may never again be the mightiest. But we can be . . . simply the best.' Campbell had every right to feel pleased with himself. The build-up to the speech had gone according to plan and the subsequent coverage had commandeered acres of newsprint. Seasoned journalists at Westminster had known few equals when it came to the deft foot-work which was required in selecting passages of a speech to be trailed in advance and then determining which of the newspapers were most likely to make best use of them. Campbell could rarely be faulted. He seemed to know instinctively how to raise expectations to Blair's advantage and, once the speech had been delivered and jour-nalists were assessing what it meant, he was unstinting in his efforts to hammer home the messages which Blair wanted to get across. Once the objective had been agreed on, and Campbell knew what Blair wanted to achieve, there was no stopping him. In government, as in opposition, he was having great success in driving forward the news agenda; but, as the weeks turned into months and, as the cabinet began making the 'hard choices' of which Blair had spoken so fre-quently, a new task loomed: where Campbell had yet to be tested was in his ability to identify the compromises or evasions which might prove troublesome and which, if revealed publicly, might backfire and damage the Prime Minister.

Certainly, in the first months of the regime, Campbell had shown few signs of being fazed by the difficult moments which the govern-ment had faced. He had a masterly understanding of the diversionary tactics which could deflect media interest and help ministers regain the initiative. But all press officers dread the explosive news stories which have been on a slow fuse, smouldering away for months, and then erupt into a conflagration that spreads unexpectedly hither and thither, setting off bush fires in its wake. By their very nature they tend to detonate without warning, usually at the worst possible moment, and invariably present a minefield for the unwary. Having been caught off guard, and finding at that precise instant that no one in the relevant government department or party bureaucracy seems to be fully up to speed on the intricacies of what exactly has been going on, the duty press officer faces a dilemma. Is it best to come clean and plead ignorance initially, or do no more than admit that internal enquiries are under way, in the hope of buying time to think things through? Or are there ways of throwing the news media off the scent? Are there threats which can be made to intimidate persistent journalists? Strong-arm tactics do sometimes work as a last resort. As a former tabloid reporter, Alastair Campbell had in the past been on the receiving end of the full repertoire of both stonewalling and intimidatory tactics. Now that he was in the driving seat of the Downing Street press office he could decide, or at least advise, on which direction to take. If the choice was not his own, and he found himself overruled, he would realise that he must not let his own conduct exacerbate the problem. At moments of crisis, when no one in the government has a route map, belligerent behaviour by a Downing Street press secretary or prevarication by a party press officer might only fan the flames. Campbell's aggressive techniques had suited Labour well in preparing for the general election; it remained to be seen how productive they would be in facing the new challenges of government.

The million-pound donation to the Labour Party from the Formula One boss Bernie Ecclestone was an unexploded political time-bomb which the combined mine-detecting forces of Downing Street and Millbank Tower had failed to uncover, and its emergence into public view in November 1997 sparked off an inferno which singed not only the government's reputation as a whole but the Prime Minister himself. For once, New Labour's famed spin doctors had no spin. To begin with their tactic was to bluster and prevaricate in the mistaken belief that concealment might work. But once journalists began picking away at the story, as they inevitably would, all the right leads were there, and it was only a matter of days before the final detonation and the word 'sleaze' was being thrown at the Prime Minister. There was no advance warning, and hence there was no emergency media strategy in place to cope with the aftermath; and yet, as is so often the case when it comes to political hindsight, the tell-tale warning signs were there if only they had been recognised and understood in time.

In making their election pledge to ban tobacco advertising, the Labour Party had taken on some of the world's most powerful vested interests. Cigarette manufacturers had always employed the best lobbyists and marketing consultants that money could buy. Through their multi-million-pound sponsorship deals with sports like motor racing, rugby, snooker and darts they had shown they could evade restrictions on their promotional activities. Nevertheless, in the euphoric first few weeks after Labour's election victory, the new Secretary of State for Health, Frank Dobson, was not going to be content with half measures. In the middle of May he told the annual conference of the Royal College of Nursing at Harrogate that the government was about to publish a bill that would ban 'all forms of tobacco advertising, including sponsorship'. Sports which were heavily dependent on sponsorship money would have to recognise that by helping to promote the sales of tobacco they were 'harming the health of many of their own spectators and viewers'. After the speech Dobson told journalists that it would apply to Formula One: 'My understanding is that if a car is running at the grand prix here, it won't be carrying tobacco advertising.'

Initially newspaper reports said the English Sports Council and Formula One were not unduly worried as they understood the ban would not affect existing sponsorship contracts, which could be completed. But the following month, after the public health minister Tessa Jowell had attended a meeting of the European Union Health Council at which Britain signalled its support for a European directive banning tobacco advertising, the fightback began. Bernie Ecclestone was quoted in the *Independent* as predicting that an immediate ban would result in Europe losing eight Formula One events and that the loss of sponsorship, worth an estimated £40 million, would be a 'disaster' for international motor racing. The subsequent two months clearly saw intensive lobbying by sports bodies, because in late August 1997 the *Daily Telegraph*'s political correspondent, John Hibbs, reported that a 'senior government source' had confirmed that sponsorship contracts which had already been entered into, and which in some cases were scheduled to continue to 2001, would not be affected. 'Labour back-pedals on tobacco sponsorship of sport' was the headline over Hibbs' front-page splash, which said that 'a period of grace' for tobacco sponsorship was being seen in Whitehall as a 'victory' for the sports minister, Tony Banks.

In fact the negotiations were still under way. Ecclestone and Max Mosley, president of motor sport's governing body, the Fédération

Internationale de l'Automobile, met Ms Jowell in mid-September; then, in mid-October, after the Labour party conference, they went to Downing Street to lobby the Prime Minister. A week later Blair had talks at Chequers with the German Chancellor, Helmut Kohl, who announced subsequently that a place would be kept for the United Kingdom on the committee running the EU central bank. Germany and Italy had already decided that the proposed European directive on tobacco advertising was impractical, and the *Guardian* reported later that some ministers believed that 'Kohl's was the key voice which prompted Labour's U-turn'.

On 4 November news of the government's final decision emerged in Brussels, where it was revealed that Tessa Jowell had written to the EU Health Council submitting a draft position paper which stated that Britain proposed to exempt Formula One from the sponsorship ban and would seek instead a voluntary code to reduce the promotion of cigarette brands at racetracks. The government had decided to join other member states in proposing the exemption to avoid both losing its Formula One Grand Prix and damaging the Formula One industry, which made 80 per cent of its cars in Britain and employed 50,000 people in connected industries. Health campaigners were horrified. Clive Bates, director of the anti-smoking group ASH, said the British climbdown was a devastating setback. Motor racing was central to tobacco promotion because 'glamorous and heroic drivers and their fast cars' had great appeal to teenagers. Then, that evening, the story took a sudden lurch and changed direction. Unexpectedly, political correspondents at Westminster found that control of the steering wheel had passed to them from their colleagues in Brussels: Ms Jowell herself had become the top line in the story with what appeared to be a previously unreported conflict of interest. She had, it emerged, a family link to motor racing: her husband, the City solicitor David Mills, had been a non-executive director of a Formula One company, Benetton Formula, until his resignation the previous May, the day after Frank Dobson told the Royal College of Nursing that the government's ban on tobacco advertising would extend to sponsorship.

There had clearly been quite a flurry that evening as the government worked out its response. In his report next day the *Daily Mail's* political editor, David Hughes, said the Department of Health had taken the extraordinary step of issuing a statement at 1.30 a.m. to explain why Frank Dobson and his permanent secretary, Sir Graham Hart, were satisfied that no conflict of interest arose. According to this statement, Ms Jowell had informed the department of the connection when she became a minister, and Mills had resigned as a non-executive director at his own suggestion. Although he remained a legal adviser to Benetton Formula, he had declined to act in that capacity on any issues concerning tobacco sponsorship.

The story had broken in the British papers on Wednesday 5 November, and Ms Jowell's embarrassment at having to reveal her husband's link to grand prix motor racing was only one of the leads waiting to be followed up during the rest of the week by reporters on the Sunday newspapers. Until the government revealed its hand to the EU there had been no mention of the visit which Bernie Ecclestone and Max Mosley had paid to 10 Downing Street in mid-October. Formula One's success in lobbying the Prime Minister, and in persuading the government to make an awkward and controversial U-turn, had opened up an entirely new dimension to the story. The two men who controlled the world's richest sport were no strangers to politics. Ecclestone was rumoured to have been a generous con-tributor to the Conservative Party. Mosley was immediately identi-fied as one of Labour's financial backers and, because he was a regular donor, giving the party over £1,000 a year, he had become a member of Labour's exclusive One Thousand Club. The challenge facing the Sunday newspapers was to discover whether Ecclestone had financial links to Labour.

I was on late duty that Saturday evening when the Press Association started listing the contents of the Sunday papers. They all had follow-up stories. Some were worded carefully, but the *Sunday Telegraph*, *Sunday Times* and *Mail on Sunday* were categoric in asserting that Ecclestone had definitely switched his loyalties to Labour shortly before the general election and that he had given a substantial sum to the party.

Labour's duty press officer that evening was the chief spokesper-son, David Hill, who told me, as I had half expected he would, that there was nothing new in the story. 'The Sundays have been grubbing around on this all day... It's Conservative Central Office who are egging them on and trying to stoke up a story which isn't there... I can show you a message on my pager from the *Express* saying Central Office are asking the paper to demand an official Labour response.' I let Hill finish his diatribe against the Tories and his attempt to put the blame on to the spin doctors at Central Office, and then tried again to see if I could extract any hard information. He said Mosley's donations were 'old news': he had been a member of the One Thousand Club for eight years and his financial support had been in the public domain for a long time. When it came to Ecclestone, Hill would not budge. He said there was no record of his contributing to Labour in 1996. If he had given money to the party in 1997, and if it amounted to £5,000 or more, his name would be listed in the accounts when they were published at the 1998 party conference, but in the meantime Labour's finance department would not divulge 'internally or externally' any information about individual donations. When I protested and said it seemed ridiculous for Labour to suggest that information which it had in its possession in November 1997 was not going to be released until October 1998, Hill told me that he would be pointing out to the BBC's journalists and editors that the 'Labour Party had heard that Ecclestone was extremely litigious' and it would be unwise to link his name to political donations. Although news bulletins that Sunday had no alternative but to stick to the wording of Hill's statement, his attempts to persuade journalists not to mention Ecclestone's name were in vain and the story was given further impetus when the shadow Secretary of State for Health, John Maples, demanded to know more about the possible donations and why it was that Frank Dobson had broken his word and retreated from the ban on tobacco sponsorship. By the following Monday morning, 10 November, Labour were being accused by the newspapers of a cover-up.

As the early reporter that day, I had to explain on *Today* what was known about Bernie Ecclestone's links with the Labour Party. Later in the programme the presenter, John Humphrys, asked the Chancellor of the Exchequer if he could confirm that Ecclestone had donated money. Brown, who had been anxious to expand on a speech he was about to give to the annual conference of the Confederation of British Industry, was annoyed at being diverted. He urged *Today* to wait until publication of the party's accounts. 'We have said we shall publish the list of donations at the appropriate time. Everything should be above board, but it should be done in an orderly way.' Charlie Whelan, annoyed that Humphrys had kept asking questions about Ecclestone, rang me to complain, ridiculing my own contribution to the programme earlier that morning. 'Your interview was classic . . . breathless, unintelligible nit picking and who the fuck is Ecclestone anyway?' Whelan was clearly not the only *Today* listener to be annoyed by my efforts to give the programme an account of what happened: Alastair Campbell gave me a nasty look as he arrived to take the 11 a.m. lobby briefing. Before answering questions he gave a rundown of the Prime Minister's speech to be delivered that evening to the Lord Mayor's banquet, in which, he said, Blair would be returning to the theme that Britain could be 'a beacon to the world'. When asked if he could confirm that Ecclestone had given money to the party, Campbell stuck rigidly to the line David Hill had adopted on Saturday evening. Anyone who gave Labour £5,000 or more did so in the full knowledge that the party operated 'a policy of openness' and would identify the donor in the annual accounts. 'It might be inconvenient for journalists, but the Labour Party's finance department does have its own rules.' Alex Aiken, the Conservatives' head of news, had issued a statement that morning reminding journalists that William Hague intended publishing a list of all donations to the Tory party of over £5,000, so I asked Campbell if Labour would be able to hold back publication of their list until October 1998.

At the very mention of what the Conservatives were saying, Campbell interrupted me halfway through my question – and kept doing so as I tried to repeat it. After failing to finish the question for a fourth time, I changed tack and said that it was a pity the briefing was not being televised because his interruptions would have provided a marvellous illustration for the viewers of what the Prime Minister's press secretary had described as the 'policy of openness' being pursued by the Labour Party. Needless to say, when I was finally allowed to put my question Campbell gave me short shrift and said that, like other journalists, I would have to wait until the list was published at next year's party conference.

Perhaps I was unwise to have riled him at a lobby briefing in front of the other political correspondents, but his reaction had not gone unnoticed. John Williams, the *Mirror's* political editor and one of Campbell's former colleagues, said it was always a mistake for press

officers to show reporters how rattled they were. Although Campbell
had held the line in insisting that the news media would have to wait
for almost a year before obtaining a list of people who had given substantial donations to Labour's election campaign, there had been no
outright denial of Ecclestone having made a contribution, and the
focus of the story had shifted on to the possible reasons for Labour's
equivocation and sensitivity. In an interview for *The World at One* I
explained how David Hill had warned BBC journalists the previous
weekend of the danger that Ecclestone might take legal action if his
name were linked in any way to political donations. By early afternoon the story had already started to slip down the running order of
radio and television bulletins, which were waiting for news from
Boston, due at 3 p.m. British time, about a fresh judgment in the trial
of Louise Woodward, the British au pair convicted of the second-
degree murder of eight-month-old Matthew Eappen. Then, out of
the blue, political journalists were called to a news conference to be
given by David Hill at 5 p.m. in the House of Commons press gallery.

Hill confirmed that Labour had 'accepted a substantial donation'
from Bernie Ecclestone towards the cost of the general election campaign in January 1997. He explained that once the government had
made its decision the previous week to exempt Formula One from
the ban on tobacco sponsorship, Tony Blair had asked the party to
seek the advice of Sir Patrick Neill, the new chairman of the
Committee on Standards in Public Life. Sir Patrick had advised that
the donation should be returned and – Hill said – the party would act
on his advice immediately. Hill would still not reveal the size of the
donation but said Ecclestone's name would be appearing in the list of
contributors who had given the party donations of £5,000 or more
during 1997. He said that Sir Patrick had told the party's general secretary, Tom Sawyer, that although he did not criticise Labour for
having accepted the donation, in order to avoid 'even the appearance
of undue influence on policy' it should be returned and the party
should avoid taking any further money from Ecclestone in the future.
'We received Sir Patrick's advice an hour and a half ago and the party
has recognised the need to take swift action and to say so publicly.'

Sir Patrick was only too happy to give journalists an account of
what had happened. He told me he was surprised at the speed with
which Labour had acted. 'It was stiff medicine. I told them at 2 p.m.

and they announced it at 5 p.m.' Sir Patrick said he did not know the size of the donation at issue, but assumed it was somewhere between £50,000 and £100,000. 'I didn't ask Labour how much money was involved because it would have been the same if it had been a halfpenny.'

Next day, 11 November, the front pages of the morning papers were dominated by the release of Louise Woodward after Judge Hiller Zobel reduced her conviction to involuntary manslaughter. Even so, the inside pages were packed with unfavourable reports of Labour's hurried response to Sir Patrick Neill. 'Blair hands back Ecclestone cash in sleaze storm' was the headline in the *Daily Mail*, which said it had been 'an astonishing development in the cash for favours row.' In a leading article, the paper said Blair had 'naively swallowed' the case which Formula One had made to be freed from the tobacco ban, and the only conclusion a normal citizen could draw from the decision to hand back the money was that the government had a 'guilty conscience' – an impression which it felt had been intensified by the timing of the announcement to coincide with saturation media coverage of the freeing of Louise Woodward.

Far more worrying for the government than the criticism of the leader writers was the claim by *The Times* that Ecclestone's donation amounted to £1.5 million, far more than had previously been suggested. A party spokesman told the Press Association that this figure was a 'wild guess', but when facing questions at the 11 a.m. lobby briefing that Tuesday, the Prime Minister's press secretary displayed none of the belligerence of the previous morning. ITN's political editor, Michael Brunson, asked him straight out if *The Times*' estimate was correct. Campbell said he was not at liberty to divulge the figure. 'I am not denying it is a sizeable sum ... At no stage have I denied that.' He explained why the party had been so keen to seek contributions from big business. 'For Labour to run the kind of general election campaign that we did this year, professionally organised, you have to have money. And we make no bones about it, we wanted to involve business leaders in the fund-raising because of the one-sided impression that it's always the trade unions who give us lots of money.' Campbell said the government had no complaint about Sir Patrick's ruling on returning the money, but it did give rise to serious questions. Did it mean ministers would have to trawl through every decision to see if there was any conflict? He said that in the case of the tobacco ban, Blair had asked Sir Patrick for his advice because Ecclestone was 'so significant' in Formula One. 'But what do we do next? What happens if animal welfare groups give us money, or the trade unions, and then we provide time for a fox-hunting bill or we agree to a minimum wage? Obviously Sir Patrick's committee is going to have to look at party funding from top to bottom.'

Campbell seemed contrite and somewhat weary of the whole business, almost as though he was acknowledging that he was power-less to stop what in terms of media management had become a runaway train, a news story that was out of control. He must have known what was coming next. Sports reporters had been pursuing Ecclestone all day, asking him repeatedly to reveal the size of his dona-tion. When they finally cornered him, he gave a one-line answer and mentioned the sum of a £1 million, a figure confirmed by the party shortly after 4 p.m., by which time health questions had finished for the afternoon in the House of Commons and Tessa Jowell had already left the front bench. Labour said Ecclestone's £1 million had gone towards the £27 million which the party had spent in the two years up to polling day, but it would be repaid. However, if officials at Millbank Tower had hoped their final confirmation of the figure would draw a line under the affair they were sadly mistaken. Wednesday's newspapers were full of fresh allegations of a cover-up. In the briefing which David Hill had given on the Monday of that week, he had made no mention of the fact that the letter seeking Sir Patrick Neill's advice had stated that since the election Ecclestone had 'offered a further donation' to the Labour Party. Under the head-line 'Labour hit by row over cash gift No. 2,' the *Sun* said Blair had only himself to blame for having been 'smoked out' by the newspa-pers. 'Why did Downing Street deceive us for days about the size of the donation? Then last night came the revelation that Ecclestone offered Labour a second big donation after the election ... For a party that revelled in censuring Tory sleaze, these were ridiculous own goals.'

A leaked copy of Tom Sawyer's letter to Sir Patrick Neill was soon being circulated among political correspondents in the press gallery. What it revealed was that the advice which Labour had been seeking referred not to the £1 million but to the possibility of a second donation: 'The position which we have adopted thus far has been to refuse this further donation, but we wish to be advised whether this is a position which we need to maintain. This approach distinguished between a pre-election donation which, of course, was not a factor in the government's decision, which was taken exclusively in the national interest as the government judged it, and the receipt of post-election donations where an appearance of a conflict of interest might be thought to arise.' The unstated implication was clear: Labour had every intention of keeping the original £1 million and would have done so but for Sir Patrick's unexpected instruction that the party should return it. Moreover, the leaked letter had thrown up another line of enquiry: it was only faxed to the Committee on Standards in Public Life late the previous Friday, whereas Blair had said the decision to seek Sir Patrick's advice had been taken two days earlier. A group of journalists from *The Times* were with the committee's press officer, Peter Rose, at 6.45 p.m. that Friday evening when he was telephoned by Jonathan Powell, Blair's chief of staff, and told that a letter in the name of the party's general secretary was being faxed to Sir Patrick from Downing Street. When the *Mirror* showed the text of the letter to Ecclestone, he said it was untrue: he had not promised Labour a second donation. 'It's a million per cent nonsense ... I haven't offered one single penny more than the donation I made last January.' Ecclestone also denied that he had ever given money to the Conservatives; and, in a letter to *The Times*, he said that Labour should be allowed to keep the £1 million and that it was a 'gross, insulting and irrational' restriction on his freedom for Sir Patrick to have ordered Labour to return it.

When I was asked on Saturday's *Today* to describe what was going on and to explain why the offer of a second donation was so significant, I said it appeared that the party's fund-raisers had been seeking a further contribution from Ecclestone for some months. Labour's annual accounts for 1996 had described the continuing attempts the party was making to obtain more one-off donations as part of a 'high-value donor programme', and when I checked this out with Jo Moore, the chief press officer, she admitted that Ecclestone's version was correct. 'Our fund-raising department was in discussion with some of Ecclestone's advisers about a second donation but nothing was agreed.' In my *Today* interview I said that the attempt to secure a further contribution from Ecclestone appeared to have been under way during the summer and autumn, at the very same time that ministers were considering a possible exemption from the tobacco sponsorship ban for Formula One.

My report was subsequently challenged by one of the Downing Street press officers, Tim Allan, who was a special adviser and who deputised in Campbell's absence on issues affecting the party. He said that Labour's fund-raisers had approached Ecclestone's advisers after the election but that discussions took place before any conflict of interest arose. 'When the government decided at the end of October to exempt Formula One, it was at that point that we decided we could not accept the second donation... Listening to your report it seems you are suggesting this is like something from the Nixon tapes... Can't you understand this isn't Watergate, the second donation never happened.' I explained to him that as Formula One was known to have been lobbying the British government to get an exemption since mid-June 1997, the party could only clear up the confusion about a possible conflict of interest if it was prepared to say when the post-election fund-raising had actually started and when it finished; but Allan was in no mood to discuss the matter with me any further. I had already been rebuked once that week by No. 10 over my report on Monday's *World at One* about David Hill's warning that Ecclestone was litigious and that journalists who used his name in the funding context could face legal action.

Jonathan Freedland of the *Guardian* referred to that broadcast in an article on 12 November entitled 'Suddenly the red rose doesn't smell so sweet'. He said the 'bloom was coming off the New Labour rose faster and more dramatically than anyone predicted', and he deplored Hill's conduct in trying to warn off journalists by implying that Ecclestone would sue. 'Downing Street says Jones's account of events is "complete bollocks" – and yet several journalists say Labour issued similar denials to them.' A BBC producer who spoke to Freedland at the *Guardian* later that day, in order to arrange an interview, said Freedland told her that Alastair Campbell had rung him at seven-thirty that morning to complain, but he had replied that if the Downing Street press office wanted to make a complaint it should contact his editor.

Most political commentators were in no doubt that it had been

Tony Blair's worst week as Prime Minister. Downing Street had been implicated in almost every twist and turn of the story and, by being forced reluctantly to confirm what had happened, bit by bit, Labour had only fuelled suspicions of a cover-up. There seemed no way out other than to admit that mistakes had been made; but, with the weekend almost upon them, Labour's spin doctors did not have much time to play with. Alastair Campbell and Peter Mandelson would have needed no reminding that the week's embarrassments would all be raked over again in the Sunday newspapers, which might well come up with further damaging disclosures. If the Prime Minister's press secretary and the minister without portfolio were going to attempt to redirect the story, there was not long to signal their retreat and they would have to create something of a sensation to achieve it.

Mandelson, who had the job of coordinating government presentation, used a series of interviews at the end of the week to pave the way for what would eventually turn out to be a spectacular climbdown. His first appearance was on Friday's *Newsnight*, which the night before had shown an empty chair in the studio to highlight the fact, lamented by the presenter Jeremy Paxman, that for the fourth night running 'no ministerial bottom' could be found for the chair that *Newsnight* had set aside in order for the government to respond to the questions raised by the Ecclestone donation. This was followed by an appearance on the Saturday edition of *Today*, in the course of which Mandelson insisted that the government had acted with 'great scrupulousness and great transparency'. When John Humphrys asked why the government was not prepared to say 'sorry' for misleading the public about Ecclestone's gift of £1 million, he complained that journalists were not prepared to give the Prime Minister any credit for returning it and for deciding that no further donation should be accepted. 'I think there's something very worrying indeed about the desire of some of the media to try to place the Labour Party in the same sort of sleazy context as the Conservatives were behaving. That is not justified, there is no wrongdoing, nobody has been able to claim that we have done anything that is improper or certainly not in any sense corrupt... Are you saying Labour is not entitled to carry out fund-raising? We are a David fighting a Goliath. Where do you suggest Labour gets its funds? We can either go back to relying entirely on the trade unions, or we look at other means.'

Later that morning, when asked by an interviewer for ITN if he was prepared to acknowledge that mistakes had been made in the way Labour had grudgingly owned up to getting a £1 million donation from Ecclestone, Mandelson suddenly became much more conciliatory: 'Yes, it is true. The government has a duty to inform the public. Where those criticisms have been fairly levelled at us, then we must learn the lessons and do better and differently in the future.' The about-turn was finally confirmed when Downing Street told the Press Association at 4 p.m. that Saturday that the Prime Minister had agreed to make a hurriedly arranged television appearance next day. Blair would be interviewed by John Humphrys on the BBC's Sunday political programme, *On the Record*, and would explain what had happened and answer the allegations which had been made.

Campbell had briefed political correspondents on the Sunday newspapers earlier that Saturday afternoon, in plenty of time for their first editions. As was only to be expected, the story led the Saturday teatime news bulletins on radio and television. According to the rundown I was given by the duty press officer in Downing Street, Campbell could hardly have been any more forthcoming in the guidance he gave journalists on what to expect: 'The Prime Minister will seek to a draw a line under the Formula One affair. He will admit that the episode has been one of the worst weeks for the government since the election and that it has not been handled well... He will make it clear that the party's procedures failed and that we allowed the appearance to grow that we were lobbying for cash at the same time as we were being lobbied on policy, and appearances are as damaging as reality. We should have been completely open about the donation the moment the exemption was agreed...We have actually done no wrong, but we have behaved as though we have.'

An hour later I managed to speak to Campbell on the phone to check out a reference in the Press Association's version of the Downing Street briefing to the effect that Blair had not been 'terribly focused' on the Formula One affair and that his attention had been diverted by the latest developments in Iraq and the need to keep in touch with President Clinton. Campbell explained that the point he had been trying to get across was that whereas the news media had concentrated on Bernie Ecclestone and his £1 million donation, the Prime Minister had lots of other things to attend to. 'You guys have been obsessed with this story, but of course I never attack the media, it gives you too much importance.' Campbell was scathing about my interview on *Today* in which I had explained how the party appeared to have been seeking more cash from Ecclestone while Formula One was lobbying for the exemption. 'What did we get from you on *Today*? Shock, horror and you trying to reveal things, but of course that is how you operate in that collective herd instinct you have at the BBC, a herd instinct that we have to live with.'

Notwithstanding his reprimand to myself and *Today*, Campbell was frankness itself when it came to acknowledging that Blair's only escape route, at least in terms of news management, was to throw out some red meat on which journalists could gorge themselves. 'The Prime Minister is aware of the importance of public goodwill. He knows that he cannot take it for granted and that the opposition are saying that he acted improperly. The best way to deal with innuendos like that is to do a few rounds with John Humphrys on TV and remind the people who elected him of the big picture, of better schools, hospitals, jobs and industry, on which the government is delivering.' I was taken aback by the comprehensive nature of Blair's intended apology and to begin with I did not quite appreciate the reasons for Campbell's utter confidence that it would have the desired effect. On reading through my notes I realised that if Blair delivered what his press secretary had told me, it would amount to an extremely personal expression of regret. Campbell had said that Blair wished to apologise because he recognised that his 'personal popularity and integrity' were essential to the government's long-term standing. 'Labour are confident that after the interview, the British public will still see Tony Blair as they elected him: young and principled, with a real understanding of their hopes and needs.'

Campbell's briefing certainly did the trick when it came to the Sunday headlines, generating a stream of front-page reports which helped prepare the ground for the Prime Minister. 'Blair goes on TV to say I'm sorry' was the banner headline across eight columns of the *Sunday Telegraph*'s front page. The *Observer*'s headline was also well on message: 'Blair: Sorry, we blundered', while the *Express* went for: 'Blair: I was wrong', and said in its front-page report that the Prime Minister would admit he had 'bungled the Bernie Ecclestone affair'. The inside pages of the Sundays, however, told a different story, and explained why Campbell had been so intent that Saturday afternoon on trying to blunt what he and Mandelson had realised would be some dire coverage for the party. 'Did you lie to us Tony?' was the headline over a two-page investigation in the *Independent on Sunday*, which accused the Prime Minister of prevarication and of taking refuge in 'a charade of outraged dignity at the despatch box' when he was challenged in the House of Commons the previous Wednesday. 'The question must now be asked: has he forfeited the trust on which the whole grandiose edifice of his new Jerusalem was built?' The *Sunday Times* said Downing Street's 'truth-dodging' had been deplorable. 'It leaves the Prime Minister mired in controversy, groping for answers that his spin doctors cannot provide.' The blame for what the *Observer* believed was a 'faultline in the culture of New Labour' was placed on the concentration of decision-making in the hands of a small clique whose preoccupations were news management, image and keeping the right-wing press on side. 'Blair lacks tough, clever political thugs, in tune with the party's values and moods, whose concern is strategy and policy ... Messrs Mandelson, Campbell and Powell do not possess a monopoly of political wisdom, nor of the right to make judgements about the overall direction of a great political party.' The same theme was pursued by the *Sunday Telegraph*, which considered Blair had become the victim of his obsession with presentation. 'He who lives by image dies by image.'

After the dramatic terms in which Campbell had trailed the interview, I could not wait to discover how far Blair would go with his apology. Whereas I could see him admitting that there had been mistakes in the way he had handled the affair, I did not think he would go so far as saying 'sorry' for taking Ecclestone's money because he had put so much effort into attracting financial support from big business and, as Campbell had explained at the lobby briefing, he was anxious to get the proportion of Labour's income derived from the trade unions down below the 50 per cent mark.

Production staff at *On the Record* had been told only that Saturday afternoon of Blair's readiness to be interviewed at Chequers the next day, and it was apparent from the way John Humphrys shook his hand that he could hardly believe his own good fortune: here was Blair embarking on a hastily arranged television appearance with the viewers having been told in advance that he was going to eat humble pie and apologise to the country for his worst blunder to date in governing the country. No previous Prime Minister had begun an interview in such circumstances; and the tactic of saying 'sorry' could be seen as a high-risk strategy. No Prime Minister who wants to retain credibility can afford to make a habit of apologising to the nation too often, and for Blair to have had to resort to such a ploy after only six and a half months in office suggested a fair degree of desperation. However, in the final months of the Conservative government Blair had repeatedly taunted John Major for his failure to apologise to the country for the misdeeds of Tory MPs, and there was every chance that considerable political kudos could be gained from a well-timed expression of regret. Campbell understood the psyche of the news media. He knew that journalists were frequently driven by a relentless urge to hold recalcitrant public figures to account, and that they took great delight in tracking down those on whom blame could be pinned for catastrophies and mishaps. Once the media pack have forced a climbdown, or extracted an apology, they might glory in their victory for a day or two but then they usually let go of the story and look for someone else to pursue. Therefore, saying 'sorry' is a quick and easy way to satisfy the newspapers and newsrooms, and as a presentational device it can rarely be bettered. It might mean some momentary loss of face, but this is usually more than compensated for by the efficiency with which an apology can draw a line under a difficult or embarrassing story. However, when the moment comes, when there are headlines at stake, there can be no half measures: the hounds have to taste blood, so come what may, at some stage the victim has to deliver the crucial word.

Humphrys took his time going for the kill, knowing that either way he was on to a winner. If, as predicted, the Prime Minister said 'sorry', the interview would be quite a coup in its own right; but if by any chance he did not live up to the advance billing and played hard to get, Humphrys would get his chance, as Campbell had said he would, to 'do a few rounds' with the Prime Minister. After a few opening questions about the Prime Minister's latest telephone conversation with President Clinton, and after Blair had been given an opportunity to reiterate Britain's support for the United States over Iraq and to express the readiness of the two nations to use force against the recalcitrant Saddam Hussein, Humphrys got down to business and asked him how he had got into the position of being told to hand back Bernie Ecclestone's £1 million donation. Blair said he had not handled it well and he wanted to apologise. 'Perhaps I didn't focus on the seriousness of this in the way I should. He made a donation before the election and we thought that he had made a firm commitment to a further donation to the Labour Party... Once we had made the decision on the directive, I said that at that point, that we could not accept any further donations.' Blair was adamant that Labour had been entirely justified in taking Ecclestone's donation and that it had not influenced the government's decision to exempt Formula One. 'No, I am not saying it was wrong to accept the money. I am not saying it was wrong to meet him... What was wrong was that we should have focused on this much earlier and it should not have come out in dribs and drabs... I apologise for the way this was handled... I am sorry about this issue... I should have realised it was going to blow up into this kind of importance.' Although Blair clearly had no regrets about taking the money, he had used the word 'sorry' – although only once, in relation to the way the matter had been managed. No one could deny that he had been at pains to show humility and remorse.

The most striking passage in the interview was Blair's highly personal appeal to the public to trust him. 'I have honestly done what I thought was best for the country...I would never, ever, do something wrong or improper or change a policy because someone supported or donated money to the party. I didn't in this case... I think most people who have dealt with me think I am a pretty straight sort of guy, and I am... In the end the country has got to look at me and decide whether the person they believed in is the same person they have got now, and it is.' The ease and fluency with which the Prime Minister expressed regret, almost as if he were pleading for the public's forgiveness, came as no surprise to Claude Moraes, director of the Joint Council for the Welfare of Immigrants and an aspiring Labour parliamentary candidate. Moraes, who had been a frequent visitor to Blair's office at the House of Commons at the time he was shadow Home Secretary, before becoming party leader, described to me how much he had appreciated the advice and encouragement which he had received. 'Blair said I shouldn't give up trying to find a seat and he advised me always to be pleasant and approachable and to learn how to say sorry. That was one of the tactics he advised.'

Notwithstanding a few snide cracks, Alastair Campbell's advice to the Prime Minister to make a clean breast of it had clearly paid off. Most of Monday morning's papers went hard on the apology. 'Sorry for such a fiasco, says Blair' was the headline in the *Express*. Some of the nationals were more taken by the Prime Minister's attempt to restore his credibility. 'Blair: I am still worthy of your trust' was the *Daily Mail*'s preference. However, the Prime Minister's straight talking did not win over the *Mail*'s columnist Peter McKay, although he acknowledged that most viewers were probably happy with it. 'Blair looked and sounded like a plausible, highly regarded sixth former who, because he'd never been caught fiddling before, deserved the benefit of the doubt on this occasion.' Nor did all the editorials reflect the assessment of the headline writers. The *Sun* said the Prime Minister had played the ace that he had up his sleeve. 'For Blair, trust is a trump card. But one that he should not be tempted to play too often.' The *Independent* agreed, and said the 'trust me' plea which Blair had made was 'that of the transgressor through the ages' and lost currency over time as 'each successive layer of innocence is stripped away'.

A few cautionary words from the leader writers were nothing for the Downing Street press secretary to be worried about. He had achieved his objective: he had taken the sting out of the story, the heat was off the Prime Minister and by the following day the coverage was far less intense and devoted for the most part to the wider issue of whether new controls were needed on party political funding. Echoing Blair's apology, Campbell told the lobby that he wished he could have been more open from the start. 'The whole facts surrounding this case should have been out as soon as this decision was made... the lot, the whole story. In retrospect, that is obvious.' Given Campbell's apparent exasperation the previous week as Labour stumbled from one embarrassing disclosure to the next until the £1 million figure was finally dragged out of the party, I got the distinct impression that he was saying a silent 'I told you so', as though he had known all along that prevarication was bound to end in trouble. The *Observer*'s Patrick Wintour was more explicit, asserting that Campbell had been 'overruled' after he had 'argued strongly that the party should publish everything and admit to the £1 million donation'. Nevertheless, whatever the truth about the advice Campbell had given Blair, and the Prime Minister's response to it, once political correspondents were on to the story Campbell's own belligerent conduct in the first few days of the affair, and indeed that of Labour's chief spokesperson David Hill, did Tony Blair no favours and only heightened suspicion of a cover-up.

The following week Hill admitted as much, telling me that he recognised their behaviour that first weekend had antagonised journalists unnecessarily and contributed to the public relations disaster which ensued. 'My job that Saturday night, when we knew the Sunday papers were on to the story, was to try to throw everyone off the scent, but I failed. I did say Ecclestone was litigious. I know I was turning somersaults. However, I did not say to journalists that Ecclestone had not given us any money although I know I did say everything but that. I'll sue anyone who says I actually denied that Ecclestone had made a donation because I didn't.' A description of Hill's stonewalling tactics had been included in a two-page feature published on 16 November in the *Sunday Telegraph*, whose correspondents, Tom Baldwin and David Wastell, had compiled a day-by-day account of how the government had 'dug itself deeper and deeper into the mire'. Among the documents they reproduced was a letter from Ecclestone's solicitors, Herbert Smith, which arrived by fax the previous Saturday and warned that proceedings would be commenced 'without further notice' if the paper proceeded to 'write and print any article regarding our client which is untrue or in any way defamatory'. Hill had taken some satisfaction from publication of the letter as he felt it substantiated his warning to myself and other BBC correspondents that Ecclestone was 'litigious', but he acknowledged that Labour's strategy of trying to frighten individual journalists and warn off the news media had been mistaken from the start. He considered Campbell had been unwise to adopt an accusatory tone at his lobby briefings and had only made matters worse by arguing with reporters like myself. For his own part, Hill felt he had been hampered by a lack of information. The first he knew of the possibility of a second donation was late that Friday evening when the letter seeking advice was faxed to Sir Patrick Neill. 'What I discovered had happened was that Ecclestone had indicated in May, after the election, that he would make a second donation. Our fund-raisers had apparently been talking to his advisers, but the way I was being told about all of this, as we went along, just added to the problem.'

Hill's candid assessment of the mistakes that had been made, and the insight he had given me into the stresses and strains within New Labour's celebrated team of spin doctors, showed that when it came to crisis management there were still no clear lines of communication, let alone any centralised control over what was being said. When Peter Mandelson proffered his judgement of what had gone wrong, in a speech delivered within days of Blair's televised apology, he too implicitly acknowledged that the spin machine was malfunctioning. He admitted that Labour had behaved out of character, and he sought to make amends publicly for the way the government had attempted to put all the blame on to the news media. 'We acted against our principles, that honesty is the first principle of communications; that good communications are essential to good government; and that the purpose of communication is not to stall or to hide but to put in context and explain.'

Mandelson's philosophical musings on how the spin doctors should mend their ways was a far cry from the immediate concerns of the Prime Minister's press secretary and the nuts and bolts of day-to-day news management when a government was in difficulty; but though Campbell's concerns were of a more practical nature, they homed in on the same central theme. He had expressed his annoyance at the lack of a satisfactory command structure the previous month, after the mayhem which followed Charlie Whelan's briefing outside the Red Lion and the subsequent confusion over Britain's approach to the euro. On this occasion he knew there could be no real excuse for not having had a tighter grip. Downing Street had been in charge all along and the whole story had revolved around Tony Blair and the U-turn which followed the visit to No. 10 by Bernie Ecclestone and Max Mosley. Admittedly the involvement of fund-raisers at party headquarters had been a complication; but Campbell was still a long way from achieving the objective he had set himself a few weeks earlier of ensuring that when the Blair government dealt with the news media, 'the voice from the centre is clear, trusted and believed.'

As the government's disarray over the Ecclestone affair reached its height, Robin Mountfield had been finishing off the report of the working group set up under his chairmanship to investigate the government information service. Campbell, who had been a member of the working group, was only waiting for the official stamp of approval to be put on its proposals before setting about introducing the changes he had in mind. His priority was to make it harder for political correspondents to suggest there was discord or division within the Blair administration. He wanted to stop them taking advantage of the simple but unchallengeable device of playing off conflicting but anonymous sources against one another. He hoped that by getting a clear line agreed, and by going on the record as the Prime Minister's official spokesman when delivering his guidance to the lobby, his account of what had happened would become the established version and all government press officers and special advisers would know that any conflicting or alternative accounts were unofficial, and that they should tell journalists to disregard them. Once he had the go-ahead to tighten up the lobby procedure, enabling him to exercise greater control by undermining the credibility of unreliable and unnamed sources, Campbell believed he would be in a stronger position to press on with his far-reaching plans to modernise the government information service, to 'raise its game' and set it about doing more to publicise government policies.

Campbell seemed to be in no doubt that the recommendations to which Mountfield had put his name would sanction all the objectives that he was seeking to achieve and, on the eve of the report's publication, he could not resist giving the afternoon lobby a taster of what to expect. He said some senior journalists had been consulted as part of the review, and that the changes which were to be introduced would be set out next day in a written parliamentary answer from the Prime Minister. When asked if he was again in danger of upsetting the Speaker, Betty Boothroyd, by openly trailing the contents of a parliamentary reply the day before it was to be delivered, Campbell just grinned and retorted: 'I have never, ever trailed things which should be relayed to Parliament first . . . ' His final words were lost in laughter, but he shrugged it off, asking 'Tell me the last time I did?' and then, without waiting for an answer, passing quickly to a diversionary tactic. He had seen me sitting in the lobby writing down his asides and he jumped in immediately with a reminder. 'Nick Jones, you'd better remember to turn up tomorrow. The Mountfield Report is going to keep you going for years.' Campbell had taken a couple of swipes at me earlier on in the briefing, saying first that one rather boring answer he had given would definitely make it in 'chapter eight, volume seven of Nick Jones's next book', and then, on being asked about an article in the London *Evening Standard* by the defeated Conservative Michael Portillo, which claimed that the 'aristocracy of the government information service had been carted off to the professional guillotine under the direction of the Prime Minister's press secretary', that he was sure that would do for 'chapter six, volume six of another of Nick's books'. At this point in the proceedings, after groans all round, my brother George Jones, who was chairing the lobby, added to the general ribaldry by volunteering a sympathetic rejoinder: 'Nick seems to be getting to you, Alastair?' Campbell, who never missed a trick, sighed wearily. 'I know, I did try to read Nick's last book but I only got to chapter three.'

My invariable tactic on such occasions was to lie low and say nothing. I understood why Campbell wanted to poke fun at me. While he was convinced that he would be able to exercise greater control if the guidance he gave to the lobby was on the record, he knew that such a change might have the effect of strengthening the argument of the handful of journalists, of whom I was one, who had campaigned for the press secretary's briefings to be recorded and televised, an option which Campbell had resolutely rejected and which he knew was opposed by most lobby correspondents.

Mountfield's report, as expected, was entirely on message: it read like a checklist of all the directives which Campbell had already issued during the autumn in his letters to the directors of information. Given the accusations that had been levelled at Downing Street of failing to be impartial, and of politicising the information service, it was essential that the shake-up which Campbell was seeking to push through achieve credibility within the civil service and win the respect of the parliamentary authorities in the House of Commons. The Mountfield Report was instrumental in endowing Campbell's plans with the necessary authority, making a cogent case for modernising working methods and procedures within government press offices in order to meet the demands of a 'fast-changing media world', and insisting that this could be achieved while retaining a 'politically impartial service'. Campbell's desire to be identified henceforth as the 'Prime Minister's official spokesman' was accepted, as was his wish not to be referred to by name, which the report said would build up an official 'too much into a figure in his own right'. Mountfield agreed that the twice-daily lobby briefings should be held on the 'assumption they are on-the-record' but off camera so as to ensure that ministers continued to be 'the public face of the government'. The report also accepted the need for measures to ensure that authentic government guidance, especially from the centre, carried due authority. In his written answer welcoming the report, Tony Blair said the improvements which were being introduced would make the government's information and communication service 'more effective and authoritative' and, by tailoring its development to the 'needs of the twenty-four-hour media world', would render it 'fit for its purpose and fit for the future'.

On arriving in the lobby room that afternoon to outline the effect of the changes to journalists, Campbell placed a microphone and tape recorder on the table in front of him and said that in future it would be his practice to record his briefings. There was no intention of transcribing each session in full, but he wanted a record of what he had said to be available in the Downing Street press office. A report on the guidance that he had given would then be supplied to every government department, and as a result the line he had authorised would be clear to everyone. 'We think this will achieve greater clarity and avoid the position where one anonymous source denies another anonymous source. It will also draw attention to the fact that there are journalists who make up quotes and try to suggest they are coming from ministers' friends or advisers. I hope editors will now question where these stories are coming from.'

Peter Mandelson gave his support to the change in a speech to the parliamentary press gallery. He said it would now be clearer when someone was speaking officially on behalf of the Prime Minister or a government department, and that should enable the public to put spin in its proper place. 'Nobody will be happier than Alastair if journalists reported more words from ministers and demanded less explanation of the blindingly obvious which is then presented as spin.' Mandelson used his speech to reminisce about the days when the 'weapon of spin' was all that he had at his disposal on being appointed Labour's director of communications in 1985. At that time Labour was lumbered by the 'Bennite legacy' and change could come about only incrementally, step by step. 'Spin – or presentation – bought us the time and space to change the underlying reality. There was nothing dishonourable about this ... I must confess, although I hate being described so now, I was originally quite flattered to have the term "spin doctor" applied to me.'

Robin Mountfield was equally enthusiastic about another of Campbell's initiatives: the creation of a twenty-four-hour media monitoring unit, of the kind which the Labour Party had developed in the run-up to the 1997 general election. So many new ministers had complained about the lack of an up-to-date media summary when facing early morning radio and television interviews that a monitoring service had already been established on a trial basis. According to Campbell, the aim of the unit was to keep departments informed as to the stories which were running in the news bulletins and to summarise how they were being treated by the newspapers. An overnight summary would be available each morning, listing the contents of the newspapers and breakfast programmes, and this would be updated after lunch and during the day. The unit would help government departments to deliver a round-the-clock response on the issues of the day, but its staff would not brief journalists nor would they engage in rapid rebuttal.

The part of the Mountfield Report which I read with the greatest interest was the section which set out the steps that were being taken to coordinate media handling across government departments; steps which would, as the report put it, give 'strategic coherence' to the 'bigger picture of broader government themes and messages'. Strenuous efforts had been made by both the Thatcher and Major administrations to coordinate government presentation across departments. In his day, Sir Bernard Ingham had relied on a meeting of the heads of information each Monday afternoon to work out the priorities for the week ahead. When the former Deputy Prime Minister, Michael Heseltine, took charge of presentation in the final years of the Conservative government, he placed far greater emphasis on a meeting held first thing each morning at which the Downing Street press secretary, senior government officials and party representatives went through the day's business. Since the change of government, Peter Mandelson, the minister without portfolio, had followed Heseltine's practice in chairing the 9 a.m. meeting in order to discuss immediate presentational issues. Mountfield said this was a tailor-made forum for allocating responsibility for dealing with current stories and it enabled Campbell to start his day knowing that the lines had been set and would not subsequently require time-consuming clearance with the No. 10 press office. 'This capability for rapid response is firmly founded upon players who are up-to-the-minute on the Prime Minister's thinking and so able to deal with stories confidently and robustly.'

The one surprise in Mountfield's report was the announcement, which had not been trailed in advance, that Campbell was to be assisted by a new strategic communications unit which would be based in No. 10, with a staff of six, and would give him control over advance planning, so as to make sure that the presentation of major announcements was not left to chance and that the government's 'essential messages and key themes' were sustained and 'not lost in the clamour of events'. Once the members of the unit had been appointed in January 1998 more details were given; to the Commons by the Prime Minister and to the lobby by his press secretary. Blair told MPs that the unit would improve strategic planning and would ensure that announcements, launches of white papers and other initiatives were consistent with 'the overall thrust of government policy', making certain that such events were 'scheduled, launched and followed through to maintain impact and to convey the central story and themes of the government in all its communications'. Campbell told the lobby that the unit would stand aside from day-to-day events and coordinate the government's media strategy for the medium and long-term. If Blair was due to make an important speech in a month's time, on education or welfare reform for example, the unit would draw together all the key messages which the government was seeking to communicate on that theme. 'The government must never stop communicating and because we are thinking strategically, it means that if we do have a difficult time, or an individual minister is getting a bad press, then the unit will help us get through unscathed...This is a gap in the government's armoury and the unit will make sure departments drive through the bigger strategic messages.'

Of the unit's staff of six, two were politically committed journalists: David Bradshaw, a former political correspondent on the *Mirror* who had worked at the Labour Party's media centre at Millbank Tower during the election campaign, and Philip Bassett, a former industrial editor of *The Times* who was known to have given Blair advice in the past and whose partner, Baroness Symons, was parliamentary under-secretary of state at the Foreign Office. Bradshaw and Bassett were both prolific writers and their former colleagues in the lobby knew that their great value to Campbell would be in helping him to sustain the seemingly never-ending flow of articles which were appearing in newspapers under the by-lines of Tony Blair and other senior ministers. When teased about his apparent inability to cope with the voracious appetite of the press and the need to employ more newspaper hacks in Downing Street to churn out Blair's columns in newspapers like the *Sun* and *Mirror*, Campbell took it all in good part. 'Yes, that's right. David Bradshaw will be like a departmental word machine. If anyone wants 600 words on x, y or z, whether it's the *Western Mail* or any other paper, then David can do it.' Control, however, would be maintained: when the lobby inquired who in No. 10 would have the task of keeping Bradshaw and Bassett in check and perform the unenviable chore of subbing down all their innumerable articles, Campbell admitted rather sheepishly that this would be his responsibility.

Some months later, after the 1998 budget, articles appeared in 120 local newspapers under the by-line of the Chancellor of the Exchequer, Gordon Brown, each tailored to address local issues. It was rumoured that Bradshaw had written them all. Later that week, the *Observer*'s gossip columnist Demon Ears spotted the 'balding, brooding figure' of Bradshaw in Downing Street and remarked that he looked exhausted, despite being 'famed for his ability to churn out the words in double-quick time'. Philip Bassett, who had always specialised in reporting labour and industrial affairs, told me a month after joining the unit that there was a tremendous pace to the work there. 'In my first week in No. 10 I saw policy papers going across my desk which would have been front-page leads in any newspaper, but you have to restrain yourself, and damp down your natural instincts as a reporter. Of course you mustn't lose your journalistic sharpness because you've got to know how things will play in the news media.' He seemed to have lost the cynical detachment that marks out most journalists; indeed, I was struck by how committed and engaged he seemed to be, as though he must have wanted for some time previously to contribute to the New Labour project. 'Yes,' he said, 'it is the right thing for me... I wanted to do something positive and once I agreed to join the unit things moved very fast, but that's what happens under Blair.' Bassett said the great challenge to the unit was to think how policy and presentation could mesh together. He cited as an example the problem which the new government had encountered over pit closures when it was known for some months that the coal contracts with the power stations were coming up for review. 'In opposition Labour were very good at thinking ahead, and working out in advance what the presentational problems or opportunities might be. You can't always do that in government because everyone is so busy, so it's right to have an arm's-length unit, that is separate from the press office and the policy unit, and which can think through what's coming up.'

Bradshaw and Bassett both had the status of special adviser but, unlike Charlie Whelan and his ilk, they did not give out information or talk about their work to journalists. On one occasion, shortly after his appointment, I did see Bassett hovering outside No. 10, listening in to a briefing being given to journalists by the TUC's head of campaigns, Nigel Stanley, about talks between Blair and a TUC delegation, but such sightings were rare. So strict was the code of confidentiality within the unit that attempts by former colleagues to speak to Bradshaw or Bassett on the telephone were rebuffed by the No. 10 switchboard, which would not put through reporters' calls. The contrast could hardly have been more marked with most other special advisers, who were only too keen to brief the news media on what their ministers were doing. Many of them, indeed, had been so forthcoming and talkative that their activities had merited investigation by the Mountfield working group. It found that in some departments there had been a breakdown in effective coordination between the special advisers and the civil service press officers. Under a code of conduct which Tony Blair had agreed shortly after the new government had taken office, the special advisers could engage in political advocacy where the interests of 'the government and the party overlap', but only in relation to activity that involved the 'development of policy and its effective presentation'. Ministers were urged to ensure their advisers and information officers developed a 'trusting and confident relationship with each other'. Once a minister had endorsed the message to be delivered, there should be agreement on the 'lines to take' and one side should not keep the other in ignorance about statements, guidance or briefings. Mountfield had noted in his report that certain senior journalists had lamented the loss of the impartial and trusted information service which had been provided in the past by some government departments; but, except for observing that 'some press offices can be a less reliable reflection of ministers' views than special advisers', the working group had not taken any further steps to investigate the complaints and did not think them worthy of further comment.

The whole thrust of its report was directed towards modernising the information service and instructing departments how to deliver the government's message in an age when the news media were 'diversifying and multiplying as never before'. Guidance on raising professional and technical standards was supplied in a newly revised manual entitled *Press Office Best Practice*, which was published as an annexe to the report and set out in the clearest terms how the information service would be expected, in Campbell's words, to 'raise its game'. Press releases should be structured to 'grab the agenda'. As white papers and other documents approached release, civil service information officers should be poised to start a 'ring-round' of newsrooms so as to stimulate advance interest in the forthcoming publication. They should begin 'trailing the announcement during the previous weekend'. Departments were warned about the need to avoid breaching parliamentary protocol: an 'announcement of new policy must always meet the needs of parliamentary propriety' and reach all MPs via an answer or statement. Ministers were also reminded of the need to 'uphold the impartiality of the civil service' and to refrain from asking civil servants to act in a way which would conflict with the civil service code. Nevertheless there was no mistaking the path which civil service press officers were being urged to take: the information service would have to become proactive and go on the offensive, to undertake the aggressive selling of the government's policies and achievements.

Amid all the exhortations to information officers to 'grab the agenda' and 'stimulate interest' in the announcements which the government was due to make, there was no advice as to how this task should be divided up between the special advisers who could engage in 'political advocacy' and the civil servants who could not 'join the political battle'. If the task of 'trailing the announcement during the previous weekend' is to be accomplished with any degree of success, it has to excite the Sunday press, a feat which requires a fair degree of stealth and cunning. Competition is so intense that Sunday newspapers demand exclusives, and the temptation is to hype the story by applying political spin in the hope that this will interest journalists, engage the attention of their editors and guarantee a good showing. Potentially underhand activity of this nature can present a dilemma for civil servants. Should they object if they think the special advisers have gone over the top? Whose responsibility is it within the department to police the hard sell that is required to grab the agenda? Should there be more reflection on the complaints made by the Speaker and opposition parties about the tactic of trailing government announcements?

On these issues the Mountfield working group was entirely silent. Its report made no mention whatsoever of the reliance which the Labour government has placed on exploiting the Sunday newspapers, nor did it examine or assess the techniques which have to be used when seeking to pressurise Sunday journalists and influence the stories they write. Indeed, the report's most glaring omission was its total failure to acknowledge the existence of the exclusive and separate lobby briefings which are held solely for the Sunday newspaper correspondents. The Sunday lobby is one of the tightest closed shops in British journalism, and as all broadcasters, news agency reporters and daily newspaper correspondents are excluded from it, the rest of the news media have no way of verifying the briefings given to Sunday journalists in the run-up to the weekend about current political stories or forthcoming announcements.

Perhaps there was no reason why Robin Mountfield, as the permanent secretary for the Office of Public Service, should have involved himself with the concerns of aggrieved journalists who consider their ability to obtain objective information has been put at risk because of the preferential treatment and access offered to one section of the news media and not another. Presumably he was unaware of New Labour's favourite technique of providing one newspaper with an exclusive article or interview which, with the right spin, is then destined to become the only version that is available to all other news outlets. The very existence of the working group was only revealed publicly in the wake of the confusion surrounding the Chancellor of the Exchequer's remarks about the timetable for joining the European single currency, information which was supplied exclusively to what at the time were considered to be Gordon Brown's two favourite newspapers, *The Times* and the *Sun*. If Mountfield thought any lessons were to be learned from that ill-fated attempt to trail an announcement and grab the agenda, he obviously felt they were not worth sharing with the rest of the civil service.

My conclusion on reading the working group's recommendations was that the media strategies which New Labour's spin doctors had finessed in opposition were destined to become standard practice in government. It seemed to me that the working group had failed to put in place the safeguards that would be needed to 'uphold the impartiality of the civil service' and that it had ignored the need to ensure equal treatment for all sections of the news media, which had to be regarded as one of the foundation stones for a policy of openness. The explanation for these failures and omissions seemed pretty obvious. Heightened competition within the news media has suited Alastair Campbell and his legion of special advisers. They wanted the maximum freedom to go on exploiting those news outlets and journalists who, in return for privileged access and information, were prepared to apply the spin which the government wanted. Mountfield appeared to have done Campbell's bidding: civil servants would become the spin doctors' accomplices and the Prime Minister's press secretary would have free rein to go on manipulating the news media as best as he could in the service of Tony Blair.

5 Of books and businessmen

Alastair Campbell's unceasing efforts to control and centralise what was being said about the government on Tony Blair's behalf were predicated on the assumption that the Prime Minister's closest colleagues in the cabinet would respect that discipline and refrain from speaking out of turn or fuelling speculative and damaging stories in the news media. No group of ministers could be expected to hold the line for ever; but if there was no shared sense of responsibility among those at the very top of a government, then disaster beckoned.

However much senior politicians like to pretend that they can survive without lashings of favourable publicity, the reality is that almost all of them avidly devour their press cuttings. They do want to know precisely what is being said about them on radio and television and whether their speeches or announcements have succeeded in securing a prominent position in the news bulletins. For Labour's rising stars and future ministers, exposure in the media had been one of the few consolations available to them during their long years in opposition. Once in government, however, publicity-seeking politicians usually have to learn the hard way that they must moderate their headline-grabbing behaviour. The interviews and access which they happily offered to journalists while in opposition cannot be controlled so easily once they have ministerial status, and whereas the odd slip-up might not have mattered in those bygone, free-wheeling days, the same risks cannot be taken once every word and expression is going to be pored over and analysed for the slightest sign of a shift in government policy. Young and inexperienced ministers consequently tend to be warned to keep their distance from all journalists unless they are seeking to promote a clearly defined objective. Their older and wiser colleagues tend to be just as wary, and even when they do cooperate with the media on less formal occasions and invite questions from newspaper reporters or broadcasters they are careful not to stray off their subject, get trapped into talking about issues which are way outside their field of responsibility or let slip news of any indiscretion by one of their team-mates. The greatest taboo within any new government is to say or do something which could be seen as undermining a fellow minister.

In the afterglow of an election victory the bond of collective achievement and responsibility is strong, and the shared goal of delivering party policy is usually enough to overcome even deep-seated personal differences. Prime Ministers like to believe that the thrill and responsibility of ministerial office should temper, at least temporarily, the appetite of individual ministers for personal publicity. In 1997, this hope proved somewhat optimistic – though the first hundred days of the new Labour government, packed as they were with announcements and initiatives, could hardly have been any more stimulating. Gordon Brown, newly installed as Chancellor of the Exchequer, had filled his early days at the Treasury with a succession of trumpeted innovations, most famously his instant grant to the Bank of England of the power to fix interest rates, which had taken the financial establishment by storm; and, within two months of taking office, he had had to deliver Labour's first budget. Yet, although Brown was already commanding huge amounts of publicity, he craved even more exposure. Egged on by his indiscreet press secretary, Charlie Whelan, and apparently oblivious to the dangers of cooperating in media enterprises which would take months to complete and might come to fruition in the future at moments of maximum embarrassment over which he would have absolutely no control, he had spent his initial weeks in the Treasury happily playing to the cameras for a fly-on-the-wall television documentary that rebounded on him in the autumn with highly damaging consequences.

Brown was also cooperating with a venture which he hoped would provide far weighter recognition of the contribution he had made to Labour's 1997 election victory. In the heady months of early summer, when it seemed the new government could do no wrong, the new Chancellor was only too pleased to grant interviews to the *Independent on Sunday*'s political correspondent, Paul Routledge, who was working on what they both hoped and believed would be a political masterstroke – the first authorised biography of one of the big hitters in the new cabinet. Routledge knew his book would be eagerly awaited. Brown's decision to stand aside for Tony Blair in the 1994 Labour leadership election, in circumstances which had not been fully explained, continued to provoke endless speculation in the news media, which Brown had done little to damp down. Caught off guard by journalists whom he had known for years, he could still appear moody and churlish; his brooding sense of unhappiness seemed to well up despite his success in achieving one of the great offices of state and having been credited as New Labour's foremost election tactician. For some reason Brown was incapable of relaxing his slavish application to the task of self-promotion. In his early years on Labour's front bench, Brown's journalistic output had been prolific. He was by far the most responsive and cooperative senior politician I had ever met and, as Labour embarked on the long haul back to government, the party's publicity staff were unable to keep up with his avalanche of press releases, newspaper articles and non-stop television and radio appearances. I wondered whether he was trying to prove to himself now that, although he might have lost out to Blair and failed to get the number one job, he was still top dog when it came to exploiting the news media.

Alastair Campbell had every reason to be wary of what might be afoot in the Treasury, even perhaps to suffer the odd nightmare over the next publicity wheeze Charlie Whelan might be about to concoct. Nevertheless, as 1997 drew to a close, and as Blair's ministers recovered their poise after the shambles over the European single currency and the humiliation of having had to hand back Bernie Ecclestone's £1 million donation, the Prime Minister's press secretary could have been forgiven for thinking that Messrs Brown and Whelan must have made some New Year resolutions and were not going to spring any more public relations disasters on an unsuspecting government. Labour's first eight months in power had been a rollercoaster ride: the highs had been tremendous, but on the occasions when something had gone wrong they had hit the ground with a bump. Campbell's own ability to bounce back in such circumstances, and his imagination and flair in finding new ways to promote Tony Blair, had never ceased to amaze me. What beforehand might have given every indication of being a rather predictable news conference could suddenly, if Campbell was involved, be turned on its head. Like a magician he could go on pulling rabbits out of the hat and smile with satisfaction as the journalists went scurrying back to their offices to file stories which had come at them out of the blue.

Downing Street briefings the day before publication of the New Year Honours list provide a wealth of material, but because of a strict embargo, forbidding publication of the details until after midnight, they tend to be pretty relaxed occasions. Political correspondents had been primed in late December 1997 to expect the announcement of honours for service personnel and royal household staff who had been involved in arranging the funeral of Diana, Princess of Wales, but we were unaware, or had overlooked the fact, that the Prime Minister had asked for the New Year Honours to do more to reflect excellence in public service and that the priority for his first list would be to acknowledge the importance of education. Campbell revealed that out of a total of 976 awards, fifty-eight honours would go to education and that for the first time three serving head teachers in state schools would get knighthoods: as he put it, 'Sirs for Sirs'. He could see that he had caught our interest. When I asked if Blair intended there to be a 'people's honours list' every year, Campbell pulled a straight face and told me that I should stop believing everything I read in the newspapers. Emboldened by his good humour, I asked if there was any chance we could refer to the knighthoods for head teachers in broadcasts that afternoon and evening, looking ahead to publication of the list the next day. To my surprise he readily agreed – but only on condition the names were kept under embargo. Campbell had jumped at the chance to set the agenda once again; and, as I realised afterwards, he was obviously delighted to get as much publicity as he could for the boost to head teachers after the criticism the Prime Minister had attracted from the teaching profession over the harsh words that he had spoken in the government's drive to raise classroom standards, and the unease prevailing about Blair's strong personal support for the controversial work of the chief schools inspector, Chris Woodhead.

The next morning, most of the tabloids headlined the knighthood conferred on Elton John in recognition of his rendition of 'Candle in the Wind' at Diana's funeral, but the *Guardian* duly gave priority to the awards for head teachers under the headline 'Blair's new class of

honour'. The Prime Minister and his family were seeing in the New
Year in the Seychelles, where they enjoyed a week's holiday and were
entertained to dinner by Richard Branson, head of the Virgin organisation; but Campbell had made sure that the Prime Minister's interests at home were not overlooked, and the headline over a by-lined
column in the country's biggest-selling popular newspaper was a
reminder that business was going on as usual: 'Tony Blair sends a
message to *Sun* readers from the Seychelles'. The accompanying
leading article could hardly have been any more flattering: 'The *Sun*'s
biggest wish today is that the Prime Minister who so inspired us in
1997 will carry the nation to greater heights in 1998.'

Campbell's enslavement to the world of *Sun*speak was total. His
ability to think and write in tabloid terms was of incalculable help in
explaining the government's intentions in language which was acces-
sible to the general public. Once he had found a way of encapsulating
the issue of the moment in a populist expression, or of working in an
allusion to a popular film or event, the key phrases would turn up at
lobby briefings and then be used in the Prime Minister's speeches and
newspaper columns. Blair's first major engagement in early January
was to be an official visit to Japan, providing Campbell with an
opportunity to try his hand at a *Sun*-style makeover for the Japanese
Prime Minister, Ryutaro Hashimoto. The trip had been preceded by
renewed demands from British former prisoners of war for compen-
sation for their suffering in Japanese labour camps. Although Blair
had indicated in advance that he did not wish to discuss the ex-
servicemen's financial claims when he met Hashimoto, he promised
to renew Britain's demand for an apology, which inspired the *Sun*'s
political editor, Trevor Kavanagh, to suggest to the Japanese that this
could be done through the columns of his newspaper. Campbell
instantly seized on the idea, and the possibility of using a signed article
in the *Sun* to apologise to the war veterans was the first subject the
Prime Minister discussed at his forty-five-minute meeting with
Hashimoto. Blair's departure from Tokyo was delayed for twenty
minutes as officials of the two governments discussed the precise text.
According to the *Daily Telegraph*'s chief political correspondent,
Robert Shrimsley, the 'final version was faxed to the British Prime
Minister's plane over Northern Siberia'. The next day Kavanagh had
his front-page splash under the headline: 'Japan says sorry to the *Sun*'.

Above a photograph of the two premiers shaking hands, the strap headline trumpeted Kavanagh's scoop: 'Japanese Premier writes for the rising *Sun*'. The piece was said to be Hashimoto's 'first article for any newspaper in the world' and a tribute to the *Sun*'s eleven million readers, who were seen in Japan as 'the pulse of the British public'.

Sharp-eyed journalists were not fooled: they instantly detected the guiding hand of Campbell in the praise the Japanese Prime Minister heaped on his British counterpart: 'Tony Blair and I are both determined to achieve a more compassionate yet efficient society and to take the tough decisions required. He is a new star on the world stage ... Livingstone, Darwin and Weston, the discoverer of Japan's alpine beauty, were some of my childhood heroes. I always wondered what it was about Britain that gave birth to so much talent.' But Robert Shrimsley's account in the *Daily Telegraph* of what had gone on behind the scenes as 'Blair's aides ghosted Hashimoto's apology' and arranged for the article to be 'infused with some of the favoured phrases of Alastair Campbell' resulted in a prompt letter to the paper's editor from the Prime Minister's press secretary. Campbell insisted the article was Kavanagh's idea, but he did own up to the help he had given: 'While it is true that I advised the Japanese about the *Sun*, its style, and the way such an article might be expressed, and while it is also true that there were a number of subsequent drafts and discussions, the words were very much under Hashimoto's total control.' Campbell's modesty in steering Hashimoto towards celebrated phrases like 'tough decisions' and 'a more compassionate yet efficient society' was too much for the *Guardian*: 'The government of Japan are not the only ones to owe Alastair Campbell. The English language itself is in his debt.'

Blair's visit to Japan yielded a wide variety of front-page stories for the correspondents who went on the trip. Charles Reiss, the London *Evening Standard*'s political editor, had the front-page splash for his account of how the Prime Minister had stayed up until 3 a.m. making telephone calls from Japan in 'a night of frantic long-range diplomacy' to save the Northern Ireland peace talks. Other newspapers headlined Blair's promise, in a speech to Japanese businessmen, to go 'the full Monty' in his attempts to modernise the British economy and to push through the government's plans to reform the welfare state. Blair's reference to the film of that name was particularly timely as it was just about to open in Japan. Ewan MacAskill, the *Guardian's* chief political correspondent, said the mainly Japanese audience laughed immediately when Blair said that when it came to putting the British economy on a secure footing for the long term, 'we intend to go, to use the vernacular, the full Monty'. Blair added a helpful footnote, explaining that the film's title was 'a very English expression . . . an expression of absolute determination'.

The Prime Minister was well aware just how much determination and persistence would be required if the government was to overcome opposition to its plans to reform social security, and a concerted attempt to build up interest in his mission to sell the idea of welfare reform had begun. To lay the ground for his intended overhaul of the system, Blair was to take part in a 'welfare roadshow', touring the country to explain personally why the social security system was not helping the poorest people in Britain. Campbell made sure that the Prime Minister took full advantage of an opportunity to trail this scheme when he was interviewed for *Breakfast with Frost* in Tokyo before his departure. Blair told viewers: 'I shall go out and fight for my position and say what I believe in.'

On the return flight from Tokyo, Campbell briefed reporters on the 'welfare roadshow'. It was hoped the new campaign would repair the damage which had been inflicted on the government by the severe mauling ministers had experienced the previous month, in December 1997, when forty-seven Labour MPs defied a three-line whip to vote against the decision to cut the rate of child benefit for new claimant lone parents. The revolt was the biggest since Labour had been elected and far larger than the cabinet had anticipated – though Blair had been given full warning of the depth of backbench unease in a letter sent to him by the Labour MP Chris Mullin, backed by the signatures of over 120 of his fellow MPs.

As the day of the vote approached, Campbell's deputy, Tim Allan, insisted that the story had been completely over-hyped. He told the lobby that the government had no intention of withdrawing the benefit cut for new single mothers. 'The idea there is going to be a three-figure rebellion is fantasy.' David Hill, the party's chief spokesperson, was equally dismissive, predicting that at most only eight or nine Labour MPs would rebel. The vote was to take place on the evening of 10 December; early that afternoon there were two resignations in protest at the government's treatment of single parents. Malcolm Chisholm, the Scottish Office Minister for Local Government and Transport, resigned from the front bench and Gordon Prentice gave up his unpaid job as parliamentary private secretary to the Minister of State for Transport, Dr Gavin Strang. By the 4 p.m. lobby briefing the Prime Minister's office was having great difficulty playing down the size of the imminent revolt. Nevertheless Campbell remained combative when I asked what he thought the government would do in the face of a tightly knit group of Labour MPs who seemed prepared to defy a three-line whip. 'I don't agree with the suggestion that they have safety in numbers. Any Labour MP who believes the response of the chief whip might be lessened by the fact there might be more voting against than less should think again.' I had predicted in a broadcast on *The World at One* that several parliamentary private secretaries might resign rather than vote with the government and I could sense Campbell's irritation with my question. 'I suppose we're now going to have to put up with Nick Jones getting all excited about this again on the *PM* programme and hear of the extraordinary developments he's witnessed as parliamentary private secretaries talk to their ministers.' I made no response, but thought his attempt to rubbish my report was a sure sign that the government was in trouble.

The scale of the subsequent rebellion was far greater than the figures alone suggested. In addition to the forty-seven who had voted against the government, another fifty-seven Labour MPs had abstained, of whom fourteen had indicated their defiance publicly by remaining in their seats when the division was called. After their failure to support the government two more parliamentary private secretaries, Michael Clapham and Neil Gerrard, resigned, and a third, Alice Mahon, was sacked.

Late that evening there was considerable speculation in the members' lobby as to whether the chief whip, Nick Brown, would be able to take disciplinary action against such a large group of rebels. Initially there were suggestions that they would each be called in to be interviewed, but Clive Soley, chairman of the Parliamentary Labour Party, assured me that he did not think action would be taken because so many Labour members were involved. His assessment proved to be correct. Later, Nick Brown sought to calm tempers and promised he would not launch a wave of reprisals. Dennis Skinner told me that the whips had been powerless because they could not blame the revolt entirely on the left as Tony Blair had hoped. Of the forty-seven rebels, twenty-two were members of the left-wing Socialist Campaign Group; but the other twenty-five were drawn from right across the party. Skinner thought this breadth of opposition showed the extent of anger on the back benches; and he said that he knew the government was worried because he had seen Peter Mandelson briefing journalists in the members' lobby late that evening, looking 'particularly evil'.

The revolt was a personal setback for the Secretary of State for Social Security, Harriet Harman, whose refusal to reconsider the benefit reduction had angered many MPs. On the afternoon of the vote she had done a series of BBC interviews and when I spoke to her in the Millbank studios she had no qualms about the looming confrontation. She rejected a complaint by Clive Soley that if only she had given some advance warning and had consulted more widely within the party, a damaging vote could have been averted. 'I don't think we could have avoided this. The trouble is some Labour MPs don't like facing up to hard choices and it's a good job I'm having to do it because no one has more experience of this than me. History will be on my side. In a few years' time we'll think it right that more single mothers should go to work and we'll wonder what we were arguing about.'

Ms Harman's resolute stand was reinforced next morning by the Prime Minister in a by-lined article in the *Sun* headed: 'We warned you that New Labour would be different'. Blair said he had made it clear to the voters that the days had gone when Labour saw the 'solution to poverty as more money on the giro cheque ... I said we would not flinch ... These were not fancy phrases to please the crowd ... One of the hard choices was pushing through the cut in benefit for new lone parents so that they are put on the same benefit level as married couples.' This was Blair's second signed article in the *Sun* in two days, following a piece the previous day headlined as some 'tough talking' to the IRA in which the Prime Minister warned the Provisionals that if they returned to violence there would be no place for them at the negotiating table. The speed with which the second article had been prepared and supplied to the *Sun* illustrated the quick turn-round which the Downing Street press office could achieve and the importance which was attached to using simple, straightforward language in a tabloid newspaper to put across Blair's position.

Campbell was anxious to mount a fightback against the hostility which the government had encountered and the criticism which had been heaped on Ms Harman's head. On the eve of the vote she had been interviewed on *Today* by John Humphrys, who reminded her that she appeared to have changed her mind. He quoted from a speech she gave in the House of Commons in November 1996 criticising the Conservative government and asserting that the way to get lone mothers out of poverty was not by 'cutting the amount on which they have to live year by year and plunging them further into poverty'. Humphrys kept challenging Ms Harman to say whether she had wanted to bring in the cut or had just been told to do so. In response she insisted that Labour had chosen the path along which they were going and the government was offering lone mothers 'opportunities they have never had before'. At this point, after he protested that she had not answered the question, Humphrys said her answers were 'Alice in Wonderland stuff'.

Humphrys' clash with Ms Harman provoked a complaint to *Today*'s editor, Jon Barton, from David Hill, who said the Secretary of State had been interrupted so frequently that she was never permitted to develop a single answer. Hill's letter, which revealed that Humphrys' conduct had been discussed first at the daily 9 a.m. meeting in the Cabinet Office to plan government presentation, which was chaired by Peter Mandelson and attended by Alastair Campbell, and then again among staff on the party's 'press front line' at Millbank Tower, said that staff at party headquarters were considering whether to suspend cooperation with *Today* when it made bids through Labour to interview government ministers. 'The John Humphrys problem has assumed new proportions . . . In response we have had a council of war . . . We need to talk as this is serious . . . We will now give very serious thought to any bid to us, in order to make sure that your listeners are not going to be subjected to a repeat of the ridiculous exchange this morning . . . No one seeking to find the Secretary of State's explanation would be any wiser at the end of the "interview" . . . Frankly, none of us feels that this can go on.'

A leaked copy of the letter was released to the press by the Liberal Democrat MP Norman Baker, who condemned Labour's 'outrageous attempt to bully *Today*'. In response to press enquiries, Jon Barton published his reply, which rejected Hill's complaint and said Ms Harman's first answer was 'almost one minute long'. Most newspapers lined up behind Humphrys. The *Guardian* said his interview was a disciplined cross-examination of a cabinet minister. 'It took the Tories seven years in government to declare war on the BBC. The Labour Party has done it in seven months.' An equally robust defence was mounted by the *Daily Mail*, which said it would be a disgrace if the BBC, which had 'played patsy to Labour's spin doctors for too long, caved in to such bullying'. Ms Harman was supposed to be a 'grown-up politician, capable of looking after herself', and if she could not stand up to Humphrys, 'could the aforesaid spin doctors please explain why she is running a major department of state?'

In the aftermath of the backbench rebellion over the benefit cut, the Prime Minister's ability to deliver the personal commitment which he had given in Labour's election manifesto that his would be 'the party of welfare reform' was repeatedly questioned by the Conservatives. On 15 January, the day on which the Prime Minister launched the 'welfare roadshow' in Dudley, William Hague used a lunchtime speech to the parliamentary press gallery to taunt Blair over the contradiction the government presented: New Labour had a history of opposition to welfare reform, yet Blair was still trying to say his was the only party that could achieve it. Blair, said Hague, so far from leading an administration of 'principle and purpose', was presiding over a 'government of polish and press releases'; and he predicted that welfare reform would become 'New Labour's Vietnam'.

After all the ill-feeling generated by the revolt, Campbell was determined that Blair should be allowed to begin his 'welfare roadshow' with a clean slate and get the chance to put afresh the case for a fundamental review of social security payments. To help explain the reasons for changing the system, the Department of Social Security had published seven 'welfare reform focus files' which set out the facts and figures concerning the most important benefits. The day before the Prime Minister's speech in Dudley, Campbell told the 4 p.m. lobby briefing that the government believed it was vital that the debate was based on 'facts and not fiction, myths or scare stories', and the 'focus files' would establish that foundation. He then gave a foretaste of what Dudley could expect to hear from the Prime Minister. One of the statistics Blair intended to use was that 'benefit fraud was costing the country £4 billion a year, enough to build one hundred new hospitals'. Campbell said the Prime Minister would stress his readiness to consult, but no one should underestimate his 'determination to see it through'.

Downing Street's control of the arrangements for the 'welfare roadshow' inevitably led to speculation that Harriet Harman was being marginalised and lacked credibility. There was no doubt that Campbell was anxious to avoid any resurgence of the controversy over benefit cuts for lone parents, and his coordination of the message that was to be put across by the Prime Minister could not be faulted. On the morning of the Dudley speech two national newspapers published signed columns by Blair, both of which included precisely the same two points which Campbell had presented to the lobby the afternoon before. Hardly a word had been changed in either of the two key sentences: 'Benefit fraud, estimated at £4 billion a year, is enough to build one hundred new hospitals... But let nobody underestimate my determination to see this through' (*The Times*); 'Benefit fraud – estimated at £4 billion a year – is enough to build one hundred new hospitals... But no one should underestimate my determination to see this through' (*Mirror*). I had always been impressed by Campbell's skill in achieving the integrated delivery of the Prime Minister's message; here, with Blair's personal standing in the country and party at stake, it seemed to have reached new heights.

However, not all Campbell's diligence could prevent media attention straying from the course he laid for it if new interests presented themselves, and even while he accompanied the Prime Minister on his engagements in Japan he was aware of one niggling blot on the landscape spoiling the view ahead to the intended smooth launch of the welfare reform campaign. Some days before the full extent of his agitation would be revealed, he was already becoming visibly irritated when bombarded with questions about Paul Routledge's forthcoming biography of Gordon Brown. Work on the book had proceeded apace since July 1997, when Routledge had finished his series of interviews with the Chancellor. Although the publishers, Simon and Schuster, were anxious to build up interest ahead of the book's imminent publication, they had not bargained for the story which broke in the *Guardian* on the day Blair addressed Japanese businessmen in Tokyo. 'How Blair broke secret pact' was the headline over the front-page story by the *Guardian*'s labour editor, Seumas Milne, which said Routledge's biography contained highly embarrassing details of the 'continuing rawness of the Chancellor's personal and political wounds' and his 'continuing ambition' to become Prime Minister: 'Brown is convinced he could have beaten Tony Blair in a contest for Labour's leadership and that the Prime Minister broke a secret pact between them.'

Campbell was hard pressed to disguise his fury when it became obvious that the revelations contained in the book were beginning to overshadow the reports which correspondents were sending back to London about the Prime Minister's visit to Japan and his preparations for the 'welfare roadshow', and he would no doubt have preferred it if the book had not been mentioned at all in Blair's interview on *Breakfast with Frost*. Sir David did, however, manage to work in a couple of questions about it right at the end of their conversation – producing a definite frisson at that moment and more than a touch of impatience in Blair's reply when he was asked what he thought of the book's central claim that Brown still wanted to be Prime Minister: 'I am doing the job and as for Gordon, he is one of my closest, closest friends and I wouldn't believe a whole lot of codswallop.'

For all its force, Blair's short, sharp riposte did nothing to halt the unfolding drama surrounding the premature disclosure of the contents of *Gordon Brown: The Biography*. Routledge was just as alarmed as Campbell by the sensational treatment which his biography had attracted, and believed Milne's exclusive was a spoiler designed to upstage the book's serialisation in *The Times*, which was due to start the following day. The venomous feud that existed between the book's author and the *Guardian*'s labour editor by far eclipsed any real or imagined stresses and strains in the relationship between the Prime Minister and his Chancellor. Both journalists had written books in the early 1990s about Arthur Scargill, the former president of the National Union of Mineworkers, regarded within the labour movement variously as a hero or as the most divisive trade union leader in postwar British history. The two books expressed their authors' diametrically opposed opinions of their subject. In *Scargill: The Unauthorised Biography*, Routledge had told the story of a 'tragic man' whose 'misplaced sense of destiny led to the devastating defeat of the mineworkers'. Milne's book, *The Enemy Within*, sought to restore Scargill's reputation by revealing details of what were said to have been attempts by the security services and the news media to destabilise the miners' leader by trying falsely to implicate him in a conspiracy to defraud the union of its money. Although it was only a sub-plot in the saga surrounding the Gordon Brown biography, the bad blood between Routledge and Milne was the key to understanding why the story caused so much mischief and ultimately provoked yet more mocking of Alastair Campbell's much-vaunted mechanisms for coordinating and controlling what Downing Street was saying.

Milne had obtained his copy of Routledge's latest biography from the Labour MP George Galloway, who had discovered that copies of it were on sale prematurely at the bookstall in Glasgow airport. Once the book was in the hands of the author's old adversary, the story wrote itself and the *Guardian* had a scoop that put both the Prime Minister and the Chancellor on the back foot. There had already been enough stories suggesting splits between Blair and Brown to alert journalists to the significance of what was regarded as an insider's account of the Chancellor's rise to power and the truth about why he had stood aside for Blair in Labour's leadership election. Routledge was a drinking companion of Brown's press secretary, Charlie Whelan; their friendship dated back to the days they had spent socialising together at trade union events and party conferences. Before being head-hunted by the Labour Party and teaming up with Brown, Whelan had been a press officer and fixer for the Amalgamated Engineering and Electrical Union. Routledge, who made his name as labour editor of *The Times* during the big industrial disputes of the late 1970s and 1980s, was a force to be reckoned with on the conference circuit, though some of the company he kept was too right-wing for Milne, who was happier with contacts on the left of the union movement. Whelan had done his utmost to help Routledge, whose publishers had been promised Brown's cooperation. All seemed set for a successful launch, and a party to mark the book's publication was due to be held in the Chancellor's reception rooms at No. 11 Downing Street. However, Brown was about to pay a terrible price for all the assistance he had given Routledge during those balmy summer days when the new Labour government took the country by storm and Blair's ministers seemed able almost to walk on water. He was already in a highly vulnerable position as a result of his eager participation in the ill-fated television documentary broadcast the previous October, which had exposed the government to damaging publicity; as far as Campbell and Mandelson were concerned, it had done immense harm to the Chancellor's reputation as a safe pair of hands when it came to handling the news media. Less than three months later, another attempt to bolster his standing was about to backfire.

The blurb on the book's dustjacket supplied Milne with all the ammunition he needed: the biography, it said, had been written with Brown's 'full cooperation'. Milne now had a golden opportunity to steal a march over Routledge, and set about his task with alacrity. In the first two sentences of his story he hammered home the message: that Brown had revealed his 'continuing ambition to become Prime Minister' in an 'authorised biography' which had been prepared with his 'full cooperation'. He quoted the Chancellor's press secretary as having confirmed to the *Guardian* that the book was 'authorised', bringing forth an immediate denial from Whelan in a letter to the editor published the next day: 'It is not and does not claim to be. Nor did Gordon Brown give any comments on the events highlighted by Milne.' Other newspapers were not convinced. Routledge had listed in the notes to his book the four dates on which he had interviewed Brown during the previous May, June and July, and that was seen among Tony Blair's friends and supporters as proof positive of the Chancellor's involvement. 'Revelations in Brown book start Labour feud' was the headline over a front-page story in *The Times*, which publicised its own serialisation of Routledge's biography with quotes from a 'prominent Blairite minister' who accused the Chancellor of 'deliberately reopening old wounds'. Nor did Whelan's increasingly desperate attempts to play down Brown's involvement do much to convince the *Observer*'s political editor, Patrick Wintour, who said the Blair camp were claiming that the Chancellor's allies were 'so determined to promote their man, they virtually commissioned the book from Routledge'. Another 'bitter minister' was quoted as saying that the Chancellor had been unwise to sanction the book because it suggested Blair was just 'an incidental moment in Brown's reform of Labour and march to the leadership'.

Andrew Grice, political editor of the *Sunday Times*, gave the most illuminating account of the alarm which the book's imminent serialisation in *The Times* had caused in Downing Street. Grice said the Prime Minister had 'grimaced when aides warned him' about how the biography might be interpreted by the newspapers. On the day of his departure to Tokyo, Blair had held an unscheduled discussion with his Chancellor about the trouble the book was causing. Grice's informants did not know the outcome of the meeting, but he reported that Brown's office had declined to provide a copy of the book for Alastair Campbell to read on the plane to Japan. Undeterred by the storm gathering around him, Routledge supplied a summary of his book for the *Independent on Sunday* in which he described how the 'machinations' of Peter Mandelson had 'blown apart' an understanding between Brown and Blair that, in the event of John Smith's death and a new leadership election, Brown would be the candidate. In fact, said Routledge, Mandelson was 'briefing for Blair from the outset, yet played a devious game of brinkmanship with Brown'. The scene had now been set for a momentous row. Charlie Whelan was still trying desperately to convince journalists that Brown had not spoken to Routledge about the leadership election and that all the biography did was 'reheat four-year-old gossip' about how Brown had stepped aside for Blair; but for the political correspondents, it was open season. Trevor Kavanagh, the *Sun's* political editor, took the Downing Street line in wondering why the Chancellor had cooperated with 'one of the most damaging biographies ever written' to rake over the four-year-old battle for the Labour crown. 'Tony Blair is the most popular politician on earth . . . There is no vacancy for Prime Minister . . . Yet, after barely eight months in office, the ultra-ambitious Chancellor is making waves and crying foul.'

By now Routledge believed his own credibility was at stake and he added yet another dimension to the drama in a column in the *Scotsman* in which he explained the terms on which he had written the book. He said Brown had fulfilled his promise to cooperate by providing access to his personal papers and granting four extended interviews, the last of which took place 'in a car hurtling towards Heathrow' from where the Chancellor was flying off for a holiday in Cape Cod with his girlfriend, Sarah Macaulay. Routledge said that although Brown was 'always voluble about politics' he was reluctant to talk about the leadership campaign and on this topic directed him instead to the chief whip, Nick Brown, who would have been the Chancellor's campaign manager if there had been an election. 'Nick spilled the beans about the leadership battle. He was clear that Brown could have won it, despite the machinations of the London self-indulgent political set. It was clear beyond peradventure that Nick spoke for Brown.' Routledge was contemptuous of the way he was being 'traduced' by the Prime Minister's spin doctors. 'The sneering put-downs from Tony Blair's creatures are worthless and self-serving and should be seen as such as the drama continues to unfold.'

As this comment suggested, Routledge had not been spared the lash of Alastair Campbell's tongue, who had reminded the lobby that the Prime Minister had described Routledge's biography on *Breakfast with Frost* as 'codswallop'. Blair, he said, would not be making any further comment. 'The Prime Minister thinks the book is in the trivia and detritus section of government life.' Campbell refused to be drawn any further, but correspondents who had been with him in Japan claimed on their return to have heard him complaining furiously about Brown and Whelan and attacking their misjudgement in cooperating with Routledge's book. As the week progressed, Whelan confirmed that he had been getting quite a bit of stick, and he showed friendly journalists a message from Campbell which he had kept on his pager. It had arrived the previous weekend, when Campbell was in Japan, and it was short and to the point: 'If you thought this book would do any good you have been proved totally wrong.'

Whelan seemed more concerned about the way Routledge was keeping the story going by writing articles for newspapers and doing radio interviews to justify his book. 'I have told Paul to chuck it in,' he told me, 'but he thinks his integrity is at stake. I cannot rein him in.' Having delivered his tirade against Blair's 'worthless and self-serving' spin doctors, Routledge decided he had other scores to settle, and in his next column for the *Independent on Sunday* he took a swipe at his tormentor on the *Guardian*, castigating the 'appalling incompetence' of Simon and Schuster and John Menzies in allowing the premature sale of his book at Glasgow airport, and the subsequent leak of a copy of it to the 'pseudo-revolutionary public schoolboy Seumas Milne', to enable 'the book's enemies to get their retaliation in first'.

Routledge and Whelan had taken the starring roles in the first act of the drama; but another newspaper columnist, the *Observer's* Andrew Rawnsley, was about to steal the limelight. One line from Rawnsley's column in the edition of 18 January, looking back on the week, had been catapulted to the front page where it had provided the basis for a dramatic headline: 'Blair reins in "flawed" Brown'. The *Observer's* lead, under a joint by-line of Rawnsley and Patrick Wintour, said that a senior source inside Downing Street claimed Brown had 'psychological flaws'. A second ministerial source 'close to the Prime Minister' was quoted as saying that Blair believed Brown's decision to sanction the book was 'a serious and silly move that weakens the government'. In his own column, Rawnsley described in greater detail how he had spoken to a wide range of contacts and got the strong impression that the Chancellor was 'exhausting' Blair's patience. 'According to someone who has an extremely good claim to know the mind of the Prime Minister, he still regards Brown as "a great talent" and "a great force". But he is wearying of the Chancellor's misjudgments, of which this was "a classic". It is time, in the words of the same person, for Brown to get a grip on his "psychological flaws". The government cannot afford any further "lapses into this sort of nonsense". If this is what Blair thinks – and I have very good reason to believe that it is – then the Prime Minister is right.'

Rawnsley's assertion that Downing Street was putting it around that the Prime Minister believed his Chancellor of the Exchequer had 'psychological flaws' was a sensational development and shot the story to the top of radio and television news bulletins. The unity of successive governments had been wrecked by bad blood between the occupants of No. 10 and No. 11 Downing Street, and the memories of Margaret Thatcher's feuds in the 1980s with Chancellors Geoffrey Howe and Nigel Lawson, and John Major's troubles with Chancellor Kenneth Clarke, were still so vivid that political journalists had every reason to believe they were on the point of witnessing a replay, this time involving a New Labour Prime Minister and his Chancellor. There was no way that Sunday morning of immediately verifying Rawnsley's quote or of identifying his source. Although the denials came in thick and fast, the suggestion that the Blair camp regarded Brown as having 'psychological flaws' was entirely in line with what most political correspondents had been told privately, and the story was lent added veracity by the presence of two prime suspects, Alastair Campbell and Peter Mandelson.

The story gained further legitimacy when the BBC correspondent Lance Price reported in radio news bulletins on the same Sunday that 'senior sources' had told him that while Brown was 'in a very strong position politically, that may not last for ever and nobody is indispensable'. Like Rawnsley, Price would not reveal his source; but he was delighted that the chilling phrase he had obtained that 'nobody is indispensable' was the basis for the follow-up stories in Monday's newspapers. 'Cool it Gordon' was the *Mirror's* front-page headline over a report by its political correspondent Nigel Morris saying that the Chancellor had effectively been told to 'toe the line or risk the sack'. The *Sun's* Whitehall correspondent, David Wooding, said the grim words 'nobody is indispensable' were a warning shot to Brown that he could 'wreck his long-term career unless he buries the hatchet soon'. Paul Eastham, the *Daily Mail's* political correspondent, said Downing Street's 'blunt broadside' showed that Blair suspected Brown of 'manoeuvring for power'. Newspaper correspondents had great faith in the reliability of Price's quote because he had impeccable connections inside the Labour Party; indeed, within a matter of months he had revealed his political allegiances by leaving the BBC and joining Alastair Campbell's team of special advisers in the Downing Street press office. Joy Johnson, a former BBC news editor who was briefly Labour's director of communications, told me that during her time with the party Price's reporting was regarded as being highly accurate and his stories had not caused the Labour leadership any difficulty. Price had always made it clear to me that he personally disapproved of my behind-the-scenes books on the activities of New Labour's spin doctors. He said that if I had ever participated in the kind of political discussions with Peter Mandelson which he had experienced, I would have realised how misguided I had been in my assessment of his work and his contribution to the Labour Party.

Alastair Campbell faced a difficult task at the 11 a.m. lobby briefing that Monday morning as he began the task of trying to repair the damage. He knew that the weekend stories about a breakdown in relations between the Chancellor and the Prime Minister, backed up by the unsourced claims that Downing Street was accusing Brown of having 'psychological flaws' and of not being 'indispensable', were likely to have a lasting impact on the way political correspondents viewed the Blair–Brown relationship. Big political stories in the future, such as the budget or a cabinet reshuffle, would be judged in terms of whether it was Blair or Brown who had come out best. Once journalists get a fixation of that kind the spin doctors are in trouble: they know how difficult it can be to dispel such preoccupations. If political stories are approached on the basis of there being a persistent feud at the top of the government, this tends to have a destabilising effect on the whole party because the news media will always insist on breaking down MPs and members of the cabinet into two or more separate camps of supporters. Reporters tend to build up contacts with one grouping rather than another; this in turn has the effect of generating yet more stories, and once these tribal loyalties have become established there is little if anything the party propagandists can do to eradicate tales of dissent or convince the news media that they are all groundless.

Campbell's immediate task at his briefing, then, was to try to halt the descent into faction before it gained any more momentum by dispelling any suggestion of disharmony between No. 10 and No. 11, and he was particularly forthright: 'The Prime Minister regards the Chancellor as an extremely excellent Chancellor for whom he has immense regard professionally and personally. They are not going to let all this silly stuff get in the way of the good conduct of government. All sorts of people will see this as an opportunity to try to unsettle their close personal relationship but they will fail.' He then set about trying to rubbish the unsourced quotes: 'In politics there are always people who are ready to give their opinions and who, for the benefit of journalists, will try to translate their opinions into the views of people who are higher than they are. You just can't stop it . . . If Paul Routledge had written this pretty shallow account of the Chancellor's life in his column in the *Independent on Sunday*, which is all it's worth, no one would have batted an eyelid. But because it's in a book, and because it is said to be "authorised", it becomes news and then things are said to journalists which also become news.' When asked if he endorsed Charlie Whelan's involvement in the book, Campbell stonewalled: 'I speak for the Prime Minister and the government. I don't get distracted by this stuff.' At the height of the row the previous October over the television documentary about Gordon Brown, Campbell had told the lobby that he did not believe in fly-on-the-wall films, and now, as the briefing drew to a close, he declared: 'I think people should stop writing books.' At this point he noticed that among those sitting at the front of his audience were the authors of two other political biographies. Campbell turned first to Colin Brown, the *Independent*'s chief political correspondent: 'I think your book on John Prescott was excellent.' Then he complimented the BBC correspondent Jon Sopel: 'Your book on Tony Blair was a masterpiece.' Luckily I was sitting at the very back of the room, so I kept my head down and avoided detection as the Prime Minister's press secretary delivered his personal critique of the literary achievements of the assembled lobby correspondents.

Brown also did his best that Monday morning to limit the damage. On his way into a meeting in Brussels of European finance ministers, which he was to chair, he tried again to set the record straight. 'This was not an authorised biography . . . and I am not going to be diverted by what is rumour, gossip and tittle tattle.' But the hunt was on to find the unidentified sources whose comments had so alarmed the government. Rawnsley refused to identify his informant when interviewed that day on *The World at One*, but he stuck firmly to his story. 'You can never be sure whether or not people are speaking on behalf of the Prime Minister or if they are addressing their own agenda but I think what I heard was a reflection of Blair's private views and I'm in no doubt he's angry about the book and thinks the Chancellor must be told "enough is enough". Yes, "psychological flaws" were the words which were put to me.' Once other political columnists had their chance to assess what had happened, they were unanimous in concluding that the doubling in the number of political advisers and the rush by Labour cabinet ministers to appoint their own spin doctors had fuelled private rivalries within the government and turned them into public rows. The *Economist*'s political columnist Bagehot said Blair should realise that the lesson of the whole unedifying episode was that he had given too much leash to 'freebooting ministerial acolytes' whose only loyalty was to the minister who had appointed them. There had been 'a huge yet barely acknowledged shift of power' within government from the civil service machine to ministerial special advisers and spin doctors. Departmental civil servants owed loyalty to their minister, but that did not extend to personal politics, which professionally were off limits. The incentive for special advisers and spin doctors was to further their minister's cause, and that lured them into 'promoting their man, which usually means rubbishing somebody else's'.

In his column in the *Guardian*, Hugo Young said the 'deformity' of the Blair cabinet was that it had constructed 'a world of meta-politics occupied by their truth doctors'. Young said the Chancellor's truth doctors operated in 'the half-world of manipulation and deniability' where truth itself was of small importance. 'They half-help his recent biographer, they half-read the manuscript of the book, they half-deny they have done so, they half-authenticate the outcome, while pretending wholly to repudiate any notion that the work has anything to do, on their part or his, with Brown's positioning vis-a-vis the Prime Minister... the time has come to stop complaining and send Dr Charles Whelan undeniably packing.'

One recurring theme in the columnists' thinking as to what might have motivated Brown's desire to go on reinforcing the myth that he had been robbed by Blair of the prize to which he was entitled was that it forced the Prime Minister to offer his Chancellor compensations. Anne McElvoy, the *Daily Telegraph*'s columnist, commented on the freedom Blair had allowed Brown to build an alternative power base in the Treasury; she also thought the Chancellor's hold over the Prime Minister helped explain why the Paymaster-General, Geoffrey Robinson, had not been moved sideways after revelations about the 'intriguing nature of his financial affairs'. A steady stream of stories about the tangled business life and tax arrangements of Labour's millionaire minister had begun appearing soon after the general election and continued unabated as journalists went on uncovering further details about the network of companies with which he had been associated.

Robinson was like few other politicians I had met. For over twenty years, until he was appointed a minister by Blair, he had one of the lowest profiles of any MP at Westminster, and he had deliberately eschewed self-promotion. Few embattled ministers have managed to keep their jobs in the face of a sustained onslaught of the kind which he had to endure, and Robinson's ability to withstand continued vilification was in part a measure of the effectiveness of the strategy which he had pursued through most of his political career in keeping the prying eyes of the news media at bay. By having gone to such lengths for so long to avoid personal publicity, by refusing to court the company of journalists or seek exposure on radio and television, he had limited the amount of information which was available publicly about his business affairs and private life. Because he rarely gave newspaper interviews or took part in the usual round of political publicity stunts, newspaper libraries had fewer press cuttings and photographs than was usual for an MP with his length of service, and there was a similar shortage of footage in television archives.

As I knew from my own experience, Robinson's lack of interest in promoting himself through the news media was evident right at the start of his political career, in fact, from the very moment he won the safe Labour seat of Coventry North West in a by-election in 1976. Robinson had been chief executive of Jaguar Cars in Coventry before deciding to stand as a parliamentary candidate, and he was considered at the time to have been quite a catch for the Labour Party. I had been sent to report the declaration of the result for BBC Radio and, according to the instructions I had been given, my task next morning was to go to Robinson's hotel and escort him personally to the BBC's studio, which was situated beneath the newly constructed Coventry Cathedral, so that he could be interviewed live down the line by the *Today* programme in London. However, when I arrived at the hotel where he was staying, I was told that he had changed his mind. Despite my own entreaties, and a supportive plea from a local party official, he refused to leave his room and said he was not interested in the publicity he might get from a BBC interview. Needless to say I got the blame, because *Today*'s editor refused to believe that a former businessman of Robinson's standing, who had just won an important by-election, would have decided of his own volition to have missed an opportunity to appear on national radio to publicise his success.

Such determination to avoid drawing attention to himself did not go unnoticed at Westminster. Andrew Roth, author of *Parliamentary Profiles*, used four words to sum up his outlook to political life: 'rarely heard, low profile'. The Coventry member's infrequent appearances and lack of contact with the news media made life difficult for journalists. Joe Murphy, who was on the Coventry *Evening Telegraph* before becoming the *Mail on Sunday*'s political editor, said he never met Robinson in the two years he was political editor of the MP's local paper. 'He was pretty invisible but we did used to get press releases from him.'

However, the closer Robinson came to the New Labour leadership, the more media attention he began to attract. His entrepreneurial flair had made him a wealthy man and the technology company he founded in 1981, TransTec, was a runaway success. After Tony Blair was elected party leader in 1994 and New Labour began to make increasing overtures to big business, Robinson became a close ally and aide of the then shadow Chancellor, Gordon Brown. In 1996 Robinson put up the money to purchase the ailing *New Statesman*. According to the *Independent*'s columnist Paul Vallely, Brown's 'lieutenant Ed Balls played a significant role in the plot to secure the *New Statesman* as an organ for New Labour'. Robinson gained further prominence that year when Tony Blair and his family spent their summer holiday at the Robinson family's villa in Tuscany. Then, after Labour won the election and Robinson was given responsibility as a Treasury minister for implementing the windfall tax on the privatised utilities, he found himself on the receiving end of considerable publicity on the financial pages.

Revelations about his business and tax affairs began appearing within a few months of his taking office, after it emerged that he was a discretionary beneficiary of a £12 million offshore trust based in the tax haven of Guernsey. The *Independent on Sunday*'s assistant editor, Chris Blackhurst, had established that Robinson was linked to the trust and he had started asking whether this put the Paymaster-General in conflict with the government's stated intention of reducing tax avoidance. Blackhurst told me that he had tried for two days to speak to Robinson or to get a response from the government, but that he got nowhere until the very last moment, when on the afternoon of Saturday 29 November the Treasury finally put out a general statement to the Press Association and the other Sunday newspapers, thus depriving the *Independent on Sunday* of its exclusive story. 'The Treasury released Robinson's response at 5.50 p.m., right on edition times, and that alerted papers like the *Observer* and *Sunday Times*. Obviously until they saw our first edition they did not know the full extent of the story. Robinson had purposely left it as late as possible before responding. He would not speak to me and was only prepared to discuss it with the editor, Rosie Boycott, so I had to give her the questions to put to him.'

The Treasury statement issued on Robinson's behalf and setting out his financial affairs explained that on his appointment as a minister all his beneficial interests were transferred to a blind trust, including nearly £18 million of shares in his company TransTec. All dividends were taxed in the normal manner. The Orion Trust, registered in Guernsey, had been established for his family by the late Mme Joska Bourgeois, a Belgian national and a long-standing family friend. Since he was only a discretionary beneficiary of this trust, he had been advised by his solicitors and the Treasury's permanent secretary, Sir Terence Burns, that there was no need to include this potential benefit in his blind trust. The following Monday, Alastair Campbell told the lobby that once Robinson had been asked to join the government his financial interests had been put on a proper footing, and the Prime Minister continued to believe he was 'an extremely able and effective minister'.

Blair's declaration of support had little effect on the newspapers, and the next weekend there were fresh disclosures, the *Sunday Times* claiming on 7 December that Robinson was linked to offshore trusts in the tax haven of Bermuda and the *Observer* revealing that the Orion Trust had purchased shares in TransTec after Robinson became Paymaster-General. The allegations were now so far-reaching that Robinson was forced to take fresh advice and, in order to avoid potential embarrassment to the Prime Minister, he did not appear on Monday morning at the launch of the government's newly established Social Exclusion Unit. Although the Treasury insisted he had another engagement, the documents handed out to journalists showed there was a gap in the guest list where his name should have been and where it had obviously been erased. That evening his solicitors, Titmuss Sainer Dechert, demanded an immediate apology from the *Sunday Times* and the *Observer* for printing articles which constituted 'a most serious libel', and the two editors were told that if they persisted in publishing defamatory statements, the Paymaster-General would launch libel proceedings.

Robinson had embarked on a highly hazardous course. If the *Sunday Times* and the *Observer* refused to back down, he would have no alternative but to go to court; and in his haste to hit back at the two papers he seemed to have overlooked the fact that if he started libel proceedings he would almost certainly be forced to resign. Ministers can take legal action to clear their names and remain in office if the allegations which are in dispute affect their private lives or are of a personal character. If the proceedings go to the heart of a minister's political or financial integrity, however, the convention is that he or she has no option but to resign from the government at least until the matter has been resolved. John Major's ability to continue as Prime Minister was not considered to be under threat when he launched libel proceedings in 1993 against the *New Statesman* and the satirical magazine *Scallywag*, which had printed unsubstantiated allegations linking his name to the caterer Ms Clare Latimer. Within four days the *New Statesman* had issued a grovelling apology. But ministerial resignations from Major's government were unavoidable in the aftermath of the allegations of financial irregularity which had been made by Mohamed Al Fayed, the owner of Harrods. Jonathan Aitken, Chief Secretary to the Treasury, and the corporate affairs minister, Neil Hamilton, both left the government in order to pursue libel proceedings.

The timing of the legal threat was also less than optimal. Newspaper lawyers say that as a rule editors are at their most vulnerable if a libel action is started before publication, when there is the greatest chance of preventing offending material from being printed. If a writ is issued subsequently, with the intent of restraining a paper and gagging other journalists, it can fail to have the desired effect if there is already a large amount of information in circulation, as was certainly the case in this instance. The statement which Robinson had volunteered the previous weekend, and which had been issued on his behalf by the Treasury, had not only given legal protection to the news media to repeat the basic facts, but had also supplied journalists with innumerable potential leads and an opportunity to investigate Robinson's hitherto unpublicised connection with the late Mme Bourgeois.

As the week progressed, and as it became obvious that neither the *Sunday Times* nor the *Observer* was going to apologise or refrain from continuing to publish the results of their investigations into his financial affairs, Robinson decided he had no alternative but to change tack and mount a charm offensive in the hope of re-establishing his credibility. After the row the previous month about Bernie Ecclestone's £1 million donation, and Tony Blair's achievement in effectively drawing a line under the controversy by the simple device of saying 'sorry', the Paymaster-General seemed to believe that if he answered questions about his financial affairs, and opened up to a degree about his vast wealth, he might be equally successful in limiting damaging exposure, and that he might manage to put a stop to further embarrassing disclosures.

In some quarters, this new tactic seemed to yield results. Robinson could not be faulted on his willingness to go the extra mile as the journalists' questions became ever more intrusive and, bearing in mind his somewhat beleaguered position in having been unable to follow through his threat of legal action, the coverage he received in some of the Sunday papers on 14 December was largely sympathetic. 'Robinson comes clean on links to offshore fund', was the *Sunday Telegraph*'s headline over its report about how the Paymaster-General, 'sitting in an armchair in his Treasury office', broke his silence and protested his innocence. 'I've done nothing wrong, nothing illegal, and I take no salary for the job I do in the Treasury. I pay all my taxes in the United Kingdom, about £1.4 million in the last five years.' The headline over a three-page report in the *Express* was far more personal: 'I am worth about £30 million'. Robinson did not deny reports that Mme Bourgeois had left him £9 million and, in response to another question, he calculated what he was worth. 'Let's tot up what we've got in the UK. We've got shares worth about – ha, they may be a bit undervalued at the moment – about £20 million, say. There's the houses... All in my name! All declared! All paid for from UK sources! I don't know – £30 million – something like that.'

However, Robinson's decision to start answering questions had the opposite effect on the two newspapers which had been threatened with legal action. The *Observer* said it deplored the way the government had made offshore tax avoidance more acceptable and the paper had no intention of giving way in the face of empty threats from the Paymaster-General. 'Today we offer no apology. We did not libel him, and we stand by our original article. Nor do we expect to be sued next week.' The *Sunday Times* said it would not be inhibited by Robinson's blanket threats of libel proceedings: 'Even if he is squeaky clean, he has been exposed as a hypocrite of the first order. That is sufficient cause for him to resign as a minister.' Robinson had taken a gamble in agreeing to answer questions about his financial affairs: the government would be able to say that it showed he had nothing to hide, but there was no certainty that the newspapers would be satisfied with his assurances.

At the next Monday morning lobby briefing Alastair Campbell appeared to be nowhere near as sure of himself as he was after Blair's apology over the Ecclestone affair. On the time-honoured principle that attack is the best form of defence, he launched into a complaint about the way Sunday newspapers had 'spent massive resources flying reporters around the world trying to dig up dirt' on the Paymaster-General. 'The *Sunday Times* Bermuda story was balls. The *Observer* story has bitten the dust. But the media are playing a game and still want to whack him about a bit. If the newspapers can dredge up enough innuendo, they think they can decide who's in the government. That may have happened under John Major but it's the Prime Minister who judges what is right and wrong, and who is in his government, and he thinks Geoffrey Robinson works effectively and brings added value as a minister.'

The two weeks which preceded Robinson's about-turn in his approach to the news media had provided an instructive illustration of the questionable tactics which Labour's spin doctors were prepared to employ. Charlie Whelan had assumed the role of chief protector to the Paymaster-General and, at the start of the second week, when Robinson threatened libel proceedings, he was determined to make it as difficult as possible for television and radio reporters to cover the story. On the morning of 8 December, as Robinson consulted his lawyers about the allegations in the *Sunday Times* and the *Observer*, Gordon Brown had an engagement at the Connaught Rooms where he was addressing a TUC conference. Whelan knew that the reporters waiting on the doorstep, who had failed to catch the Chancellor's attention on the way in, would try again on his departure and would have another go at asking him questions about Robinson's tax affairs. A BBC television producer, James Helm, who was standing there beside his cameraman, said Whelan signalled to them that Brown was on his way out of the building. When Helm moved forward to ask a question, Whelan unplugged the microphone lead to the camera. Undaunted, Helm tried put his question, but at this point Whelan stood in front of the cameraman.

Helm said that although it was a relatively jokey encounter, and there had been some good-natured joshing beforehand, there was no doubt that Whelan had acted deliberately to prevent him from putting his question to the Chancellor. Whelan told me later that he did not consider he had behaved improperly in unplugging the microphone. 'The arrangement was quite clear. Gordon was only going to give the television crews a leaving shot. Questions were not going to be asked. That was the deal. We knew that if television had the sound of reporters' voices on tape, asking the Chancellor questions and him not replying, that would look bad.' On subsequent occasions, if there was any likelihood of friction during doorstep filming of the Chancellor, Whelan would take great delight in reminding me and the assembled company of his brush with Helm, and would warn the reporters and television crews that he meant business if anyone stepped out of line. 'It's my job to protect the Chancellor and if you or anyone else tries to ambush him, I'll do the same to you and unplug your microphones as well.'

Whelan cultivated his tough guy image assiduously, but fortunately for me his protection duties did not involve following Robinson's every footstep. The day after the confrontation outside the Connaught Rooms I was pleased to see he was not on guard duty outside the door of the room where the House of Commons standing committee discussing the Bank of England Bill was meeting. Robinson sat there throughout the morning session but said nothing, leaving others in the ministerial team to do all the talking. In my view this reticence reflected the difficulty he would continue to face whenever he appeared in parliament or if an attempt were made to ask him to speak publicly on controversial issues affecting taxation. His credibility had been so damaged by all the publicity surrounding his business and financial affairs that he could no longer be presented with authority as the acceptable public face of the government. David Heathcoat-Amory, one of the Conservatives' finance team, went further, and said he thought the Paymaster-General's silence in the committee room showed that he could no longer be seen publicly as having been responsible for taking financial decisions, and therefore he could not function properly as a Treasury minister and would have to resign.

My report for *The World at One* that day about Robinson's evident discomfort at the standing committee session had angered Alastair Campbell, who parodied my broadcast for the benefit of the assembled journalists at the 4 p.m. lobby briefing, deriding my account of what had happened as 'pathetic'. As the Prime Minister's press secretary was clearly in a mood to hand out plaudits, I thought I would ask what would happen if Robinson went ahead with his libel proceedings. Would he abide by convention and follow the example of Jonathan Aitken and Neil Hamilton in resigning from the government? My question had caught Campbell off guard, and he paused for a moment before replying. 'The Prime Minister doesn't believe the Paymaster-General has done anything which merits the course of action you suggest. There is a world of difference in his case. Geoffrey Robinson does not draw a salary and he intends to pay his own costs.'

I had already been on the receiving end of Campbell's taunts once that day, at the morning briefing. On entering the room, seeing me sitting there with pen poised, he sighed and told the lobby that 'as Nick Jones is here, I'll have to watch my Ps and Qs again'. One of Campbell's favourite jokes was to suggest that because of my presence he was less forthcoming than he would like to be. At one point in the briefing, he stopped himself in full flow, remarking with a flourish, 'I nearly said what I thought . . . ' He then paused and checked that I had my pen in my hand before continuing: 'I'll repeat that for Nick Jones, "I nearly said what I thought." That'll do for chapter twelve of the encyclopaedia of spin doctors, to be read by eleven people, all of them called Jones.' For some reason Campbell was in a particularly bouncy mood that morning and, after challenging one correspondent about the accuracy of his story, he volunteered an assessment of his own record for reliability in his days as a political editor. 'When I left being a part-time propagandist to become a full-time propagandist, my colleagues at the *Daily Mirror* went through all my stories and found only one story which was wrong, so that wasn't bad.' He then proceeded to laugh at his own joke; but he would not reveal what the inaccurate story was about.

For all the bravado of the Prime Minister's press secretary and the foot-in-the-door artistry of the Chancellor's special adviser, even they must have realised they were beginning to sail close to the wind in their defensive tactics on behalf of the Paymaster-General. The code of conduct for special advisers, and the rules requiring civil servants to be impartial, did put some limit on what could be done to help a minister who had become embroiled in a highly charged political controversy. Certainly Robinson was in increasing need of help if he was to survive. The Conservatives were on the point of making a formal complaint to the Parliamentary Commissioner for Standards, Sir Gordon Downey, about Robinson's failure to declare in the Register of Members' Interests that he was a discretionary beneficiary of the Orion Trust. Peter Lilley, the shadow Chancellor, was also doing all he could to exploit Blair's embarrassment at having appointed a Treasury minister who might benefit from a £12 million trust in the tax haven of Guernsey, when Brown had told the 1996 party conference that a Labour Chancellor would 'not permit tax reliefs to millionaires in offshore islands'. Another of Lilley's lines of attack was that the government had been hypocritical in allowing Robinson, who had not declared that he was the possible beneficiary of an offshore trust, to announce details of the Treasury's plans for a new individual savings account, and the linked decision to impose a cap for tax relief of £50,000 on existing savings schemes, such as Peps and Tessas.

In attempting to defend himself against the mounting accusations, Robinson laboured under a grave handicap. Many of the disclosures about his business and tax affairs, and the complaint that he had failed to make a full declaration of his financial interests in the register, related to the period before he became a minister. The rules for civil service information officers are precise. They can handle media enquiries concerning issues which arise 'in the course of, or as a direct result of, the minister's official duties' and, 'if the minister wishes', the press office can handle an enquiry that 'concerns a matter so minor that it would be petty to refer it elsewhere'. However, in the normal course of events, a minister's 'personal or private issues' would be dealt with by a constituency office or party headquarters. Press officers are exhorted to remember that presentation of government policy and action 'must be done in furtherance of the government's activities rather than building the image of a minister'. The guidance to information officers, and a reminder that ministers and special advisers must not ask the staff of departmental press offices to 'act in any way which would conflict with the civil service code', had been included in the Mountfield Report, published in November 1997, which had sanctioned the changes which Alastair Campbell had been seeking to enable the information service to 'raise its game'. Mountfield's working group, of which Campbell had been a member, considered there was no danger of the information service being politicised, and its report said these rules did 'not constrain information officers from providing the kind of service' which ministers could properly expect in respect of the 'vigorous exposition of ministers' policies and of the reasons ministers themselves use as a justification for those policies'. None the less the code of conduct was clear on the point that press enquiries of a personal nature had to relate to issues arising 'in the course of, or as a direct result of, the minister's duties' if departmental press officers were to respond to them; and, as Mountfield's report was issued the week before the Robinson story broke, the warnings and safeguards were fresh in my mind.

I considered that questions about Robinson's personal tax affairs and the registration of his interests in the years before he became a minister fell clearly outside the limits of what departmental press officers could legitimately handle; if not, they were certainly on the borderline. In my view, the way journalists' enquiries on these matters were handled by the Treasury would provide the first test of Mountfield's assurances that information officers would be able to remain impartial under the edict which Campbell had issued that in future they must respond 'quickly, confidently and robustly' when a story went wrong. There were several pertinent issues at stake. Would journalists' calls be referred to Millbank Tower for the Labour Party to answer, or would the Paymaster-General get the full support of the Treasury's public relations machine? What would be the response of civil servants who might find themselves getting drawn into the rough and tumble of defending a minister at the centre of a heated political controversy?

As the Robinson affair unfolded, I talked to Charlie Whelan and the Treasury's press officers and waited to see what would happen. On the evening Robinson's lawyers demanded apologies from the *Sunday Times* and the *Observer* I was working in a television edit suite, preparing my report for the *Nine o'Clock News*, when Whelan asked to speak to me. Sounding agitated, he said the conversation would have to be off the record and he could not be quoted, but he wanted me to understand that Robinson had no control over the Orion Trust in Guernsey. 'Robinson doesn't own or control it so you mustn't say it's his trust. That is where the papers are going wrong.' Earlier that day

I had noticed a degree of hesitancy on the part of the press office. When I asked for some guidance as to when Robinson was likely to complete his conversations with his lawyers, I was told that as it was 'his private business' no comment could be made. That evening, the Treasury issued a short covering note attached to copies of the letters which Robinson's solicitors had sent to the *Sunday Times* and the *Observer*. The duty press officer, playing strictly by the rules, said the Treasury was making no comment on the contents.

As the months went by I detected a growing note of weariness in the voices of the Treasury's press officers, faced with persistent questions from the media as the Conservatives stepped up their calls for Robinson's resignation and more stories emerged about his business background. In January 1998 Robinson was cleared by the Committee on Standards and Privileges of any wrongdoing in respect of Peter Lilley's complaint that he had failed to register the Orion Trust in the Register of Members' Interests. The committee said there was 'no case for saying Robinson had breached the rules of the House' – but it did make the point that there were occasions when 'interests of this nature would be better registered'. Some weeks later fresh complaints were made to Sir Gordon about Robinson's failure during the 1980s and 1990s to register payments from directorships in a number of companies operated by the late newspaper tycoon, Robert Maxwell. The subsequent investigations dragged on for months, and were widened again in June 1998 after the Conservatives said there was evidence Robinson had received £150,000 from these sources in 1991. On checking to see if Robinson was responding to this latest claim, I was told by the duty press officer, whom I shall refer to as information officer X, that the Treasury was making no public comment, as the complaint affected the Paymaster-General's position well before he became a minister. However, information officer X said he had been told to assist journalists if they asked for information. He said he could only talk to me on an off-the-record basis. 'I cannot be identified as a Treasury spokesman but I have been supplied with a copy of a letter which Robinson received from the Registrar of Members' Interests in 1991, confirming the declaration of his directorships, and I have been asked to fax that to journalists if they would like to see it.' After asking him to fax me a copy, I enquired if the figure of £150,000 was correct. He said that was the figure which was being quoted. It had appeared first in the *Express* and it was 'not at odds with the one–off figure which was paid to Robinson' but he had been told to tell journalists that if they made mention of the figure having been confirmed, they should attribute it to 'friends of the Paymaster-General' and not to the Treasury.

For my report for *The World at One* that lunchtime I stuck rigidly to the formula we had agreed and reported that 'friends confirm the figure of £150,000 is close to what he received, but that the amount had not been declared because it is only in recent years that this has been required'. Information officer X had been straightforward and matter of fact in responding to my questions, and I had valued his professional help. None the less I had half expected the Treasury to refer my call, and others like it, to Millbank Tower. As our conversation continued I think we both knew that the information which I was being given should more properly have been issued by the Labour Party; but journalists working for television and radio need information instantly if they are to meet their deadlines, and I had gone straight to where I knew I would get the quickest answer.

The investigation into the complaints about Robinson's failure to declare payments from Robert Maxwell's companies were not completed until July 1998, when he escaped with a mild rebuke. Although the Committee on Standards and Privileges said it did not uphold the complaints about the non-registration of paid director-ships, Robinson had not met all the requirements. However, his conduct did 'not reach the threshold which would justify the imposition of any penalty by the House'. Robinson's ability to hang on to his ministerial post, and to the public support of the Prime Minister, puzzled newspapers like the *Independent*, which said it failed to square up with Blair's assertion the previous week that the government was 'purer than pure'. When Blair took to the airwaves to speak up for the beleaguered Paymaster-General, he wanted people to believe his government was different; but it was becoming 'increasingly difficult to trust him'. By allowing the Robinson affair to fester, the paper said, he had shown 'a worrying lack of judgement'. And yet, despite some harsh editorials, Robinson kept his job in the July cabinet reshuffle. The *Sun* claimed that Blair was about to sack him because of the 'sleaze row surrounding his business deals' but backed down after a bitter argument with his Chancellor, who stepped in at the last minute to save his closest political ally. 'Robinson's presence in the government does Blair no favours. That decision was wrong. And it may come back to haunt him.'

After a third inquiry into his affairs in November 1998, following complaints about a failure to register interests in two other companies, Robinson apologised personally to MPs in a fifty-four-second statement from the House of Commons despatch box. He said the register had been amended and the shareholdings and directorships were now a matter of public record. 'No attempt was made by me at any time to use my position in this House to advance any commercial interest. The oversight concerning registration, for which I apologise, is entirely my responsibility.' The brevity of his remarks caused surprise, and the next day's newspapers criticised it as being far too perfunctory. 'Has he no shame?' was the bold headline in thick type across the front page of the *Express*, which said the 'insouciance with which he appeared to treat the experience' was scandalous. 'If Robinson had any sense of propriety he would have made a statement not just of apology but resignation.' Within a week of what the *Sun* called a 'grovelling apology', the Conservatives were making renewed calls for him to be sacked after the *Sunday Times* revealed that companies with which he had been connected were being investigated by the Department of Trade and Industry for incomplete or inaccurate records between 1988 and 1992.

There had now been a full twelve months of embarrassing revelations about the Paymaster-General, and he was no nearer to clearing his name. His two attempts at turning the tide of vilification had both failed. By declining to follow through his original threat of libel proceedings he had given the newspapers carte blanche to dig deeper and deeper into his financial affairs and, instead of gaining any advantage from his about-turn and brief moment of openness, he had supplied journalists with fresh leads and had ended up putting facts and figures into the public domain which were subsequently used against him. As the months dragged by, and as Robinson showed no sign of resigning in the face of his messy stand-off with the news media, I could not help but recall a conversation with the former Conservative Chancellor of the Exchequer, Norman Lamont, which had taken place some months before he was given a life peerage in

June 1998. Lamont, who took much of the blame for Britain's hasty withdrawal from the European exchange rate mechanism and was sacked by John Major in 1993, was no stranger to press vilification. In November 1992 the *Sun* caused consternation when it reported that Chancellor Lamont had been sent 'five legal warning letters by Access' for not making the required monthly payments and that one of the unpaid items on his credit card account was a bill for £17.47 for a bottle of Bricout Brut Reserve champagne and a packet of Raffles cigarettes, which he was said to have purchased at a Threshers off-licence near Paddington. The basis of the report was subsequently proved to be false and two sales assistants at Threshers admitted they had fabricated the story. When we discussed Robinson's experiences, Lamont told me he could not understand why the tabloids had not hounded the Paymaster-General in the same way. 'I was pilloried from pillar to post for an alleged scandal about a bottle of champagne and a seventeen quid bill on my credit card but Robinson is involved in a twelve million pound offshore trust in a tax haven and doesn't get anywhere near the same treatment.' I explained to Lamont that perhaps most *Sun* readers could relate to a fuss about an unpaid bill at the off-licence but found it harder to grasp all the intricate details surrounding Robinson's financial affairs. His indignation reflected the burning resentment which Conservative MPs continued to feel about the way they had been harassed over sleaze, and explained why the Tories would not relent in their pursuit of the Paymaster-General.

Admittedly Lamont's travails at the hands of the tabloids were in a league of their own; but they had thrown up one unexpected and surprising parallel with Robinson's experiences. The derision which he suffered over an unpaid credit card account had followed a somewhat saucier saga the previous year which had erupted when the *News of the World* disclosed that he was evicting from his basement flat a tenant who it emerged was a sex therapist trading under the name of Miss Whiplash. Because of the threat this story presented to his authority as Chancellor, Lamont immediately sought the advice of the leading libel lawyer Peter Carter-Ruck. The Treasury's press office fielded enquiries from journalists on his behalf. Subsequently it emerged that the Treasury had paid a £4,700 contribution towards Lamont's total legal bill of £23,000, most of which concerned the eviction and was paid by the Conservative Party. The Treasury said the taxpayer had met the cost of instructing Carter-Ruck, issuing a press statement and handling subsequent press enquiries. Inaccurate newspaper stories about the eviction of Miss Whiplash and Lamont's credit card account had to be corrected immediately because the allegations were potentially damaging to the Chancellor's reputation and it was 'important quickly to put the record straight so as to retain full confidence in the office of Chancellor'. Gordon Brown, who was then shadow Chancellor, was dissatisfied with the Treasury's explanation and in December 1992, he demanded an emergency statement in the House of Commons. Public money, he said, should not have been used in what was essentially a private matter, and the government had no justification in using Treasury press officers to answer journalists' questions about legal action which the Chancellor was taking in a private capacity. 'The rules make it absolutely clear that public funds could be justified only in the conduct of public duties that involve a minister's official responsibilities. The press handling of a private eviction is not one of these.' On rereading Brown's 1992 interpretation of the government's rules in the light of my own experience in June 1998, I considered I had every reason to conclude that asking Treasury press officers to fax journalists copies of Robinson's declaration for the 1991 Register of Members' Interests, made six years before his appointment as Paymaster-General, constituted a breach of the code of conduct.

When assessing the various factors and circumstances which might be said to have swayed Alastair Campbell's judgement as he thinks through the government's media strategy each day, there is usually no contest as to which has probably been the most influential. More often than not his benchmark in deciding what to do next has been the attitude adopted by the *Sun*. If Rupert Murdoch's biggest-selling newspaper is supportive of the line being taken by the Prime Minister, which has been the case, by and large, throughout the twenty months of the Labour administration, then the Downing Street press secretary can look ahead with confidence and begin planning his next move. If the *Sun* has veered off course and is acting unpredictably, Campbell has to take notice; for Blair and his ministers have invested so much time and effort into tailoring the government's news agenda to win favourable treatment from Murdoch's newspapers that serious points of conflict have to be addressed.

Campbell's preoccupation with the *Sun*'s editorial thinking is no passing fancy. In all his campaigning years as a Labour Party propagandist, striving for the downfall of the Conservatives, the key moment for him was undoubtedly that Tuesday morning in March 1997, the day after John Major had announced that the general election would be held on Thursday 1 May, when he could hold that day's *Sun* and see, there on the front page beside a smiling picture of Tony Blair, in three-inch-high capital letters, the words: 'The Sun backs Blair'. That four-word headline represented the culmination of three years' unstinting effort on Campbell's part. He had pulled off what every Labour candidate acknowledged was a seismic shift in the party's relationship with the popular press. His achievement was seen as a turning point. Editorial loyalties were already on the move, but

Blair had picked up the backing of the most influential tabloid on the very first day of the six-week campaign. A framed copy of the *Sun*'s front page immediately took pride of place on the wall of the war room at the Labour Party's headquarters in Millbank Tower.

The lasting impact of Campbell's accomplishment cannot be over-estimated. The strong and productive working relationships which he has established with so many of the key executives in Murdoch's two British enterprises, his publishing company News International and his television operation British Sky Broadcasting, have carried through from opposition into government. There are numerous instances down the years of British Prime Ministers having worked hand in glove with newspaper proprietors, but in terms of the sheer intensity and regularity of the two-way contact, political historians would be hard pressed to find an example to match the degree of cooperation which has been established between No. 10 Downing Street and the Murdoch empire.

For Campbell himself, the bottom line has always been patently obvious. His twin objectives since Blair became Prime Minister have been to do whatever he thinks necessary to ensure that the Labour Party continues to retain the *Sun*'s support through to the next general election, while trying at the same time to persuade Murdoch's newspapers to moderate their strident opposition to the European single currency, and to acknowledge the strength of Blair's argument in wishing to see Britain play a greater part in the development of the European Union. These are clear-cut political goals which Blair has every right to pursue and, when looked at from an historical perspective, are basically no different from the political ambitions of those former Prime Ministers who had equally close links in their day with businessmen who owned important daily papers. In her years in Downing Street, Margaret Thatcher was shown unswerving loyalty by some of the country's most influential news-paper proprietors, who shared many of her political aspirations and who made sure their editors printed stories which were sympathetic to the Conservative cause.

But there are aspects of the Labour government's relationship with the Murdoch empire which are significant and distinctive and which do, I think, set it apart from its predecessors. News International, which publishes *The Times*, *Sunday Times*, *Sun* and *News of the World*, controls a combined circulation which far outstrips rival companies and, put together with his television interests, gives Murdoch an unprecedented grip on the British news media. Then there is the very presence and status in 10 Downing Street of Alastair Campbell. This is without doubt the key differentiating element. Never before has a British Prime Minister had as his right-hand man and constant companion a gifted tabloid journalist of Campbell's calibre; nor has any previous Downing Street press secretary ever enjoyed the political freedom which Campbell has been able to exercise on Blair's behalf. I would suggest that the aspect of the relationship which has to be regarded as unparalleled has been the opening up of unprecedented lines of communication between a British Prime Minister and the world's most politically driven media magnate. The volume and intensity of the two-way communication are beyond comparison. Murdoch's newspaper and television executives have at their disposal in effect a hotline to the Prime Minister's official spokesman, the Downing Street aide who has by far the closest relationship with Blair and who, over the full extent of the working day, usually spends more time with him than any other official. For his part, Campbell can make contact instantly with some of the most powerful editors and executives in the country's biggest media conglomerate.

Any detailed assessment of the strength of this partnership will undoubtedly take time, and my attempt to gauge its effectiveness so soon into the new government's term of office is inevitably no more than an initial appraisal. None of the principal players has given much away and both sides have commanded great loyalty from those in the know. Nevertheless, when I piece together the results of my research, based on my own observations and conversations, I am in no doubt that the relationship is unique and that it does raise important questions about the degree of cooperation that can legitimately exist between a democratically elected government and a media business whose aims and objectives are bound to be different and would be regarded by many outside observers as incompatible. An obvious point of potential conflict would have to be those moments when the profit-making imperatives of Murdoch's newspapers and television channels do not coincide with the interests of the government and its public duties and responsibilities. Is there a danger that the judgement of Tony Blair's media supremo could be influenced by the years he spent working on newspapers? Do his tabloid instincts mean that he can still get caught up in the thrill and excitement of putting together an exclusive story and pulling off a scoop? And, most importantly of all, does the Prime Minister's official spokesman find himself being pulled along by the deadlines and demands of Murdoch's newspapers to the detriment of Blair's colleagues in the government?

My attempt to explore the issues which I have raised starts at that emotional moment when Campbell was told the news he had been waiting to hear for so long. I knew from my own conversations with him during the election campaign that he was surprised that the *Sun* came out publicly in support of Labour so far ahead of polling day. The full impact on him of that announcement emerged in a BBC Radio programme, *Power and the Press*, which was broadcast on 30 April 1998. Campbell told the presenter, Anthony Howard, that the first inkling he had of the paper's decision was when he received a message on his pager from Stuart Higgins, the *Sun*'s editor. Higgins wanted to arrange a photograph of Blair holding an early copy of the paper carrying the headline 'The Sun Backs Blair', so that it could be published on the front page alongside their endorsement of the party leader, who was trumpeted as 'the breath of fresh air this country needs'. After Campbell described the arrangements which had to be made with the *Sun*, there was a slight pause, before he added emphatically: 'Yes, it was for me a great moment.'

Gaining the *Sun*'s backing was one thing; keeping it after the election, however, was another. Labour's former deputy leader Roy Hattersley, another contributor to Howard's programme, said he believed the *Sun*'s support had proved to be a severe constraint on the new government. If Blair had not been so fearful of offending the Eurosceptic prejudices of Murdoch's newspapers, he thought, the Prime Minister could have been far more positive from the start of his administration about the need to join the European single currency. Howard shared Hattersley's assessment and, in an interview for *Breakfast News* the next day, he said he thought the Labour government's failure to join the first phase of the euro would come to be seen as Blair's fatal blunder, a mistake influenced by the fear of Murdoch's newspapers.

The most visible manifestation of what I believe has developed into an unprecedented level of collaboration has been the publication of a constant stream of signed articles by Blair and his ministers in Britain's biggest-selling daily and Sunday newspapers, the *Sun* and the *News of the World.* The preparation of these by-lined columns is often a joint effort. Drafts and suggestions go backwards and forwards as the Prime Minister's wordsmiths and Murdoch's journalists combine forces to prepare the punchiest prose and the snappiest headlines. Exclusive interviews and photographs have to be thought through well in advance, as do other combined promotions. Campbell's strategy of trying to persuade the *Sun* and the *News of the World* to publish as many by-lined articles as possible dates back to the weeks immediately after the Labour leadership election in the summer of 1994. The priority at that moment, as he saw it, was to take immediate advantage of the media honeymoon which Blair was enjoying. In an interview he gave to Roy Hattersley which was published in the *Observer* in February 1998, Campbell explained why the readiness of the tabloid newspapers to look at Labour afresh once Blair had been elected was an opportunity that had to be seized: 'We had to exploit that very quickly and we did. We started to offer interviews and articles to people who maybe we wouldn't have offered them to in the past, especially the *Sun* and the *News of the World.*' Friendships have blossomed amid the toil and trouble of meeting each day's deadlines and, in recent years, Campbell and his colleagues have become regular attenders at the social events of News International's editors and executives.

Close working relationships have had another spin-off, too: high politics is not always the driving force among the journalists and special advisers to whom the task of churning out Tony Blair's signed articles in the *Sun* is delegated, and for hard-pressed, lowly paid special advisers and political activists, the possibility of a lucrative job in one of Murdoch's companies hovers as a powerful lure. If the initiatives which needed publicising were not considered to be politically sensitive, and therefore did not require the personal attention of either Alastair Campbell or the *Sun*'s political editor Trevor Kavanagh, their assistants got a chance to demonstrate their tabloid skills and could then get a buzz from seeing their handiwork appear in print under the Prime Minister's by-line. Brightening up an article on the importance of computer training involved several days' close liaison between the Prime Minister's press office and the *Sun*'s newsroom in April 1998. Blair was about to launch a £600 million investment programme to improve information technology in schools and the National Health Service, but when the *Sun* received the by-lined article which had been commissioned several days earlier from the Downing Street press office, it was considered by the sub-editors to be 'terribly boring' and unfit for publication. One of the *Sun*'s political correspondents, Martin Bentham, told me they suggested to No. 10 that the article should be personalised. 'As we knew that Blair didn't use a computer himself, and that he prepared his speeches in long-hand, we thought it would be much better if it was approached in that way, so that the readers would know what Blair thought himself about trying to use a computer.' Campbell's deputy, Tim Allan, was one of those instructed to knock the article into shape and make it more readable. When it was finally published under the headline 'Britain will lead way in computer revolution', Blair's column had a far snappier introduction: 'Let me break the first rule of politics and lapse into total honesty: I very rarely use a computer. I write my speeches in long-hand and others type them up.' The article had an altogether lighter touch: 'It is time to stop the culture in which a lot of people think the Internet is something which Italian strikers shoot at.' Bentham said the joke about the Internet and Italian football had been Tim Allan's contribution to the rewriting of the article and Allan was delighted when it was picked out by a BBC political journalist, Max Cotton, for inclusion in his report for the 7 a.m. news on Radio Four.

However, Bentham also told me that having to accommodate so many of the Prime Minister's articles in the *Sun* was regarded as something of a mixed blessing by the paper's correspondents at Westminster because it often cut down the amount of space which they were allocated for political news. Joy Johnson calculated for *British Journalism Review* that in the first eight months of the government, the *Sun* published fifteen of the twenty-three by-lined newspaper articles put out in the Prime Minister's name; three had appeared in the *News of the World*.

Nevertheless, the *Sun*'s journalists appreciated the favoured status which they had been accorded by Campbell and they valued the advance knowledge which they obtained through the detailed planning and preparation which went into Blair's columns, and which sometimes gave them a significant advantage over other political correspondents. As they knew at first hand the care which might have gone into the wording of what Blair or one of his ministers wanted to say, they ended up having a far better grasp than some of their counterparts as to how far the government intended to go on particularly sensitive or controversial issues. Other lobby correspondents envied the privileged position of the *Sun's* journalists, and especially the access which was granted to its political editor, Trevor Kavanagh, who worked closely with Campbell on a succession of exclusive stories, such as the Japanese Prime Minister's apology to British prisoners of war. The obvious imbalance this created at lobby briefings became a running joke. If correspondents on the *Sun* knew that their paper was about to get an exclusive article or interview they usually sat tight and said very little, leaving it to other correspondents to ask the questions and incur the wrath of the Prime Minister's press secretary. Occasionally Campbell might shake his head or mutter a few words of disapproval if he disagreed with the way the *Sun* had approached a particular story, but he never unleashed on Kavanagh or his colleagues the kind of abuse which he heaped regularly on the heads of some other recalcitrant correspondents. After one of my particularly bruising encounters, Bentham came over to commiserate as we left No. 10 and tried to cheer me up. I said rather ruefully that Campbell would probably be on the phone in the next half hour dictating Blair's next article to Trevor Kavanagh. Bentham laughed and could not resist a jocular rejoinder: 'You do know, don't you, that we only go along to the No. 10 lobby briefings now for show?'

Tim Allan's help in thinking up a joke about the Internet and Italian football to insert into Blair's article on computer training was one of his final acts of collaboration: three days later he was signed up to become director of corporate communications for Murdoch's television company, British Sky Broadcasting. The *Sun* said that Allan, who was twenty-eight, had 'walked into an £85,000 a year post' at BSkyB after earning £35,000 a year for his 'round-the-clock job' as Campbell's deputy in Downing Street.

Allan's departure had been rumoured for some weeks, and during this period he often sounded rather peeved whenever he had to speak to me, always insisting that any information which I obtained from him on party issues must be attributed to 'a senior Labour source'.

One possible cause of his annoyance was the way I had reported a lobby briefing which he had given in Campbell's absence about the latest in a series of *faux pas* by the accident-prone Lord Chancellor, Lord Irvine of Lairg. In an interview for the *New Statesman* on press intrusion, published on 6 February, Lord Irvine had said he wanted the Press Complaints Commission to step up its pressure on newspapers which broke the Commission's privacy guidelines and he favoured the introduction of a mechanism for 'prior restraint' on newspapers which were shown to be on the point of breaching personal privacy without justification. If the Commission knew that a newspaper was about to publish details about someone's private life where revelation was not in the public interest, the aggrieved person should be able to seek an injunction to stop the story being printed, and it would be up to the newspaper to prove that publication would serve the public interest.

Lord Irvine's proposal produced an outraged response in the newspapers. They had been criticising him for weeks for his comparison of himself to Cardinal Wolsey, the all-powerful Lord Chancellor to King Henry VIII, and for going ahead with the refurbishment of his official residence in the Palace of Westminster at a cost initially estimated at £330,000, which included £59,000 on hand-made wallpaper copied from Pugin's original designs. 'Get your tanks off our lawn, Mr Blair' said the *Mirror's* front-page splash, over a leading article which accused the Lord Chancellor of 'an outrageous and disgraceful attack on press freedom'. Lord Irvine was described as 'a wealthy, privileged man whose pompous bullying arrogance' appeared to know no bounds and who wanted to bar newspapers from 'exposing anything about the life of a politician'.

When the story broke Campbell was in Washington where Tony Blair was having talks with President Clinton, and the lobby briefing that day was taken instead by Tim Allan. If the official spokesman was away the task usually went to the deputy press secretary Allan Percival, who was a civil servant, but if the enquiries involved issues which were considered to be of a political nature, Tim Allan stood in for Campbell. Lord Irvine's unexpected public foray into the controversial issue of press intrusion, and the condemnation of it in the newspapers, had caused consternation in the government. David Hill, the Labour Party's chief spokesperson, was so alarmed he spent the morning advising journalists that the Lord Chancellor was entirely 'off message' and that the government had no plans to introduce a law on prior restraint, so as to curb the tabloid papers. 'We have no intention of bringing in a privacy law. We are not in the business of trying to gag journalists.' At the 4 p.m. lobby briefing Allan repeated Hill's line and said that Tony Blair had 'no desire to bring in a privacy law either by the front door or by the back door'. However, he also said that the government had not taken a final view on press intrusion and that Lord Irvine would continue having discussions with the Press Complaints Commission on ways of strengthening voluntary self-regulation. Allan's insistence that options were still open puzzled the assembled journalists and, in view of the confusion, I asked him if he could name any other member of the cabinet who had spoken up in support of Lord Irvine's ideas. I said that from what I had heard the Lord Chancellor was entirely on his own in advocating prior restraint and in suggesting a public interest defence to stop publication. Allan did not appear to demur at my assessment of the position within the cabinet and, as he did not volunteer any names for me of possible supporters of Lord Irvine, I took his response as confirmation of what I was saying.

Next day the newspapers went hard on Allan's line from the briefing that Blair would not countenance a privacy law 'either by the front door or by the back door'. A large zip had been superimposed across Lord Irvine's mouth in a photograph used by the *Express* which reported the Prime Minister's 'embarrassing slapdown to the Lord Chancellor' under the headline: 'Gag the press? Angry Blair zips up Lord Irvine instead'. As I discovered later that day, Allan had been distressed to find that his guidance to the lobby had been responsible for prompting another savaging of the Lord Chancellor. However, he should not have been surprised at the way his briefing had been treated: lobby correspondents considered he had taken a calculated step in personalising the story, and they interpreted his remarks as indicating that Blair was issuing a personal put-down to the Lord Chancellor. Allan was a political appointee, and journalists understood the significance of those occasions when one of the Downing Street special advisers gave the briefing. They had specific authority, unlike the civil service information officers, to respond to stories which had a 'significant political dimension' and, as set out in Robin

Mountfield's report on the information service, they could be described in the news media as 'an official spokesman' when 'the Prime Minister's official spokesman' was absent. In view of the clarity of Mountfield's guidelines I had no hesitation in reporting on *The World at One* that 'an official spokesman' for the Prime Minister had admitted that no other member of the cabinet supported prior restraint and that Lord Irvine appeared to be in an isolated position.

Immediately after the broadcast I received a message on my pager to 'ring Tim Allan urgently'. He challenged my report, saying I had no authority to claim that Downing Street was 'admitting that no one in the cabinet supported' Lord Irvine and I had broken lobby rules by attributing that statement to the Prime Minister's office. 'You know that is not what I said. Our line is that no decisions have been taken. We have not said that there is no other cabinet member who supports Lord Irvine.' I could tell by his voice that Allan was in an agitated state. Nevertheless I stood my ground and reminded him that he had failed to name anyone in the cabinet who supported Lord Irvine when I had specifically challenged him to do so. If he was still unable to give me the name of a minister who backed the Lord Chancellor, then I had no intention of withdrawing what I had reported. I pointed out that all the newspapers were interpreting his briefing in the same way and that the *Daily Telegraph*, for example, had been categoric in its assessment, saying that 'Tony Blair had authorised an unprecedented rebuke to Lord Irvine, one of his closest personal and political allies.' The *Guardian* too, I pointed out, had published an equally forthright opening to its lead story: 'Tony Blair unleashed the whole of the Downing Street and party machine against his blunder-prone mentor, Lord Irvine.' At this point in the conversation Allan went on the offensive. He said that I was mistaken, that I had breached the propriety of lobby conventions and that I was trying to attribute to Downing Street what I had probably picked up from a Labour Party spokesman.

In order to verify the accuracy of my assertion that Lord Irvine was on his own in calling for the legal remedy of prior restraint, I checked it out with the head of information in the Lord Chancellor's Department, Sheila Thompson. Because of his dissatisfaction with the press coverage he had been receiving, and his doubts about the ability of his staff to respond to it, Lord Irvine had announced the previous month that he intended to bypass her by appointing a director of communications to take charge of publicity for his department. None the less, in view of the ridicule which her boss had attracted for comparing himself to Cardinal Wolsey and for favouring Pugin-style wallpaper, Ms Thompson had built up considerable experience in fielding difficult calls from journalists. She told me that so far as she knew no other member of the cabinet had advocated prior restraint on newspapers. 'I was there for his *New Statesman* interview and the Lord Chancellor was not roaming around on this. He was quite clear that there were two ways of bringing in greater control, either by the Press Complaints Commission getting their act together or by introducing prior restraint.'

Tim Allan's departure from Downing Street, and his achievement in becoming BSkyB's director of corporate communications at the age of twenty-eight, was raised at Question Time on 20 April by the Tory MP Tim Collins, a former director of communications at Conservative Central Office. He said Blair should come clean about his links with Rupert Murdoch because Allan's appointment suggested that 'a revolving door relationship is emerging' between Downing Street and Murdoch's companies. Steve Richards, the *New Statesman*'s political editor, said the government should beware of the perception that would be created when politicians asked: 'What was Murdoch up to in poaching someone from the heart of Downing Street?' Allan got his chance to respond when interviewed by Kirsty Wark on *Newsnight*. He blamed political journalists for creating a needless fuss through their obsession with spin doctors. 'We've had enormous success as a government with our policies and programmes but *Newsnight* loves nothing more than to talk about spin doctors. It's true there've been times in the last twelve months when we haven't had a perfect press but the Prime Minister isn't obsessed with spin. Yes, he keeps in touch with events but he doesn't read the newspapers every day. It was John Major who used to read them all the time.'

The odd awkward question or two about the appropriateness of a special adviser in Downing Street being hired by BSkyB did nothing to dampen the atmosphere at a farewell party for him in the No. 10 drawing room, hosted by the Prime Minister. Their working relationship went back to 1992, when Blair was shadow Home Secretary, and had continued throughout his campaigns to become party leader and then Prime Minister. Allan had made many friends among political correspondents at Westminster and he played in the friendly football matches which were a regular fixture for some of the journalists and special advisers. According to the political diaries there was an exceptionally good turnout for the party. Peter Oborne, writing in the *Express*, said Blair was in 'dazzling form' and 'playfully taunted Allan for some of the blunders he had inevitably made' during the years that he had worked for him at Westminster, although he also praised his readiness to be tough with journalists when the need arose. There were tributes to Allan in *Sunday Business*, which said his 'closeness to Alastair Campbell won him the soubriquet the "sorcerer's apprentice" in the run-up to the election'; according to the *Observer*'s diary, when it came to his own speech Allan was 'lavish in his praise for Campbell, saying "he taught me everything I know".'

Social events at No. 10 provided political correspondents and newspaper executives with an opportunity to cement their working relationships with Campbell and the rest of the Downing Street press officers. Although he was rarely seen accepting hospitality from journalists, and was said to turn down scores of lunch invitations, Campbell did attend the thirtieth birthday party of Rebekah Wade, the *Sun*'s deputy editor, on 29 May. A few days later the paper's editor, Stuart Higgins, resigned. There was much comment subsequently about the way in which the *Sun* had delivered its pre-election support for Tony Blair under Higgins's editorship and about what the guests saw in retrospect as the valedictory speech Higgins gave at Ms Wade's party.

Campbell's regular contact with the editorial executives of News International, and his determination to retain the *Sun*'s backing for Blair, could cut both ways: there were times when Murdoch's newspapers wanted favours in return for their cooperation with the government, when they were desperate to enlist the assistance of 10 Downing Street. Although little has been revealed publicly about those occasions when the Prime Minister's official spokesman has found himself under pressure to respond to the demands and deadlines of News International, there was no doubt that he was placed in a difficult position in the summer of 1997, when he was approached by the *News of the World* on the morning of Friday 1 August and told that the paper was ready to strike a deal with the Downing Street press office over the way it wanted to handle its exclusive story about the affair between the Foreign Secretary, Robin Cook, and his secretary, Gaynor Regan.

Exactly three months into his premiership, Tony Blair and his press secretary faced a defining moment: how would they respond to what the *News of the World* would no doubt seek to claim was the first major sex scandal to hit the new government? Was the Blair administration going to try to break free from some of the most distasteful dictates of the newspapers, or, like its predecessors, would it give way in the face of the agenda being pursued by Rupert Murdoch's tabloids? John Major had been pilloried for his failure to act swiftly when his ministers were caught out having extra-marital affairs. In the long wait for the general election, Labour had gained immeasurable advantage from the damage inflicted on the Conservative Party by the kind of sexual disclosures which appeared so regularly in newspapers like the *Sun* and the *News of the World*. But, after Labour's landslide victory, there was a new mood at Westminster, and Blair had an unrivalled opportunity to take a bold stand in response to the abhorrence felt by politicians and other public figures over press intrusion into their private lives. Many of the young, newly elected Labour and Liberal Democrat MPs had an enlightened and tolerant approach to personal relationships; and the much depleted band of Conservatives, after their party's shattering defeat and the mauling which they had received in the pages of the popular press, were in no mood to launch a hue and cry over the alleged sexual misdemeanours of their fellow parliamentarians. If a new Prime Minister was going to take on the tabloids, this was the moment. If Blair had been so minded, he could have ordered his official spokesman to tell Murdoch's newspaper empire that his government would have nothing to do with the squalid little deal which the *News of the World* had been touting around the Downing Street press office that Friday morning. He could have said that, as Prime Minister, he had the utmost confidence in his Foreign Secretary, whose private life was his own business as long as it did not impinge on his duties as a minister of the crown, and there was no evidence that it had. Robin Cook and his wife Margaret, who were on their way to a three-week holiday in America, would have been airborne within a matter of hours, so there was little, if anything, that the newspaper could have done about it.

Blair had the opportunity to stand firm, and take a risk on Cook's behalf, because circumstances at Westminster were entirely different from those prevailing under Major. His government had an unprecedented mandate and, after the momentous events of its first three months in office, there was no danger of its authority being undermined. The political atmosphere had changed out of all recognition when compared with the previous parliament, and the likelihood of any MP seeking to make political capital out of the kind of personal disclosures which were the speciality of the *News of the World* was negligible. Indeed, the most likely reaction of virtually every MP would have been to urge the Prime Minister to tell the paper to do its damnednest because they would have been happy to give him an absolute assurance that they would ignore it. A discreet telephone call to the offices of William Hague and Paddy Ashdown could easily have secured their cooperation in ensuring there were no maverick attempts to exploit newspaper speculation about difficulties in Cook's marriage. And there were other tactical factors working in Blair's favour, if he had wanted to seize his chance. As the summer recess had just started most MPs were heading off for their holidays, so there would have been very few of them around Westminster in any case, and the journalists too had been packing their bags: political news would be slipping down the agenda during the following few weeks.

The events that unfolded that fateful Friday were to be cataclysmic for the Cook family, for Gaynor Regan and for their friends. Unlike the break-up of many other political families, the trials and tribulations of Robin and Margaret Cook were not going to be a one-day wonder. They would continue to engage the interest of the tabloid newspapers for month after month. For well over a year rarely a week went by without Cook hitting the front pages, usually as a result of fresh disclosures about his troubled married life or because of developments in his relationship with Gaynor Regan and the events surrounding their subsequent marriage. His notoriety dogged him in his official duties as Foreign Secretary, whether escorting the Queen on overseas tours or hosting lavish receptions for visiting foreign dignitaries. Cook had become an easy target for journalists: the slightest misunderstanding, mistake or omission would be headline news.

As neither Cook nor Campbell has gone on the record to give a step-by-step account of precisely what they said to each other during their conversations over the *News of the World*'s approach, there has to be a degree of conjecture about what happened, but the basic facts are not in dispute. Cook was told to ring Downing Street while he was being driven in a Foreign Office car towards Terminal Four at Heathrow Airport, where the couple were about to catch their plane to Boston en route for a riding holiday in Montana. After speaking to Campbell, Cook escorted Margaret to a VIP lounge, told her of the *News of the World*'s story and said the holiday was off.

Campbell's role in the lead-up to the final denouement has already secured him a place in the mythology of spin doctoring, credited by most newspapers with having issued an infamous ultimatum to the effect that the Foreign Secretary had an hour to decide whether to stay with his wife or announce the break-up of his marriage. While Campbell has been wholly justified in protesting at the way his telephone call has been so badly misinterpreted, he has acknowledged that he did negotiate a 'deal' with the *News of the World*, although he has insisted that its sole purpose was to give Cook, his wife and Regan sufficient time to sort out their affairs. Whatever his motives, it remains the case that the Prime Minister's official spokesman was taking action in response to the demands of Murdoch's biggest-selling Sunday newspaper, and that events were being dictated by the publishing deadlines of the *News of the World* rather than the best interests of the Cooks and Ms Regan.

The first detailed account of what ensued after Cook spoke to Campbell appeared in December 1997 when *The Times* published an extract from an interview which Margaret Cook had given to Linda McDougall, wife of the Labour MP Austin Mitchell, for her book *Westminster Women*. The Cooks, Ms McDougall said, had flown down from Edinburgh together, and it was not until Cook had shut the door of the VIP lounge at Heathrow that he told Margaret that the *News of the World* had 'got the story'. Ms McDougall told me subsequently that in checking out her story she had managed to speak to someone who was in the same room as Campbell that Friday afternoon as he waited in Downing Street for the Cooks' plane to land at Heathrow and as he prepared to speak to the Foreign Secretary. She had often wondered since what might have happened if Campbell had been unable to communicate with Cook and if the couple had left for their holiday as planned without 'being pressurised'.

Campbell gave his side of the story to Kevin Toolis in an interview for the *Guardian* in April 1998. Toolis said the accusations that the Downing Street press secretary had ordered Cook to 'end his marriage and cancel his holiday' were entirely false. 'In reality, Campbell managed to do a deal with the newspaper to buy Robin Cook some time to think – a few hours – before the story inevitably broke.' A far fuller account was given by John Kampfner in *Robin Cook*, the first biography of the Foreign Secretary, published in October 1998. He said that the *News of the World* told Campbell it would make the details of its revelations known by the following Saturday morning, leaving the Cooks a little over twelve hours to sort it out. The deal on offer was quite explicit: 'Campbell had been phoned on Friday morning by the *News of the World*, who agreed not to contact Cook himself, Margaret, Gaynor or the children, provided a statement was issued in response to the story. Campbell told Cook that, for what it was worth, clarity in news management was the only way they were going to get out of it. Cook interpreted "clarity" as meaning he should make a choice one way or the other and told Campbell that he knew he could not go on with the holiday with Margaret, being pursued by photographers and reporters. Nor could he ditch Gaynor. Campbell was not surprised by the response.'

The brutal finality of these events was vividly retold by Margaret Cook in *A Slight and Delicate Creature*, her book on the break-up of their marriage. They were met at Heathrow by Cook's special adviser, David Mathieson, who was 'on edge' and told her husband that Campbell wanted to speak to him urgently. 'Robin impatiently lifted the car phone and dialled…Robin had become very still and silent.' She described what happened in the VIP lounge: 'Robin said chillingly, "I am afraid there won't be any holiday, Margaret. It's cancelled. The *News of the World* is running the story of my affair with Gaynor, on Sunday. I can't leave the country. I think you and I should part."' Mrs Cook said she had no idea what kind of ultimatum her husband was given by Blair and Campbell. 'They clearly wanted to avoid the image of Robin as having a "bit on the side" and dropping her as soon as the affair was revealed. The image of a genuinely impassioned love affair was one the public might more easily be persuaded to accept. The cynicism in such behaviour was appalling.'

The *News of the World*'s tactics followed the usual pattern for managing the publication in a popular Sunday paper of an exclusive story about a sex scandal. Campbell was no stranger to the procedures involved and he knew all about the kind of 'deal' which was on offer. Surprise is always an important element: the victim should not be informed until the last possible moment, usually Saturday morning, in order to leave only a few hours' thinking time before the print run starts late on Saturday afternoon. In that short, concentrated period many a far-reaching decision has been made in haste. In Cook's case there seems to have been a longer lead time, no doubt because a powerful intermediary was on the scene in the shape of the Prime Minister's official spokesman and the *News of the World* could afford to be more flexible than it might otherwise have been, hoping no doubt that Campbell would prove to be a useful conduit for passing on information and might even exercise some useful persuasion on their behalf.

It is at this point, when contact is first established, that a degree of sharp practice can enter into the equation. The dodge which newspaper executives often employ is to talk up their story in this initial discussion without ever actually producing any of their evidence. Instead they offer a deal and promise not to harass the victim or the family if those concerned are prepared in return to make a statement. To the uninitiated it might appear that the newspaper is somehow seeking to play fair, but the ploy can amount to a pretty blatant deception. Once the victim has issued a statement which takes even the slightest step towards confirming the story, the newspaper can use that one tiny element of verification to justify the publication of other far more questionable material which might otherwise have been too risky to print.

By piecing together what happened in Cook's case from the accounts of Kevin Toolis and John Kampfner, the 'deal' can be seen for what it was: Cook had agreed by the Friday afternoon to issue his statement, but it was to be the following Saturday morning before the *News of the World* disclosed to its target 'the details of its revelations'; in return, the paper had promised that it would not pursue the Cooks or Gaynor Regan. So there had in effect been no contest; the moment had passed when it would have been possible for Tony Blair to have stood firm, for his press secretary to have called the *News of the World*'s bluff and for them all to have waited to see what it dared print and whether the story was followed up subsequently by other newspapers or exploited by their political opponents. When it came down to it, what did the *News of the World* actually have as evidence of Cook's affair with Regan? Had any of the parties involved spoken to the news media? Was there any independent corroboration or other potentially incriminating material, perhaps correspondence or photographs of the couple together? Would there have been suffi- cient information to stand up the story of an affair had Cook not been prepared to volunteer his statement that he was leaving his wife?

I acknowledge immediately that there are weaknesses in my argu- ment, and that other matters came into play. The couple were well aware themselves of the difficulties in their marriage; Cook was said by friends to have realised for some time that he would rather be with Ms Regan, and Margaret Cook had known for some time of her husband's long-standing affair. There were a host of other factors influencing Alastair Campbell, too. Labour had benefited from John Major's lack of 'clarity' in handling the problems posed by the extra- marital affairs of his ministers and, as Blair's official spokesman, Campbell was determined to be decisive. He believed that if there was embarrassing information which would leak out eventually it was usually better to release it straight away rather than to sit on it.

Campbell had built his formidable reputation on the basis of having been proved right time and time again in judging the poten- tial strengths and weaknesses of news stories. He also knew that a lot of people could end up feeling hurt and distressed when newspaper journalists and photographers were on the trail of a salacious story. I would in no way seek to minimise what I am convinced would have been his genuine concern to seek to protect those caught up in the breakdown of Cook's marriage. Nevertheless, given the limited nature of the information which the *News of the World* had in its pos- session, there is no doubt that the paper's executives must have been mightily relieved that Friday afternoon when Campbell finally told them that Cook would be issuing a statement, that he would be admitting the breakdown of his marriage and that he was leaving his wife. Without Cook's statement, or some other independent corrob- oration, all that the newspaper appeared to have to substantiate its story was a diary compiled by two freelance photographers listing the comings and goings by Cook and Ms Regan at Cook's flat in Victoria; a picture of Cook carrying a black rubbish bag out of his flat; another picture of him feeding the meter for Ms Regan's car; and a photograph of her driving it away.

From the moment that Friday afternoon when the Foreign Secretary made his decision, and once he had been assured personally on the telephone by Blair that his job was safe, the 'deal' took effect and, according to Kampfner, Cook agreed that as soon as the first edition of the *News of the World* had revealed the story on Saturday evening, he would make a public statement to the news media. 'Next morning, the news management operation went into full swing. Cook discussed the wording of statements with Campbell . . . and his deputy Tim Allan.' That evening the story was out: 'Robin appeared on the steps of the Foreign Office and, to the accompaniment of flashing camera lights, announced that he was leaving his wife for his secretary.'

The story could not have broken at a more inconvenient moment for either the Prime Minister or his official spokesman, both of whom were about to leave for their family holidays. The Blairs' destination was the villa in Tuscany owned by the Labour MP Geoffrey Robinson; and, according to the *Sun*, Campbell was still taking calls over the Cooks' break-up as he drove to the south of France with his partner Fiona Millar and their three children for a two-week break. Yet despite all the various complications the arrangements for making the announcement went as planned. The late editions of the other Sunday newspapers carried not only Cook's personal statement but also a message from the Prime Minister, who said that although it was a personal tragedy for those involved, it did not affect Cook's 'capability as a truly outstanding Foreign Secretary'. In his own statement Cook said that he accepted that he was a public figure but he asked that the 'privacy of those involved be respected at a very painful time'.

The only opposition MP to speak publicly about the Cooks' separation that weekend was William Hague's parliamentary political secretary, Alan Duncan. While insisting that he was not passing any comment on the Foreign Secretary's affair itself, he said the government's handling of it revealed Labour's hypocrisy. He claimed that when Conservative ministers were in a similar predicament, the 'likes of Peter Mandelson would get a lot of people to do their dirty work, to try and condemn it and cause us embarrassment'. Duncan sought to justify his accusation about 'double standards' by pointing to a Labour leaflet issued during the Uxbridge by-election the previous week which had 'resurrected' mention of an affair involving the Conservative Party chairman, Lord Parkinson, which had happened fourteen years earlier.

Mandelson, interviewed that Sunday morning on GMTV's *Sunday Programme*, denied that Labour took advantage of the marriage break-ups of Conservative ministers. 'Labour has never made any comment, never exploited any personal tragedy of this sort...We have not and we don't intend to start now, and we don't expect the Conservatives to. Perhaps that's too high an expectation of the Conservatives.' In the event, Duncan's somewhat misjudged intervention was the only public pronouncement by a Conservative MP on Cook's affair in the immediate aftermath of their separation; from my discussions with MPs that summer it seemed clear that they all felt Blair would have been far better advised to have left the Cooks and Gaynor Regan to sort out their own affairs without asking his press secretary to intervene only hours before the couple's departure on holiday. These conversations confirmed my impression that if the *News of the World* had failed to get a response from the Foreign Secretary, and that if all it had been able to publish were the snatched photographs taken outside Cook's flat, then MPs would not have exploited the story.

Campbell's intervention, and his advice to Cook that 'clarity' was needed, was considered to be particularly ill-judged by the Tory MP Shaun Woodward, who was the Conservatives' director of communications during the 1992 general election. 'We had hoped that after all the troubles that we went through as a party over marriage break-ups and affairs, that Tony Blair would have wanted to start the new parliament with a clean slate. As the new Prime Minister, he should have been ready to stand firm straight away when the first newspaper began intruding like that into the personal life of one of his ministers, or any other MP, come to that. Campbell should have been told to inform the *News of the World* that the Prime Minister had total confidence in his Foreign Secretary and that Cook's relationship with his wife had nothing to do with the government, the newspapers or anyone else. Blair missed a real opportunity over that because we'd have backed him.'

Of all the scenarios which went through Campbell's mind as he advised the Foreign Secretary on how to respond to the *News of the World*, he could hardly have imagined that it would be Margaret Cook who would rebel against Downing Street's news management and throw a spanner into the whole operation. Within a fortnight of the break-up of her marriage she wrote to the *Scotsman* reflecting on how the 'overdriven workaholic personality' was selectively attached to politics and became strongly attracted to any person who regularly and unstintingly provided 'praise, adulation and acclaim'. Her letter catapulted the story back on to the front pages. 'Mrs Cook's side-swipe' was the *Daily Mail's* headline, and the tabloids were convinced she was on the brink of 'telling all' about her husband's affair with his secretary. Much to Campbell's annoyance, every story included reference to the way he had given the Foreign Secretary 'one hour to decide whether to leave his wife or his mistress'. His role in the proceedings was thought to have reflected badly on what was considered to be Blair's obsession with news management, and it would not be forgotten by those in the Labour Party who were already criticising what they called New Labour's 'control freak' tendency. Several days later Margaret Cook wrote to *The Times* saying she was glad her marriage 'did not fall apart' until after her two sons had started work.

Through her letters to newspapers outlining the sacrifices which she had made, Margaret Cook was signalling that she was not averse to publicity. Her action would also ensure that the spotlight of media attention would never be far away from Robin Cook and Gaynor Regan. Foreign Secretaries get used to seeing reporters and photographers at official occasions, but once their presence gets too persistent, and once a politician realises the journalists are only there on gaffe watch, looking for sleights and slip-ups, the constant scrutiny tends to be extremely nerve-racking and can have a destabilising effect on even the most controlled of temperaments. Cook's ability to withstand such pressure was put to a severe test that autumn when he was accused of mishandling British policy on Kashmir while accompanying the Queen on her visit to India and Pakistan. A few weeks later he surprised cabinet colleagues by telling *Today* that he had not ruled out the possibility of standing for the post of First Minister in the new Scottish parliament, only to withdraw the suggestion a week later, saying he was thoroughly enjoying being Foreign Secretary. In early January 1998 he announced that he intended to divorce his wife and marry Gaynor Regan. On arriving at Edinburgh Airport, he was questioned about other extra-marital affairs but stuck to his statement: 'The only relationship I have is with the woman I love and with the woman I will marry.' Campbell, who was in Tokyo with Blair when the story broke, reiterated his denial of ever having issued an ultimatum to the Foreign Secretary. He had warned Cook there 'was going to be a problem' after being 'tipped off' by the *News of the World*. 'At no time did I tell Robin Cook to end his marriage ... I said you have got overnight to decide what to do.'

Within a few weeks the story had taken off again after the *Mail on Sunday* claimed on 25 January that Cook had sacked his Foreign Office diary secretary, Anne Bullen, in order to 'create a vacancy in his private office for his lover'. At the 11 a.m. lobby briefing next morning Campbell said Ms Bullen had been appointed personally by the former Conservative Foreign Secretary, Douglas Hurd, and as Cook considered she was not the 'appropriate person' for the job, she had been replaced by a career member of the diplomatic service; the post had not gone to Gaynor Regan, who was his constituency secretary.

Downing Street's attempt to stop the story in its tracks failed utterly. Next morning the *Mirror* published an exclusive interview with Ms Bullen, who said she 'broke down in tears' after being fired and insisted that Cook was obsessed with Regan and had intended to 'give his lover my job'. At a news conference later that morning in Brussels, where he had been presiding at a meeting of European Union foreign ministers, Cook threw caution to the wind and put Ms Bullen in her place: 'I reluctantly came to the conclusion that I could not extend her contract because she was impossible to work with. One option after I decided to close her contract would have been to appoint Gaynor Regan. I quickly decided not to pursue that option.' Cook's outburst provoked an outraged response from Ms Bullen, who said the Foreign Secretary was 'rude, arrogant and terse'.

My task that day was to doorstep the monthly meeting of Labour's national executive committee, which was being held in Millbank Tower for the first time since the party's departure from its former headquarters in Walworth Road. David Hill, the party's chief spokesperson, was alarmed at the way the story was continuing to hurtle out of control. He thought Cook had been right to explain why Ms Bullen's contract had not been renewed, but the remark about her being 'impossible to work with' illustrated how difficult it was to coordinate what the government was saying. 'Ministers have to be consistent if they want to avoid creating a story. They're now having to realise that every word they utter does matter and that the odd word out of place can cause immense problems.' As she left the meeting, Clare Short, the Secretary of State for International Development, called me over. She shook her head ruefully as she looked back at Millbank Tower and said she wanted to remind me of a discussion we had had when Labour was in opposition, about the downside of spin doctors and the party leadership's obsession with presentation. 'There are some good things about this government, some very good things, but those things that we talked about in opposition, those are the things that are bad about this government.' She did not expand on her aside, but her dissatisfaction was clear.

Cook's clash with Ms Bullen was a delight for the headline writers. 'War of the secretaries' was the front-page banner headline for the *Mirror*, which led with the story for the second morning running. The *Sun* had been supplied with its own exclusive, and it reproduced a letter which Diana, Princess of Wales, had written to the Foreign Secretary two months before her death, thanking Cook for giving up his 'precious time' to brief her on various issues affecting her campaign against anti-personnel mines. The letter had been released to the *Sun* in an attempt to rebut Ms Bullen's claim that Cook had kept Diana waiting for twenty minutes. By now the saga of the sacked secretary was in its fourth day and it was obvious at the 4 p.m. lobby briefing that Campbell was in no mood for pleasantries. He lashed out wildly at all and sundry. 'The idea that Cook's secretary should be second item on the ITN lunchtime news is ridiculous and that it gets twelve minutes on *The World at One* is pathetic.' Campbell then turned his fire on Kevin Maguire, the *Mirror*'s political editor: 'Your paper has been ridiculous. A sacked diary secretary, the *Mirror* make her a heroine and then people believe her every word.' When a *Financial Times* reporter said the fact that Cook had considered appointing his mistress to a job in the Foreign Office was a matter of public interest, Campbell retorted: 'Well, the *Financial Times* had better sack Sam Brittan and get in Clare Rayner.' Michael White, the

Guardian's political editor, suggested the Prime Minister's official spokesman should 'take it easy' and remember that his briefings were now on the record, but it was to no avail. 'No, I won't take it easy . . . I'll continue to deal with the papers in the way I want to.'

On leaving the lobby room Maguire said he hoped I would give him a 'name check' in my next book. He thought Campbell had been out of order slagging off everyone except the *Sun* when it was Downing Street which had been playing fast and loose with the lobby and had made sure that the *Sun* got Diana's letter exclusively. 'Doesn't Alastair realise we're off the leash now?' He had a point: nine months into the government, political journalists were not going to stand meekly by and accept punishment from Campbell if at the same time he was orchestrating the kind of favouritism to which Maguire and other journalists objected. Next morning the *Mirror* retaliated with its own exclusive under the headline: 'Cook did keep Diana waiting'. It said a 'royal source' had confirmed that Diana did have to wait fifteen minutes before meeting the Foreign Secretary and, in a 'sensational rebuke', Buckingham Palace had made clear its view that Cook had 'behaved recklessly' in allowing a private letter from the princess to be released to the *Sun*.

Anne Bullen's protest over the way she was sacked underlined the urgent need for Cook to regularise his private life so that he could put a stop to hurtful newspaper stories and constant references to his 'mistress' and 'lover'. Within a matter of weeks, when the Cooks' divorce had finally been completed, he announced he would marry Gaynor Regan in early April, at a private ceremony to be held at no cost to the public at Chevening House, the Foreign Secretary's official country residence. To mark the announcement he posed for a photograph with his fiancée on the steps of Chevening; but the resulting publicity, and the suggestion that their arm–in–arm pose was a calculated snub to Margaret Cook, hardly helped his cause. 'The Mistress of Chevening' was the *Daily Mail's* front-page headline over a photograph of the couple which some caption writers thought resembled the famous engagement photograph of Prince Charles and Diana Spencer. The choice of Chevening for the photo-call and for a wedding the following month was said by journalists to have 'raised eyebrows' as the house was financed as a charitable trust. Stung by the renewed criticism, and fearing further unfavourable publicity, Cook brought the wedding forward, and the couple were married ten days earlier than planned at Tunbridge Wells register office. The ceremony, which was held without any public warning, was conducted at 8.30 a.m. on the day before Good Friday. The couple said they 'wished it to be a private event free from media intrusion'. Some workmen outside said they saw Cook arrive. He was wearing a green anorak and his bride was dressed in a dark suit. According to the *Daily Telegraph*, Foreign Office 'mandarins were amazed' to be told so early in the morning by Cook's special adviser, David Mathieson, that 'their boss had just said his vows'.

Mathieson, who was one of just three guests at the ceremony, must have been as relieved as the Foreign Secretary himself that the relationship with Gaynor Regan was at last on an official footing. He had spent almost a year fielding calls from journalists about the pair's tangled private life and he had found it a chastening experience. Unlike larger-than-life characters such as Charlie Whelan, Mathieson did not seem entirely at ease in the company of journalists. He complained regularly about the way the newspapers had mounted a vendetta against Cook, but he was not as streetwise as Whelan, who often succeeded against the odds in turning difficult occasions to Gordon Brown's advantage. Sometimes, in order to avoid a media scrum, a deal has to be done with newspaper photographers and television channels. Increasingly ministers and party leaders insist that semi-private events are covered on a pooled basis, with only one photographer and television crew allowed to attend. Cook's wedding in Tunbridge Wells register office was just such an occasion. With some imagination and astute planning it could have been turned to the couple's advantage but, after having been hounded for so long by the media, Cook was determined to outwit his tormentors. Allan Oakeshott, a painter, who was one of the workmen who served as stand-in reporters outside the register officer, said the Foreign Secretary 'punched the air' when he left the building and found there were no photographers waiting for him. 'I think he was glad he had missed the press and avoided the cameras.'

Two days earlier Cook had discussed his plans with Alastair Campbell and they had agreed that a secret wedding on Maundy Thursday would help minimise publicity because it would be overshadowed by the talks which Tony Blair was holding in Belfast that

Easter on a Northern Ireland peace agreement. Cook's readiness to take Campbell's advice, and to cooperate with Downing Street's strategic communications unit in preparing his speeches, was a change of tack for him, and had followed the criticism of his undisciplined attack on Anne Bullen for being 'impossible to work with'. The *Independent*'s columnist Donald Macintyre said humility had never been Cook's strongest suit, but his outburst had irritated those in the government who were faced with the 'day-to-day struggle to secure the most favourable headlines' and who felt he should have 'put himself more fully in their charge'. Campbell's relief that Cook had at last succeeded in drawing a line under a story which had caused so many problems was one small consolation at the end of what, in terms of his relationship with lobby journalists and the Labour Party, had been a disastrous month. The Prime Minister's press secretary had suffered two personal setbacks: his reputation as a reliable and credible spokesman had been brought into question after he gave evasive answers to the lobby, and the leak of faxes in which he ordered two ministers to stop briefing journalists and giving radio interviews was seen by friend and foe alike as revealing that he had exceeded his authority as an unelected adviser. Campbell had sailed close to the wind on numerous occasions when briefing the lobby, but the pace of events was usually so fast that there seemed little point in harking back to what might have been misleading answers or discrepancies in what he had said. However, when it came to Blair's links with Rupert Murdoch, he should have known he could not take risks. Information which journalists gleaned from Campbell about the government's connections with Murdoch's newspaper and television interests was of commercial as well as political interest to those newspapers which were in competition with News International's titles. If Campbell was caught out giving evasive or flippant replies so as to avoid having to answer awkward questions in this area, he could hardly expect to get away with it; and if there was even the merest hint of a cover-up, rival newspapers were unlikely to let go.

Throughout the early months of 1998 Murdoch's activities had come under increasing scrutiny at Westminster. In February the government was defeated in the House of Lords when a cross-party group of peers succeeded in amending the Competition Bill to outlaw what was known as predatory pricing. News International's policy of regularly reducing the cover price of *The Times* in order to increase its circulation was regarded as unfair competition by the *Daily Telegraph* and the *Guardian* and was said to be threatening the survival of the *Independent*. The government insisted there was no need for additional safeguards, and its defeat by the upper house heralded the start of a prolonged parliamentary struggle and repeated accusations that ministers were letting News International get away with an improper commercial advantage. A fortnight later, Murdoch was accused of demanding changes in the memoirs of Chris Patten, the last governor of Hong Kong, to avoid offending the Chinese government and to protect his television interests in south-east Asia. After Stuart Proffitt, editor-in-chief of Murdoch's publishing subsidiary, HarperCollins, had resigned in protest, the *Daily Telegraph* published a copy of a memo revealing that Murdoch had ordered the rights to the book to be relinquished because he was 'extremely worried' at what he thought were the book's 'negative aspects'. Patten sued for breach of contract and within days HarperCollins announced a financial settlement and 'unreservedly apologised' for suggesting the former governor's book had been rejected for 'not being up to proper professional standards or for being too boring'.

Murdoch's conduct over Patten's book, which had provoked outrage in the literary world and attracted widespread publicity, should have put Campbell on his guard later that month when it was revealed in Rome by *La Stampa* that the Italian Prime Minister, Romano Prodi, had been asked by Tony Blair whether his government would obstruct Murdoch's twice-thwarted takeover of Mediaset, the holding company for Silvio Berlusconi's television interests in Italy. Downing Street's initial response that evening was to confirm that a conversation had taken place but to make no comment on what the two Prime Ministers had discussed. Next morning the *Financial Times* led on the story under the headline 'Blair intervened on Murdoch bid'. When pressed repeatedly at the 11 a.m. lobby briefing to explain why Blair had been putting questions to Prodi on Murdoch's behalf, Campbell lost his temper. He did not deny the conversation had taken place, but he attacked the way it had been reported in the *Financial Times*. In case correspondents had not heard him the first time when he said the story was a 'complete joke' he spelt it out again, this time in capital letters. 'It's balls that the

Prime Minister "intervened" over some deal with Murdoch. That's C-R-A-P.' Later, on a visit to Paris, Blair did not deny that Murdoch's interests had been raised in his conversation, but he insisted there had been no special favours. 'There is no question of offering assistance to anybody. I treat Murdoch no differently from anybody else in respect of any business with British interests.'

Next day the *Financial Times* revealed that Murdoch had spoken on the phone to Blair the week before the two Prime Ministers had their conversation. Campbell told the lobby that if Murdoch had rung Blair it would have been a private conversation which he could not discuss. Downing Street maintained the same line the following morning when Campbell again rebuked the *Financial Times*, saying its story that Murdoch had phoned to seek Blair's assistance was a 'complete non-story' which was being driven by newspaper groups 'playing their games in public'. Earlier in the week there had been much comment about the failure of *The Times* to report the story; eventually its media editor, Raymond Snoddy, gave Murdoch's version of the conversations which had taken place, and in doing so he cut the ground from beneath Campbell's feet.

Snoddy's piece in *The Times* said that Murdoch had 'used information obtained directly from Tony Blair to inform his business decisions' during BSkyB's attempt to buy Berlusconi's television interests. 'Despite a number of ambiguous statements from Downing Street spokesmen over the past few days it is now clear that last week Murdoch rang the Prime Minister to see if he would find out what the political reaction might be.' Murdoch was quoted by *The Times* as saying he had not lobbied Blair but had made a 'perfectly innocent request for information', and once he heard from Blair that Prodi would prefer to see Mediaset going to an Italian purchaser, he decided not to make a higher offer.

When interviewed on *The World at One,* Snoddy pulled no punches in his criticism of the way that Campbell had briefed the lobby. 'Journalists had their stories denounced as a joke, and some of them were called a joke themselves, about a story which I now believe was completely true. It's unbelievable and outrageous and it's very close to providing misleading information.' Robert Peston, the political editor of the *Financial Times*, whose reporting had been rubbished so comprehensively, told the programme that Campbell's behaviour, in treating the whole issue in an incredibly off-hand manner and with derision, was inappropriate because Blair's relationship with Murdoch was a matter of public interest. He thought the original reference to Blair having 'intervened' on Murdoch's behalf had been justified all along. Campbell's description of his story as a 'complete joke' was in fact a 'non-denial denial': rather than denying it outright, he was trying to suggest it was a 'non-story', which was meant to sound like a denial without actually being one.

Murdoch's intervention account of the episode, which in the opinion of the *Independent* had left 'Blair in the lurch', produced a flurry of speculation in the weekend press about Campbell's position. The Liberal Democrat peer Lord McNally, who had led the Lords' revolt on predatory pricing, said the conflicting briefings from Downing Street were so serious they warranted a House of Commons statement. Among the few commentators to defend the Prime Minister's official spokesman was one of his past employers, the former *Daily Mirror* editor Roy Greenslade. In his media affairs column in the *Guardian* he said Campbell's initial description of the story as a 'complete joke' was justified. 'In a sense, I think he was right. I am convinced that Blair didn't do or say anything he shouldn't. I am also persuaded that Campbell didn't lie to lobby journalists, though he was economical with the truth because he and Blair were punctiliously observing the protocol of protecting the confidentiality of a private conversation between government leaders.'

Greenslade's support for his celebrated protégé cut little ice with the former Conservative spin doctors on whom Campbell had inflicted so much damage. The Tory MP Tim Collins, who had been the party's director of communications during some of John Major's most difficult years, told me it was always foolish when answering difficult questions about a speculative but embarrassing story to dismiss it as a 'complete joke' or 'crap', and it would have been far wiser for Campbell to have retreated into other devices – like saying 'no comment' or that 'more information' was being sought. 'A cover-up is always worse than the original problem and Campbell is now having to realise that if you live by spin, you die by spin. He could get away with it in opposition when Labour were so obsessed with thinking about how they could deliver tomorrow's headlines. A new story was coming along every day, so Labour knew they could knock trouble on the head one day and be sure it would be overtaken by another story the next day. But in government it's different and Campbell's tactic of trying to rubbish something by saying it's crap or a non-story might work for twenty-four hours but will come back and hit him in the face ten days later.' Collins raised his concerns with the Speaker on a point of order. He said the Downing Street press secretary had 'quite scandalously abused and insulted' journalists who had written 'perfectly proper and accurate stories'.

Francis Maude, the shadow cultural affairs secretary, followed up Tory protests by calling on the Prime Minister to explain why his official spokesman had given out information which was 'at best misleading and at worst deliberately false'. After Labour won the election the code of conduct for special advisers had been specifically altered in Campbell's case to give him managerial authority and, as a political appointee, he had unprecedented powers to issue orders to civil servants. Maude said that as a result of the change in status, Blair must recognise that it was unacceptable for his press secretary 'deliberately to give out false information'. When challenged next morning on *Today*, Maude reinforced his demand that Campbell should be held to account for what he had said: 'We want to know if he is doing this off his own bat. Is he specifically authorised to tell lies?' By pushing the charge a stage further in suggesting that the Prime Minister's spokesman had not simply misled journalists but had lied to them, Maude had given his target the opening he was looking for. His aim in denouncing Robert Peston's report as 'crap' and a 'complete joke' had been to rubbish what the *Financial Times* had printed. Lobby journalists understood the code: insisting it was a 'non-story' was not quite the same as denying the story categorically, which would have been an outright lie. Campbell seized his moment. Unfortunately I missed the eleven o'clock lobby briefing that morning, but the Press Association news agency said he stood his ground and rebutted Maude's accusation immediately. 'There is not a single person in this room who can say I have lied on this story. If there is, I would like them to say it now, because it is not true.' None of the journalists present took up the challenge. Campbell must have been pretty confident that he would escape without being contradicted, because doing so would have meant supporting the accusation which Maude had made. If his question had been framed differently, and if correspondents had been asked whether the lobby had been misled, then the outcome might well have been different – as he knew only too well.

When some reporters did challenge him for giving evasive replies, he again insisted that Blair had not 'intervened' on Murdoch's behalf. Prodi had put in the call to Downing Street and afterwards the two Prime Ministers said their conversation should be kept private. Campbell told the lobby he had nothing to apologise for: 'I don't regret having these lobby briefings on the record. We are more upfront and open and I make no apology for that. Nor do I apologise for having a highly proactive communications strategy.' When asked if the Downing Street press office would be keeping the tape record-ings of the disputed briefings, he said he was not sure 'as the record-ing system is a bit haphazard'. He asked political journalists to understand that in future the twice-daily meeting of the lobby would be his only means of communicating with them. 'I don't brief any more except at the lobby. Everything I now say is said at these brief-ings. I don't brief journalists singly any more. I don't have time to do it any more.'

Campbell's willingness to take on all comers was described by the Press Association's political editor Phil Murphy as a 'bullish performance' from a Downing Street press secretary whose 'driving motivation is to control journalistic output with the aim of painting the government in a positive light'. By going public in defending himself, he prompted *The World at One* to compile an item assessing his effectiveness as Blair's official spokesman. As one of the political correspondents asked to give an opinion on Campbell's ability to browbeat the media, I said that as he was over six feet tall I had found it rather intimidating when he 'towered over me' at the party confer-ence and told me my story was 'a load of nonsense'. In explaining how Campbell had a good line in amusing put-downs at lobby brief-ings, I described the way he had poked fun at me earlier that month and had accused me of 'having an orgasm over there in the corner' because I was scribbling away so furiously for my next book. I made the point to the programme's presenter, Nick Clarke, that it was the kind of jibe which the Prime Minister's official spokesman would not have been able to get away with if the briefings were being televised, as they were at the White House in Washington.

Dr Kim Howells, the Minister for Lifelong Learning, responded for the government and said my remarks were 'complete nonsense'. He and Campbell had been acquainted for a long time and were good friends. 'I know Alastair's sense of humour. He's been brilliant in the presentation of the Labour Party and its policies.' But when Nick Clarke put to Dr Howells my suggestion that perhaps the time had come to allow the guidance given at lobby briefings to be broadcast on radio and television, he was surprisingly supportive: 'If Nick Jones wants secret little briefings in dark rooms, where nobody is supposed to be quoted on anything, well say it, but if he wants the system to change, if he wants Alastair Campbell or whoever it might be as press spokesman, out there speaking in public, someone you can nail things to, then that is part of the transition to democracy too, but you can't have it both ways.' In giving *The World at One* my illustration of Campbell's behaviour I had no idea that Dr Howells was prepared to acknowledge the case for having televised lobby briefings. When I was invited to discuss my proposition later that afternoon on *Westminster Live*, another Labour MP, Ben Bradshaw, said he understood why some politicians and journalists hated the lobby system. He was all in favour of changing it. 'I would challenge Nick Jones to persuade other political correspondents to join him in campaigning to change it. The trouble is he's in a minority. Most journalists at Westminster don't agree with him because they can get their tittle tattle through the lobby and they want to keep the system as it is.'

I had taken a calculated step in publicising the ease with which Campbell could exploit the laddish atmosphere in lobby briefings and ridicule with impunity a correspondent whose reputation he wished to trash and who he wanted to suggest was deranged. One safeguard inherent in the system of televised presidential briefings at the White House is that journalists are able to put questions to the executive without having their motives challenged or lampooned. Campbell was always pleased when political commentators and columnists contrasted his success as Blair's official spokesman with that of President Bill Clinton's outgoing press secretary, Mike McCurry. However, the two men had an entirely different approach when fielding questions from journalists. Recordings of McCurry's briefings showed that whatever the provocation thrown at him by the White House press corps, he kept his cool. As his briefings were being televised, he realised that viewers expected him to address the question and not cast gratuitous slurs on the professional reputations of the correspondents or make sarcastic remarks about the basis of the points they were seeking to raise. American journalists, too, appeared on the recorded extracts to be far more supportive of each other than their British counterparts, as though they would not sit idly by if the President's press secretary repeatedly upbraided one organisation (say, the BBC) but refrained from commenting on the conduct of another (say, the *Sun*).

The brush with Campbell to which I had referred had begun after some good-natured banter when he was asked to respond to a ten-page investigation by *New Musical Express* into why the world of rock music felt 'betrayed' by Blair and why musicians were pouring cold water on the 'New Labour–Cool Britannia love affair'. Campbell said Blair would go on inviting stars from the music industry to Downing Street receptions.'I don't deny that having Noel Gallagher turning up at No. 10 to meet the Prime Minister might make the picture of the day ... but I sometimes think these guys in the music industry believe they are more in tune with public opinion than they might in fact be ... Anyway we don't accept criticism from *New Musical Express* as we are in what we describe as a post-euphoria, pre-delivery stage.' Campbell knew his joke would go down well because he was repeating a much-ridiculed line from one of Blair's speeches about the difficult tasks Labour faced in implementing their manifesto commitments.

Elinor Goodman, political editor of *Channel Four News*, asked for some examples of what Blair had in mind. Campbell said it was up to the journalists to work it out for themselves what Blair meant. When asked if he had written the line 'post-euphoria, pre-delivery stage' in Blair's speech, he knew he could play to the gallery, and he wiped away a grin:'It is the Prime Minister's phrase [laughter] ... All the best phrases are the Prime Minister's, you know that [renewed laughter] . .. I give you the facts. You can do with them what you will [more laughter].' Ms Goodman was chortling with amusement and Campbell noticed that with one exception everyone in the room had stopped writing and had joined in the fun. 'Ah, hang on a minute. Look, there's Nick Jones over there in his pre-delivery stage. No, I'm wrong, he's having an orgasm over there in the corner [more laughter].'As Campbell had enjoyed himself at my expense I naturally squirrelled away his taunt as a prime example of an amusing put-down, not imagining I would be making use of it so soon – though I realised that, rather like the television cooks who illustrate their culinary skills by producing dishes which they have cooked earlier, I could be accused of delivering a pre-prepared answer.

I knew Campbell would be furious with me because the smutty nature of his aside could be seized on by those among his opponents who took delight in reminding the Prime Minister that before working for the *Daily Mirror* his official mouthpiece had written erotic porn thrillers under the by-line 'Riviera Gigolo' for the adults-only magazine *Forum*; so once I had delivered my riposte on *The World at One* I realised I would be for the high jump at the 4 p.m. lobby briefing. Campbell gave me a dirty look as he walked in and asked the *Guardian*'s political editor, Michael White, for some assistance: 'Look, Nick Jones is over there again, will you get someone to go and hold his hand.' As the lobby chairman was late arriving, Elinor Goodman took the chair and Campbell motioned her to sit down. 'Elinor, will you stroke my thigh and get Nick Jones excited.' Ms Goodman asked Tony Bevins, the *Independent*'s political editor, to give the Downing Street press secretary his cue for another rant about the BBC, but before he could reply Michael White challenged him on the drama that morning and reminded him that no lobby journalist had gone so far as accusing him of being a liar. Campbell launched himself into a ten-minute tirade: 'Francis Maude said I was lying. But everyone in this room knows that I haven't lied... Journalists who profess to believe in the truth should be prepared to stand up and say so, if that's what they think... Blair's relationship with Murdoch is a legitimate matter of interest but it is a non-story... There are certain things the media are neuralgic about. One is Murdoch. One is Labour Party spin doctors. Put the two together and you can have an orgy of self-indulgence lasting for days... Political news is chemical, it comes and goes, it blows in and out, but it's pretty much of zero interest to the great British public... I have very few run-ins with the BBC but some of their programmes like *The World at One* are a joke; *Today* leading on Francis Maude at 8.10 a.m. was pathetic... In the end that lot at the BBC will have to come to their senses about how they cover politics... I have been to all those BBC seminars, all that BBC hand-wringing about how the public aren't interested in politics, and then you listen to *The World at One* where you get BBC people interviewing each other.' When he paused for a moment to catch his breath, George Jones, the *Daily Telegraph's* political editor, interrupted him: 'Alastair, aren't you getting obsessed? This is the second briefing at which you have just talked about yourself.' The rest of the lobby sighed with relief that someone had at last found a pertinent full stop to punctuate his rant, and the assembled company beat a hasty exit.

Campbell's suggestion that Elinor Goodman should stroke his thigh to get me excited had been subsumed within an instant into the rest of his diatribe, and in retrospect it seemed of little consequence. None the less he had used expressions which were inappropriate for a public figure of his standing, and if the briefings had been recorded his remark might well have been broadcast on television or radio and done him incalculable harm in the politically correct environment of New Labour. If a Conservative minister had used lewd language or made a similar sexual gesture, Campbell would have been the first, during his days on the *Daily Mirror*, to have demanded that the culprit should be sacked. There had been widespread coverage earlier in the month of the plea by the sports minister, Tony Banks, for the disciplining of two disgraced directors of Newcastle United football club, Freddie Shepherd and Douglas Hall, who had been trapped on video in Spain by the *News of the World* using 'sleazy, foul-mouthed' language to boast of their sexual exploits and abuse the club's supporters and their wives. If Campbell was a director of his beloved Burnley and had been caught on tape inviting a woman to stroke his thigh he might have found he had some explaining to do.

In the event no political journalist felt the need to get into an argument with him, or respond to his challenge about the truthfulness of his briefings; the newspaper coverage that morning had already meted out punishment enough. 'B-U-L-L-Y-I-N-G' was the one word take-off which formed the headline for a leading article in the *Daily Telegraph* taking Campbell to task for the twin offences of misleading the lobby and for reprimanding the Secretary of State for Social Security, Harriet Harman, and the Minister of State for Welfare Reform, Frank Field. Faxes sent to the two ministers had been leaked to the Sunday edition of the *Express* whose political editor, Simon

Walters, said they revealed the 'thuggish methods' used by Campbell to order the pair to stop ignoring his instructions.

Ever since the revolt the previous December over the cut in lone parent benefit Ms Harman had gone to inordinate lengths to try to rebuild her image, but many of her publicity initiatives had backfired and she had found herself increasingly at odds with Field over the direction which the government should take on welfare reform. Campbell was clearly exasperated by the two ministers' inept freelance efforts to publicise their ideas and opinions. His first fax, sent in January 1998, revealed his concern about their rival attempts to claim the credit for the 'welfare roadshow' being launched that day by Tony Blair. 'No matter how much we urge silence, congenital briefing goes on about who is responsible for what . . . It is time facts took over from personalities.' Campbell was determined that the publication of the 'welfare reform focus files' should not be pre-empted by either minister and there was no doubt as to who was in charge: 'I will issue the files at 11.30 a.m. at the morning briefing. I will announce membership of the welfare group.' He sent another fax the following month saying it was important that the two ministers entered a 'period of pre-budget purdah' and avoided giving interviews because speculation on welfare changes and budget issues had become inextricably linked. He also urged 'extreme caution in relation to lunches'. Perhaps the most menacing line was directed at Ms Harman. Campbell said he would be 'grateful for an explanation' as to why interviews which she had given to the *Guardian*, *Woman's Hour* and *The World at One* were not 'cleared through this office'.

In his article in the *Express*, Walters said the faxes showed how 'enforcer Campbell' had been 'in a rage again' when he discovered that in an attempt to regain favour with Labour MPs, 'Hapless Harriet' had 'blabbed to left-wing writer Polly Toynbee' of the *Guardian* and leaked budget plans to provide extra cash for childcare. Frank Field was the first to respond, when interviewed by *On the Record*. He acknowledged Campbell's right to intervene but said that after reading the faxes he had thought of correcting some of the English and sending them back. Ms Harman told *Breakfast with Frost* that she had experienced a 'slight raised eyebrow' on being issued instructions but she had not replied to the faxes. 'Alastair Campbell has got a job to do and he does it brilliantly . . . This is what a press secretary has to do to be effective and he is.'

Proof that Campbell had been caught red-handed ordering ministers to do what they were told provided a field day for columnists, commentators and ex-Downing Street press secretaries. Sir Bernard Ingham was in his element on *Westminster Live*: 'Campbell doesn't know how to behave. He should be bound by civil service rules. It is a constitutional innovation to browbeat an elected minister by fax and none of Campbell's predecessors ever did that . . . It is the responsibility of the Prime Minister to bawl out ministers who get out of line, not the press secretary.' In a comment column in the *Daily Mail*, Joe Haines said Campbell was doing nothing new but had made the mistake of putting his instructions on paper. When Haines sent memos during the last Labour government he made sure Harold Wilson signed them. 'When Alastair Campbell throws his weight around, it is Tony Blair's weight. When he speaks, writes, shouts or loses his temper, he does so on behalf of the Prime Minister . . . He is His Master's Voice . . . Every Mr Nice needs a Mr Nasty.' Paul Johnson, writing in the *Daily Mail*, said that 'New Labour specialises in New Arrogance' and that the 'domineering and insolent' rebukes of 'Parliament's bully-in-chief' and the man with the 'loudest parade-ground bark' at Westminster were 'not only unparliamentary, they are un-English . . . Campbell behaves as if he were the Prime Minister's Grand Vizier and issues commands like Tsarist ukases. The communications he despatches, even to cabinet ministers and members of the Privy Council, are couched in peremptory language and read like military orders. You will do this. You must not do that.' Kevin Maguire, the *Mirror*'s political editor, said that for the first time Campbell 'was in the soup': he, not what the government was doing, had become the story. Nevertheless, he was in no danger. 'The Burnley supporter's foul-mouthed tongue-lashings to journalists, errant MPs and rival soccer fans have made him an infamous and fearsome beast . . . But what is undeniable is his importance to the Prime Minister . . . Above all else Campbell protects his master. Blair will never find another Campbell and they both know it.'

The other great significance of the faxes was that they pointed to the eventual demise of Harriet Harman. Her desperate and foolhardy behaviour in thwarting Campbell's instructions on the need to coordinate publicity over changes to social security and welfare reform showed scant regard for the damage which had been done to the government's reputation by the revolt over the benefit cut for single mothers. 'Harman's trouble is she's clueless' was the *Sun*'s verdict at the start of the year. In February she was joined by her department's new director of information, the former BBC Moscow correspondent Martin Sixsmith, who had succeeded Steve Reardon after the latter's relationship with Ms Harman had broken down; she required, she had said, a 'change of style'. Ten days into his new job Sixsmith told me that she was anxious to rebuild her relationship with the news media. 'She is very nervous, very twitchy and even has doubts about her own ability. She realises she got off to a disastrous start and that ninety per cent of what she has to do is to introduce pretty terrible things.' As early as 13 February an exclusive front-page headline over a splash story in the *Express* by its political editor, Roland Watson, predicted that she would be sacked in the July reshuffle: 'Lost Harman faces the axe.' As there seemed to be no other option, Ms Harman began a kamikaze-style attempt to relaunch her political career. Campbell's memo had indicated that he believed her fingerprints were all over Polly Toynbee's pre-budget exclusive in the *Guardian* that the government planned to 'restore the value of the controversial lone parent benefit cuts'. In a comment column accompanying her exclusive, Ms Toynbee could hardly have been any more sympathetic to Ms Harman's plight in the wake of the backbench rebellion: 'They sent her out there to do the dirty deed in their name and take the blame. Monstered and demonised, she has taken the flak . . . But behind the scenes Harman insisted, persuaded and single-handedly changed Treasury thinking . . . Firing Harman would be rat-like injustice.'

At Prime Minister's Question Time on 25 February, after taunts from William Hague about protestors throwing eggs at Labour's 'welfare roadshows', Blair said there would be no backsliding and the *Guardian*'s story was wrong. 'There is no U-turn; there will be no change in the regulations governing lone parent benefit.' The next day, stung by another morning of grim headlines to the effect that she had been slapped down by Blair, Ms Harman walked out of an interview on *Woman's Hour* when asked by the presenter, Jenni Murray, to respond to a question about calls for her to resign: 'I'm sorry, Jenni. It's not just because you ask that question. I must go. Sorry. I have got another thing to do and I have to go to cabinet.'

Her last desperate throw was to put herself at the mercy of

interviewers on the weekly magazines. If she had thought there was any chance of recovering her authority by this means, two of the interviews, which appeared on the same Sunday in May, were cruel reminders of the danger which all politicians face when a relentless pursuit of publicity seems to be their only reward or consolation. Before doing her interview for *Observer Life*, Lynn Barber said Martin Sixsmith had asked what sort of questions she wanted to ask Ms Harman so that she could prepare her brief. 'Oh dear God, no, *please* don't let her prepare a brief! We have all heard her speaking–clock impression.' Ms Barber's deadliest thrust concerned her observation that by being a 'totally obedient Blairite' she had 'entirely lost any popularity or personal credibility she might once have had'. Ms Harman supplied her own anecdote when describing how she had agreed to do a series of BBC local radio interviews and suddenly found herself having to answer a question from Radio Cumbria about the nuclear waste disposal plant at Sellafield. 'I didn't know what the line was . . . So I kind of felt myself choosing to just sound completely ignorant. Because the people listening might think "Bloody hell! What an airhead!" but actually it wouldn't go anywhere, it wouldn't cause problems for my colleagues.' Lesley White found her in a similarly reflective mood for an interview in the *Sunday Times Magazine* when they started discussing the pitfalls she had encountered while loyally following the instructions of her seniors. Ms Harman described how in the early 1990s she had had to deal with an exasperated Jeremy Paxman on *Newsnight* when trying to ensure that Labour were not blamed for British withdrawal from the exchange rate mechanism. 'What's worse, me saying night is day and looking evasive, or us being blamed for ERM? . . . We were in story-limitation mode, so I went round every economic forum and made myself look an airhead.'

Ms Harman's foray into self-analysis read like a political obituary. She was a casualty of New Labour's obsession with presentation. As an acceptable and presentable face, she had been wheeled out when needed during those long-drawn-out years in opposition. But she faced a huge responsibility heading the Department of Social Security, and when tackling it came to the mammoth problem of welfare reform and cutting back expenditure on social security the prominence which she had gained doing the leadership's bidding proved to be of little real value.

7   No case to answer?

Few recent parliamentary investigations have had the high-profile send-off which followed the final decision to set up an inquiry into the allegations that Labour Party spin doctors had politicised the government's information and communication service. A week after the House of Commons Select Committee on Public Administration made the announcement in late March 1998, Tony Blair vindicated it with a rather injudicious answer at Prime Minister's Question Time. In seeking to defend his official spokesman, Alastair Campbell, who had been accused of misleading journalists and bullying ministers, Blair tripped himself up and appeared inadvertently to have endorsed the very point which the opposition parties were making, that the Downing Street press secretary and his colleagues were no longer abiding by the conventions designed to protect the political impartiality of the civil service. Campbell's contract as a politically appointed special adviser was tightly drawn: he could promote the government's policies and decisions in a political manner, but this did not give him the freedom to mount an offensive against the Conservatives. Blair had been mocked by William Hague over the way Campbell had been caught out giving evasive answers. When the Labour MP Gerald Kaufman said this could hardly be equated with the misdeeds of Sir Bernard Ingham, the Prime Minister agreed but then went a step too far: 'There is one reason why the opposition attack the press spokesman: he does an effective job of attacking the Conservative Party.' Blair's slip-up was raised immediately after questions on a point of order by the Conservative MP Sir Peter Tapsell, who said the answer confirmed what the Tories had been saying: that the Prime Minister's official spokesman was acting improperly. A letter from Conservative Central Office to Sir Richard Wilson, the

Cabinet Secretary, was sent off that evening demanding that the press secretary's annual salary of £87,000 should no longer be funded by the taxpayer.

Campbell had already suffered his worst drubbing since the election, and now, thanks to Blair's answer, it was official and on the record: he was getting up to precisely what he had promised he would not do, which was to abuse his position and attack the Conservatives. Although Downing Street tried to dismiss Blair's answer as an inconsequential slip of the tongue, the damage had been done and the committee's decision the previous week to call Campbell as a witness now had far greater legitimacy. Rhodri Morgan, the Labour MP who chaired the committee, found that all of a sudden its investigation promised to be one of the highlights of the parliamentary session. After the notoriety which Campbell had recently acquired for getting above his station, the prospect of a group of MPs getting the chance to grill the Prime Minister's combative press secretary gave the inquiry added status and attracted considerable publicity.

The original trigger for the investigation had been continuing concern over the reasons for the sudden departure of so many of the departmental heads of information, and the resulting fears that civil servants were getting drawn into Labour Party propaganda. Now, as a result of complaints about his own conduct, Campbell had provided the committee with a far wider agenda: Rhodri Morgan said the MPs would want to investigate the misleading answers he had given to lobby correspondents about Blair's conversation with the Italian Prime Minister and consider whether his brutally worded faxes to Harriet Harman and Frank Field were appropriate. Morgan was surprised that Campbell apparently had no compunction about issuing orders to ministers, and he thought the faxes illustrated the power of the 'control freak tendency' within the government. His committee would want to consider whether a temporary civil servant such as the Prime Minister's official spokesman should be 'talking down to ministers and administering a ticking off in this way'. The terms of Campbell's contract would have to be re-examined, along with the role of all the other special advisers, because together they seemed to represent another shift towards a presidential style of government. Morgan said Campbell's position already appeared comparable to that of a press secretary for a US President, and if moves were under way 'bit by bit' to run an operation like the White House in the Prime Minister's press office in Downing Street then it was time MPs had the chance to discuss it.

Campbell pretended to be impervious to the fuss he had created. At the 4 p.m. lobby briefing after Blair had complimented him from the despatch box for doing 'an effective job in attacking the Conservatives', he feigned complete indifference when asked for an explanation. He brushed aside a couple of questions by suggesting that reporters should read the order in council issued on his appointment, but Liam Halligan, a political correspondent with the *Financial Times*, persisted and asked whether, in his role as a temporary civil servant, he was under an obligation to refrain from attacking the Conservatives. Campbell looked away. He pretended to fall asleep and started snoring. Halligan tried again, reminding him that as press secretary he was paid nearly £90,000 a year by the taxpayer. Once roused, Campbell resorted to belligerence: 'I do a good service for you all ...' He paused, and then turned to face Halligan: '... and your eight readers. The answer to your question is that the order in council changed it. As well as being able to instruct civil servants, I can also put the government's case in a political context. So get a grip on yourself.' Michael White interjected wearily: 'Bullying does demean you, Alastair.' Campbell was not abashed: 'Oh no, I must go on bullying ... what would Nick Jones have to write in his diaries if there wasn't intimidation?' But however much Campbell protested, there was nothing he could do to stop the scope of the inquiry from being extended, and the committee's Conservative and Liberal Democrat members became increasingly voluble when expressing their determination to take him on.

Concerns which had been expressed by the departing directors of information about Downing Street's influence on the make-up of the departmental press offices were heightened when two political journalists from the *Mirror* were appointed to senior positions in May 1998. John Williams, formerly the paper's political editor, became the deputy head of the newsroom at the Foreign and Commonwealth Office and Sheree Dodd, a political correspondent, was signed up as head of news for the Northern Ireland Office. With Campbell in No. 10 and David Bradshaw in the strategic communications unit, the four ex-*Mirror* journalists could work together as a team on government publicity.

Ms Dodd's appointment coincided with a vitriolic article in the *Sunday Times* by Andy Wood, who had lost his job as director of information at the Northern Ireland Office after Mo Mowlam had complained of a 'lack of personal chemistry' and said she wanted a change of style. Wood believed he had been part of a 'collective culling' of information directors who had 'fallen foul of New Labour', and he attacked Dr Mowlam in highly personal terms, portraying her as foul-mouthed and vindictive. He thought she was 'on top neither of the detail nor the language' when the Northern Ireland Office needed 'absolute precision in language'. His 'crime' was to have gone on holiday during the first two weeks of July, the '12th fortnight' when Protestants celebrated the Battle of the Boyne, which he said were quiet compared to previous years. Wood found he was the victim of a campaign of 'bad-mouthing', and his account of his few months working under Dr Mowlam was peppered by the expletives she was said to have used: 'Mowlam used not just bad language but "dirty talk", "toilet talk", with a frequency which seemed to border on the compulsive, if not the obsessive . . . I can remember coming out of the BBC and she was f****** and w****** all over the shop . . . She had also referred to me as a w***** and anally retentive.'

Wood's description of his day-to-day contact with his secretary of state did him little good, provoking a shoal of letters from readers complimenting Dr Mowlam on her sound judgement in sacking an official who had shown he was prepared to abuse private conversations by writing about them for the newspapers. One letter came from Hugh Colver, a former public relations chief at the Ministry of Defence and briefly director of communications at Conservative Central Office, who said Wood's 'ill-judged rantings' had dealt the information service one of its 'severest blows' at what was already a difficult time for government press officers. Ministers, he said, had a right to expect that they could trust the civil servants around them. If they felt at risk on a day-to-day basis that the 'rough and tumble of departmental life' would be exposed, that trust would be undermined. Press officers for the political parties told me they thought his rebuke was fully justified.

Moreover, by agreeing to the publication of his *Sunday Times* article at that particular juncture, in early May, Wood had done his former colleagues a considerable disservice. A final decision was being taken that month on the witnesses to be called before the select committee when it started hearing evidence in June, and the directors and heads of information who had been sacked or forced into early retirement were beginning to marshal their arguments. The most devastating critique had been put forward by Jill Rutter, whose unseemly treatment at the Treasury had evoked considerable sympathy. She had since left the civil service to join British Petroleum. In a speech to the Social Market Foundation on 6 December 1997, she claimed that the permanent secretaries were in a state of 'denial' over the way the information service had been politicised by Alastair Campbell and this meant that the rest of the civil service had been 'denied a sensible debate over it'. She considered the degree of politicisation was so serious that the code of conduct for the politically appointed special advisers should be strengthened so that they were made to observe the same standards of truth as civil servants. Although Ms Rutter defended Labour's right to bring in political appointees, she contended that they should not be paid for by the taxpayer unless they were bound by the rules of public service. 'Political parties are free to operate how they like at their own expense. It is one thing for parties to manipulate, but should government do it at the taxpayers' expense?'

After her speech Ms Rutter told me that she had been deeply disappointed by the report of Robin Mountfield, which had endorsed the changes pushed through by Campbell to force the information service to 'raise its game'. 'I thought it was atrocious for a permanent secretary to write a report like that . . . It was a cop-out for the benefit of Alastair Campbell. It's fine if the Labour Party want to spend their money on publicity but it's an entirely different matter for the state to provide a huge government machine for Labour.' Ms Rutter also revealed how she had offered to stand aside as head of communications at the Treasury when Labour won the election so as to make way for Gordon Brown's special adviser, Charlie Whelan. She complained to the then Cabinet Secretary, Sir Robin Butler, that Whelan had taken three-quarters of her job. Sir Robin had replied: 'Just do the other quarter for the good of the service.' When the Treasury suggested Whelan should be given the title 'political press secretary' she said Sir Robin blocked it because he feared it would only highlight the politicisation of Whitehall.

Another of the ousted directors, Liz Drummond, who left the Scottish Office after being told her department was to be restructured, was interviewed by the Edinburgh *Evening News* for its edition of 29 December. She said the new administration was discovering to its cost that the 'slickest presentation skills' could not obliterate the absence of a clearly thought-out policy. The mess created for universities in Scotland by the introduction of tuition fees for students was still having to be untangled. 'I don't think Alastair Campbell's outfit has really appreciated the Scottish dimension.'

As both Ms Rutter and Ms Drummond were putting forward cogent arguments which seemed relevant to the inquiry, I asked Rhodri Morgan which of the former directors would be called to give evidence, the number who had left having risen to nine following the departure in April 1998 of Sheila Thompson, head of information in the Lord Chancellor's Department. To my surprise he said the committee had decided not to call any of the sacked directors – though they were free to supply written submissions. 'We agreed after Andy Wood's outburst over Mo Mowlam that we couldn't allow any of them to give evidence. It would have just become a mega-whinge and we are not an industrial tribunal.' Morgan said the committee had decided instead to call Sir Bernard Ingham as a witness. When I pointed out that Sir Bernard's stint with the government's information service ended in 1990, when Margaret Thatcher was ousted, and that he had no direct experience of Tony Blair's government, he said I had to understand that the choice of witnesses reflected political considerations. He denied that the inquiry would lack credibility as a result and said Labour MPs wanted Ingham to be called as a benchmark against which to measure Campbell, so that they could assess whether there had been any change since the election.

I was even more surprised when Morgan listed the three political editors who would be called to give evidence on behalf of the journalists. All three were from newspapers: the current chairman of the parliamentary lobby, John Hipwood, political editor of the Wolverhampton *Express and Star*, and two former chairmen: Michael White, political editor of the *Guardian*, and Peter Riddell, political columnist of *The Times*. I inquired why no radio or television journalist was being called, nor any tabloid political editor – Trevor Kavanagh of the *Sun*, for example. When I tried to explain that it was broadcasters who were under the greatest day-to-day pressure from political spin and that Downing Street was making great use of Rupert Murdoch's newspapers to push politically inspired stories I could see Morgan's eyes glazing over. 'Look we're not in the business of picking and choosing which journalists to take evidence from, that's up to the lobby.'

I knew that Messrs Hipwood, White and Riddell would do all they could to represent the views of their colleagues, but they had no personal experience of the constant deadlines of rolling news nor any real understanding of how successful Labour had become in manipulating radio and television. White and Riddell had the comparative luxury of being able to spend much of their day reflecting on what they intended to write, and although Hipwood, working for an evening newspaper, had earlier deadlines than the two national political editors, even these were nothing like as demanding as the pressures imposed by twenty-four-hour broadcast news. Nor were they having to spend their Saturday evenings, up against tight deadlines, having to assess the news value of the by-lined articles, exclusive interviews and other politically inspired Sunday newspaper stories which were being used to trail government announcements and 'grab the agenda'. Nor, unlike broadcasters, were the three print journalists subjected to non-stop monitoring of their output; nor did they have to endure a constant stream of complaints from spin doctors prepared to go to almost any lengths, at virtually any hour of the night or day, to influence the radio and television coverage of their respective parties. As I knew that Peter Bradley, one of the Labour MPs on the committee, was interested in media affairs, I asked if he was concerned that the allegations of politicisation would not be examined from the perspective of broadcasters. But he told me he did not think there was a problem: television and radio stations had the ability to break stories whenever they wished, so were in fact in a far better position than the newspapers.

Three separate sessions had been allocated for the witnesses. Bernard Ingham, the first to appear, was as forthright as usual when baited by Labour MPs intent on providing the knockabout political theatre which Morgan had hinted at. The name of the game was to blacken Margaret Thatcher's press secretary so that his misdemeanours could then be used to neutralise any subsequent attack on

Alastair Campbell by the committee's Conservative members. Needless to say, Ingham was delighted to give another airing of his exploits in Downing Street and his decidedly whiskery tales about 'moanalot' Francis Pym, 'semi-detached' John Biffen and other miscreants in Thatcher's cabinets. He berated political journalists for their 'astonishingly poodle-like' behaviour under New Labour; demanded that taxpayers should be relieved of the burden of paying Campbell's salary; and said he was not surprised that the Speaker was up in arms at the 'systematic trailing' of government announcements at weekends.

The three political editors told the committee that the first day of Tony Blair's government had not been year zero as far as they were concerned because the argument about the politicisation of government publicity tended to be cyclical and reflected the power of the Prime Minister of the day. When the Conservative MP Andrew Tyrie asked whether Downing Street's strategic communications unit was doing a 'very similar job' to that performed by Millbank Tower when Labour was in opposition, Peter Riddell agreed that the government might have found a way to get 'quite a big propaganda effort' financed by the taxpayer. 'I think there is a danger of blurring... and that the lines of a party in government do get blurred... If the Prime Minister wants to write for every paper in town, great, but it does rather devalue the currency.' Michael White thought there probably was more favouritism being shown towards certain newspapers but the *Guardian* had made a virtue of keeping a degree of distance from the government. John Hipwood said it would be 'regrettable' if the lobby's proceedings were ever televised.

When the Cabinet Secretary, Sir Richard Wilson, gave evidence the following week, he disagreed with the assessment of the three journalists that there had been no more than a gradual, cyclical movement in the government's approach to the news media. Sir Richard considered the changes under Labour had been concerted and striking: 'At the moment there is a more systematic, determined effort to coordinate, in a strategic way, presentation of the government's policies and messages in a positive light across the whole of the government, than I can remember since the time I have been in the senior civil service.' Sir Richard believed that because of the speed with which the news media received and reported information, the civil service were experiencing a 'permanent shift in gear' which would remain whatever government was in power. He agreed with the strategy which Alastair Campbell had advocated, and which had been endorsed in Robin Mountfield's report: namely, that senior civil servants had to grasp that presentation was an integral part of policy. He was convinced that the changes which had been made in the information service would lead to much improved performance and prospects. 'I predict that in five years' time this committee will not have an issue to discuss. The information service will be performing much better and the opportunities will be better.'

When Tory MPs on the committee got their chance to question the Cabinet Secretary they asked why Blair had been allowed to praise Campbell publicly for doing an 'effective job of attacking the Conservatives' when this indicated a clear breach of the rules by the Prime Minister's press secretary and confirmed that government publicity had been politicised. Sir Richard tried repeatedly to reassure them. He began by suggesting that Prime Minister's Question Time was not the best moment to draw up Campbell's job description. He thought Blair was indicating that his official spokesman was effective in attacking the Conservatives before the last election and would no doubt be effective again at the next election. When Andrew Tyrie said the answer could only mean that Campbell was also doing an effective job in government in attacking the Conservatives, Sir Richard said the press secretary was freer than a civil servant to present government policy in a political context. 'Campbell is overtly political so everyone knows where he is coming from . . . He is able to point out how the government and its policy may differ from its predecessors . . . But I do not think his job is to go over the top and attack the opposition with bricks and bottles . . . Every day I see the lobby reports. If there was something I did not like I would go to Campbell and say, "I think you ought to watch that. You are going over the line on that." Or if someone reported in the press something that he had said and I did not think it proper, I would go and say it. If needs be, I would go to the Prime Minister.' Another Conservative MP, Richard Shepherd, complained that the Cabinet Secretary had still not addressed their principal concern: that unlike most previous Downing Street press secretaries who were civil servants, Campbell was a 'particularly proactive' press officer who was engaged in a 'wider political battle'. Sir Richard denied that Campbell had become a Labour Party spokesman paid for by the state. 'He actually speaks on behalf of the government and that is a proper expenditure for the tax-payer... If he were to go wrong, I would go along and say "watch it".'

Campbell's appearance had been kept until last, and there was a real sense of anticipation at the final session as he walked in, flanked by Robin Mountfield and Mike Granatt, head of the information service. The committee's three Conservative MPs had been waiting with growing impatience, and a fair degree of trepidation, for their chance to take on a political propagandist whom their party respected but feared. In their eyes he did not have same mythical properties as Peter Mandelson because there was nothing mysterious about him. They knew from what they had seen and heard that Campbell was a formidable operator and that he was upfront with it: if it came to an argument in the committee room, he would be up there, right in their faces. And they had a respect, however grudging it might be in some cases, for his achievement: when he casually remarked that the pace of change in the media world was phenomenal and that his objective was to 'be on top of that', none of the MPs present was in any doubt that Campbell was one of the few political publicists in the country who was capable of achieving that. They could see the relentless force they were up against when he described how, after working up a big story one day, his job was to think ahead immediately to the next big story the following day and then the one after that. 'We need to be communicating constantly about the things that we said we would do and we need to be seen by the people to be focusing on them... I have got a pretty good judgement about what is getting through... and it is our job to keep focused upon what is happening out there and you do that by constantly communicating.'

The Tory MP who had the task of opening up their attack was David Ruffley, a solicitor by profession, who had been a special adviser to the former Chancellor, Kenneth Clarke. Ruffley was no stranger to Campbell. He had made a name for himself on the Tory benches through his persistent questioning of ministers about what the opposition considered were breaches in the impartiality of gov-ernment publicity. Ruffley started his questioning by asking if the committee could be supplied with a tape recording of the lobby briefing on Blair's conversation with the Italian Prime Minister.

Campbell was waiting for him. He said the recordings of lobby brief-ings were not kept for posterity, nor were there transcripts of the pro-ceedings. A recording was made simply in order to prepare a summary of the information which had been given out by the press secretary and to enable any quotes to be checked. At the height of the row about what Blair had asked Romano Prodi, political journalists had specifically asked for the tape to be kept, but Campbell made no mention of this in his answer and instead waited for his moment to begin a demolition job on his inquisitor.

Ruffley persisted in challenging Campbell: If disputes were arising, Downing Street should change its practice and undertake to keep all tapes in future. Turning to the chairman, Rhodri Morgan, Ruffley said the controversy over whether the lobby had been misled could be cleared up instantly if the committee could hear 'the Campbell Tapes'. Before Ruffley could complete his sentence, Campbell interjected:'I can see "The Campbell Tapes", that is your intended headline.' Ruffley: 'You can spot them, can you not?' Campbell:'I can certainly spot them, yes.' Campbell was equally fleet-footed when Andrew Tyrie challenged him for misleading the lobby over the report by the *Financial Times* that Blair had 'intervened' on Murdoch's behalf. Had the Prime Minister's official spokesman described that story as 'balls' and 'C-R-A-P'? Campbell: 'I may well have said that.' Tyrie: 'So can I take that as yes?' Campbell: 'Well, I cannot remember every single word that I have ever said, but it is not impossible that I would have said that.' Ruffley:'The tapes will tell us.'

In the quick fire of the questions and answers the MPs failed to notice that Campbell had done a neat little body swerve and made a significant adjustment to the original version of what had taken place three months earlier. On the day Campbell asked lobby journalists to stand up and be counted, and to say if they were dissatisfied with his briefings, he had worded his challenge with precision:'There is not a single person in this room who can say I have lied on this story. If there is, I would like them to say it now.' As the newspapers reported at the end of March, journalists were not given the chance to vote on the alternative and perhaps more appropriate charge of misleading the lobby. Political correspondents were well aware of the particular significance which attached to the word 'lie' when used in the House of Commons: an MP who accused a fellow member of lying had to be able to prove 'deliberate intent' or face a reprimand from the Speaker. So inevitably reporters had thought twice about challenging Campbell. Now, in giving evidence to the committee, Campbell was ready to take a risk, and he proved to be correct in his judgement. The MPs did not spot the difference as he repeated but blatantly reworked the words he had used when issuing his challenge to lobby journalists: 'You have been at all these briefings and you know that I have misled nobody, you know that I have lied to nobody and if there is anybody here who thinks that I have lied to or misled them, why don't you just stand up and say so? And nobody did.' His insertion of the word 'misled', and his suggestion that it was an option which the journalists had been given the chance to consider and had then rejected, was a typical example of Campbell's sleight of hand with words; and, as the questioning proceeded, he continued to outwit the MPs time and again.

When the session opened Mike Granatt had been asked, as head of the information service, what he thought was the impact of Labour having doubled the number of politically appointed special advisers. Granatt said they were playing 'a considerable role in briefing the media' and, in a well-run department, where the relationship between the advisers and the head of information proceeded smoothly, that was a 'key function'. Much later in the proceedings, Campbell was asked by Andrew Tyrie to explain why the Labour government needed seventy special advisers when there were only seven in Margaret Thatcher's first government. Campbell denied that the advisers were abusing the rules and then turned Granatt's evidence on its head: 'The term spin doctor is applied universally to all of them ... But the vast majority do not have any contact with the press whatever.' Campbell escaped again without further challenge when he asserted that he did not 'operate on a system of favourites' when dealing with lobby journalists. 'I sit twice a day on the record. That is my prime contact of meeting with journalists, and on many days it is my only contact with journalists ... I do not have people who stay behind afterwards and get some sort of special treatment.'

Campbell's response was accurate as far as it went: the obvious point which Tory MPs should have pursued was his special relationship with newspapers such as the *Sun* and the numerous, well-publicised occasions on which, well away from his lobby briefings, he had cooperated with the paper's political editor, Trevor Kavanagh. Another line of enquiry might have been to ask why he complained so frequently about the BBC but not about the newspapers published by Rupert Murdoch. Neither opportunity was taken.

Of all Campbell's unchallenged assertions, perhaps the most sweeping was his declaration that the information service was not in danger of being politicised as a result of the changes which he had advocated and which had been approved by the working group on which he had served with Robin Mountfield. 'This was not Alastair Campbell and Peter Mandelson sitting down and saying, "Let us rewrite the way we work." It was a proper considered investigation of the way that the government information service was working and how all of us might actually improve the way that we work. That is to the benefit of the government. It is not a political point. I keep reading all this stuff about politicisation. I have never seen a substantive convincing piece of evidence about politicisation.' Again, there were innumerable examples which could have been put to him. No attempt was made to question him about the 'systematic trailing' of government announcements to which Sir Bernard Ingham had drawn attention and which required civil servants to verify politically inspired, speculative stories. Nor was there any further mention of Peter Riddell's point about the way Downing Street's strategic communications unit was churning out articles of a highly political nature for Tony Blair, regularly praising the virtues of 'New Labour' and condemning the 'posturing' of the Tories for remaining the 'party of privilege not ambition'.

Before the committee could look round their two-and-a-half-hour hearing was over. It ended with the Tory MPs having failed to cause Campbell any real discomfort, let alone land a punch on him, and he emerged from the contest without a scratch. Political sketch writers were unanimous in their verdict: the Select Committee on Public Administration had been a flop. Rhodri Morgan's 'amateurish committee thrashed hopelessly around but never caught sight of their prey', said Matthew Parris in *The Times*. Paul Routledge, who had left the *Independent on Sunday*, nearly joined the *Express* and ended up as the *Mirror*'s chief political commentator, had clearly enjoyed his ring-side seat, watching as the 'villainous Alastair Campbell, the PM's snarling press secretary' took on all comers: 'Campbell, a professional to his fingertips, turned the tables on his inquisitors and left them looking fumbling and amateurish.' Campbell's ability to acquit himself so easily was regarded as the ultimate in political spin by Peter Oborne in the *Express*: 'Far from a bully, a liar and a cheat Alastair Campbell was in fact the nearest equivalent at Westminster to the Archangel Gabriel, or at any rate, a most accomplished spin doctor.'

At a party the following week Campbell relished the opportunity to tell Sue Cameron of the *Spectator* where the MPs had gone wrong in their grilling. He agreed with her that he could have made an infinitely better job of cross-examining himself. '"What would I have asked myself?" he mused. Almost immediately he found the answer. "I would have asked me if I ever said f★★★ when giving briefings. I'd have had to say yes. And then I'd have asked me if that kind of language . . . " He did not need to say more . . . Having found a potential weakness, Campbell assured me he would never have let himself off the hook the way some of those MPs did.'

The three Tory members of the committee had undeniably allowed Campbell to run rings round them at the hearing, but they refused to be a pushover when it came to preparing a report and, together with the one Liberal Democrat, Mike Hancock, fought a line-by-line duel with the six Labour MPs. Although they had no chance of rewriting recommendations which they opposed, they did bring out a minority report. Given the political sensitivities of the inquiry, and the reluctance of Labour MPs to be seen even to be contemplating criticism of Campbell, there was never any real prospect that the committee would agree on its findings. Nevertheless, a select committee's inability to publish a bipartisan report is always regarded as a setback, and the lavish praise heaped on the head of the Prime Minister's press secretary in the majority report did stretch the credulity of those who supported increased parliamentary scrutiny of government activity.

Campbell got an entirely clean bill of health in respect of those contentious issues where the committee had failed to solicit any opposing evidence. The case for televising his briefings was dismissed in a few sentences, although broadcasters had not been asked for their opinion and no advocate of the change had been given the chance to explain the safeguards provided by televised briefings at the White House. An editorial in the *Mirror*, published the day after Campbell gave his evidence, argued that opening up lobby briefings by allowing television cameras to record the proceedings would be a 'big step towards a more open democracy'. The committee's verdict was that the changes which Campbell had already introduced, including the attribution of guidance to the Prime Minister's official spokesman, 'worked well'. When it came to the claim that the press secretary 'operated on a system of favourites', the committee thought it best to wash its hands of the issue completely: 'Campbell is frequently credited with the ability to manipulate or lean on the press, but the journalists from whom we took evidence were sceptical of anyone's ability to do this... We were given no clear evidence that Campbell provides some journalists with special treatment. There are in any case procedures which can be implemented within the lobby to deal with any such allegations.' Again the committee had failed to seek any evidence from broadcasters, who would have had a different opinion from newspaper journalists about the degree to which they were being leant on by the government, and the suggestion that problems concerning favouritism should be left to journalists to sort out for themselves was fatuous. In view of the fierce competitive pressures within the news media, no news organisation was going to turn down the offer of exclusive or favoured access, and Campbell had been masterly in his manipulation of the intense rivalry which existed between newspapers, television and radio.

The one area where the report did have some bite was in respect of action to curb the activities of the record number of special advisers working for ministers. A new and tougher code of conduct was suggested to lay down a 'set of ground rules' to regulate their contact with the news media, so as to ensure that information was presented to the public 'effectively and openly'. When it came to the grievances of the ousted information directors, the committee acknowledged there were 'serious problems of morale' within the information service and recommended that civil servants should not be placed at a disadvantage when applying for more senior posts.

In their minority report, the four opposition MPs said they found Campbell's evidence in relation to the complaints about the systematic trailing and leaking of government decisions in advance of parliamentary statements 'unconvincing'. They recommended curbs on the practice of pre-briefing by special advisers and suggested fresh guidance to control their behaviour. They also asked for the role of the strategic communications unit to be re-examined as part of a wider review of party political funding, to see if it did give undue advantage to the government, and their report recommended that tapes of Campbell's lobby briefings should be routinely kept for twelve months.

Publication of these conflicting conclusions was delayed until after the start of the summer recess, but Rhodri Morgan was mistaken if he thought an early August news conference might mean less media interest in the bickering which had surrounded preparation of the two reports. The four opposition MPs claimed that the chairman's attempt to achieve an agreed and balanced outcome had been thwarted by the committee's six Labour MPs, who were said to have been 'nobbled' by the whips and told to tone down all criticism of Campbell and to vote against the introduction of any curbs on the government's publicity operation. David Ruffley said the whips' intervention to get a watered-down report reflected the government's obsession with media management. 'The behaviour of the Labour MPs is a disgrace... They are nothing more than Alastair Campbell's glove puppets.'

Morgan did his best to stand above the fray. He insisted that concern about the questionable activities of special advisers, on which both sides of the committee were agreed, had already been acted upon the previous week when Dr Jack Cunningham was appointed to the new post of Minister for the Cabinet Office. His task was to ensure greater coordination between departments, and he was put in charge of presenting the government's case on radio and television. Dr Cunningham was immediately dubbed 'The Enforcer' in newspaper reports of the July cabinet reshuffle after he revealed that one of his responsibilities would be to stem the tide of malicious briefing against ministers, much of which was blamed on unattributable briefings by the unaccountable band of special advisers. He was determined to carry out Tony Blair's instructions: 'We mustn't let anything, either personalities or individual spin doctors, get in the way of the government's clear message ... What we cannot have is the hyping of who's in, who's out, who's up, who's down, who's had a row with who, the exaggeration of bad personal relationships which from time to time has completely obscured the much more important decisions and announcements of government.' Dr Cunningham's orders to enforce discipline among the special advisers only served to under-line the equivocation in Alastair Campbell's evidence to the select committee a month earlier; but, when the press secretary gave his briefing on Blair's first cabinet reshuffle, he readily acknowledged that there was a problem and that it had to be tackled. He told the lobby he was delighted that a member of the cabinet who was 'close to the Prime Minister and valued by him' had at last been given the authority to end 'this nonsense of spinning, malice, gossip and rumour'.

In his first year in the cabinet as Minister for Agriculture, Fisheries and Food, Dr Cunningham had acquired few friends in the farming industry because of mounting anger over the government's contin-ued failure to persuade the EU to lift the export ban on British beef. Protests increased when the Ministry of Agriculture stopped the sale of beef on the bone in December 1997, and at farmers' demonstra-tions he earned the sobriquet 'Jack-Boots Cunningham'. Now, after having been 'minister for presentation' for not much more than forty-eight hours, he had to hold the line for the government on the *Today* programme amid a welter of accusations which followed the sacking of Harriet Harman and the resignation of Frank Field, the Minister for Welfare Reform. Ms Harman marked her exit from the Department of Social Security quietly and elegantly. Next day most newspapers carried front-page photographs of her smiling bravely for the cameras as she walked out of Richmond House clutching a large bunch of lilies. On the other side of Whitehall, Field's departure was turning into a presentational disaster. Having been told on his appointment to 'think the unthinkable' in looking for ways to reduce social security spending, he now seemed intent on saying the unsayable. Standing on the steps of No. 10, he announced that rather than be shunted sideways into another job he was going to leave the government and campaign for welfare reform from the back benches.

Blair's impatience at the inability of Field and Ms Harman to work together, or to develop a coherent strategy, had been the subject of speculation for months after the leaking of Campbell's faxes to the two ministers and his instruction that they should stop trying to compete with each other for publicity. 'The Disposable Duo' was the

Daily Mail's headline over its account of the demise of 'Whitehall's odd couple' whose pairing few believed would last. Theirs had become one of the most acrimonious relationships in Whitehall: David Brindle, the *Guardian*'s social services correspondent, said that despite Campbell's order to them to stop their feuding, 'advisers to each minister continued relentlessly to brief against each other'. Next day the newspapers had much fuller accounts of Field's downfall. The *Independent*'s columnist Donald Macintyre said that his ideas for welfare reform 'took up a lot of cabinet time', to the irritation of Blair as well as the Chancellor, Gordon Brown, and were not considered capable of delivering real reform. Field was incensed to find that he had been briefed against and, in an emotional resignation statement that afternoon, he said he realised it was his mistake to have accepted the job of Minister for Welfare Reform when it lacked the executive authority of a cabinet post. 'If the past fifteen months have taught me anything, it is not only that the biggest of all reforms requires an executive position for a person with convictions about welfare reform, but that the entire cabinet, especially the Chancellor, shares beliefs about that common endeavour.'

Field's attack on Brown, in the first high-profile resignation statement since the election victory, was the most visible demonstration yet of the tensions existing within the government. Campbell was rapidly in action to defuse the situation, telling lobby correspondents he was mystified as to what the proposals were which the Chancellor was supposed to have blocked and dismissing Field's suggestion that he should have been given a more senior role. 'People can't just say they want to be in the cabinet . . . It's time to get the job done and not just talk about it.' The implication of the briefing was clear: Field was all talk and incapable of delivering welfare reform. In giving Downing Street's stamp of approval to Field's denigration, Campbell opened the floodgates to every unattributable briefer in Westminster who wanted to trash the former minister; moreover, according to reports that weekend of the guidance he gave to lobby correspondents on the Sundays, Campbell was off the leash himself. Patrick Wintour of the *Observer* said that in one of the 'bitterest briefing wars' of this government, Blair's official spokesman had said Field's talents were 'not best suited to running a government department'; his proposals were 'largely at an analytical level, they never took the form of policy capable of being implemented by a government'. For the Sunday Times, Andrew Grice quoted Blair's official spokesman as having remarked that Field had 'generated lots of thinking' but that the government had no policy to implement. Campbell's readiness to pass an opinion on Field's ministerial capabilities contradicted the evidence he had given a month earlier to the select committee. In response to a question from David Ruffley, he denied having described the Chancellor as 'psychologically flawed' and said he did not know who was responsible for the phrase. Campbell then set out the principles to which he tried to adhere when giving guidance to journalists: 'Now I happen to believe that you can put across the government's case in a coherent and coordinated way without frankly briefing against anybody.'

To begin with, Field managed to restrain his anger over the Downing Street briefings. When interviewed by the Sunday papers he tried to set the record straight and insisted that the reform projects which he had put forward had been allowed to 'run into the sand and disappear into a black hole'. However, he told the *Observer* that if Downing Street continued rubbishing him, he would prove they were lying. Next morning the editorial writers rallied to Field's defence and there was trenchant criticism of the way he had been savaged by Downing Street. The *Independent* said that for Campbell to state that Field was 'not best suited' to running a department was counterproductive because it allowed unnamed sources to come in behind with a 'long string of cheaper insults: "hollow", "a disgrace", "childish and pathetic" . . . Blair and those who speak for him should have let Field have his fifteen minutes and stuck to the issues instead of the personal insults.' The *Daily Telegraph* regretted that 'character assassination' had reduced a desperately important subject to the invective of the school playground; and Roy Hattersley, writing in the *Guardian*, said Field had been treated 'shamefully by the increasingly unattractive government publicity machine'.

Buoyed up by the support he had received, Field was ready to turn it to his advantage when interviewed that morning on the *Jimmy Young Programme*. He said his dispute was not with the Prime Minister but with the Downing Street spin doctors, and he complimented Blair on having appointed Dr Cunningham to tackle the problem of 'divisive spinning' from within the government. 'I hope the spin doctors will be put in order quite shortly ... Sadly, this episode shows the need for that. In the long run, you cannot run a government like this. It's a cancer that will eat away at the heart of our very existence and undermine the way ministers behave.'

A cabinet reshuffle in the last week of July, coinciding with a last-minute rush to complete parliamentary business before the summer recess, can be a testing time for any government; but the ruthless way in which Field had been dispatched to the back benches showed that Blair could remain cool and calculating under pressure. He needed no reminding of the fury which could be provoked by a shake-up of his frontbench team. Ministers sacked from Conservative governments had turned their resignation speeches into an art form. Margaret Thatcher had had to maintain what she said subsequently was a 'mask of composure' while listening on the front bench to Sir Geoffrey Howe delivering the resignation speech which triggered her downfall. Television footage of her strained features provided a visual reminder of her discomfort and the pictures were used repeatedly in the months which followed to illustrate divisions within the Conservative Party. The fact that newspaper and television libraries have very few unflattering pictures of Blair or his family reflects the exceptionally stringent precautions which he has taken, as party leader and Prime Minister, to avoid an accumulation of images which could be used to embarrass or damage the government. Except for a few well-ordered photo-calls, the Blairs have rarely been seen relaxing together as a family and great care has been taken on their return from holiday destinations to avoid their getting caught by photographers or television crews – though their 1999 New Year holiday in the Seychelles was marred by the attentions of a freelance cameraman working for the *Sun*, who snapped Tony, Cherie and the children standing together in their swimming costumes at the water's edge. Blair has been especially rigorous in limiting the occasions when he has been filmed or photographed in the company of trade union leaders or other figures on the left of the party. As a result, newspapers and television programmes would be hard pressed to find archive material of him to illustrate stories about the Labour Party's links with the union movement.

In view of the calamitous circumstances surrounding Field's resignation, Blair had no intention of repeating Thatcher's mistake and of remaining in the chamber to hear what his departing minister might have to say. The minute Prime Minister's Questions were over and the Speaker rose to announce Field's personal statement, Blair and Brown were on their feet, walking away from the front bench, provoking consternation in the chamber. Amid protests from the opposition benches, the Speaker had to intervene. 'This House must come to order. That is disgraceful behaviour from members on the front bench.' Her strictures were echoed by the parliamentary sketch writers, who accused Blair of a grave misjudgement. 'He should have stayed, listened quietly, and left immediately afterwards,' wrote Matthew Parris in *The Times*. He said Blair decided to leave without waiting for Field's statement because he had become 'super-sensitive to the demands of image-management', but the sight of a Prime Minister and his Chancellor 'scuttling for the door looked dreadful'.

This was one public relations fiasco that could not be laid at Peter Mandelson's door; for the minister without portfolio was one of the first beneficiaries of the reshuffle and had been relieved of his responsibilities for coordinating presentation well before the start of the Field debacle. On the Monday morning when the reshuffle started, the only political editor to report exclusively and correctly that Mandelson had definitely got the job of President of the Board of Trade was Trevor Kavanagh of the *Sun*. 'President Mandelson' was the headline over Kavanagh's report that Blair's spin doctor had finally been promoted to the cabinet with a 'proper job' and a department to go with it. Mandelson had been saying for months that his days as the Labour Party's Prince of Darkness were over and that he wanted to escape from the manipulative world of media management. Nevertheless, as was perhaps only to be expected, he succeeded in promoting his own promotion with his customary flair for presentation. As soon as it was confirmed that he was to succeed Margaret Beckett, he announced that he intended to drop the title President and would be known as the Secretary of State for Trade and Industry. He said the task of creating 'prosperity for Britain's hard working families' did not require 'pompous titles'. His promotion was applauded by the *Guardian*'s columnist Hugo Young, who said that such was the damage done to Blair's 'chief merchant of perception' that it was vital to the survival of a 'talented, grotesquely maligned politician' that he got his own department.

Mandelson's delight was heartfelt. There had been suggestions that Blair was about to give him an enhanced role as Cabinet Office 'overlord' and 'media supremo', but Gordon Brown and other ministers were said to have opposed his appointment as an interfering 'troubleshooter' and, on the eve of the reshuffle, the Sunday papers predicted with great certainty that the job of progress-chaser and front-man had gone to Dr Cunningham. The *Mirror*'s political editor, Kevin Maguire, reported later in the week that on the Sunday evening Brown invited Mandelson to his flat at No. 11 Downing Street where, over a glass of chilled white wine, he 'broke the news to his arch-enemy' that he was going to get Trade and Industry and was the first to congratulate him.

Speculation about the promotion prospects of the minister without portfolio had persisted for weeks, and doubts had been cast on his chances of entering the cabinet since his involvement earlier in July in the tangled affairs of one of his protégés, the highly paid lobbyist Derek Draper, whose rapid rise to fame and fortune had made him a New Labour icon for many of the party's eager younger members. Draper's fall from power and influence was dramatic; and as he struggled to clear his name in what the news media dubbed the 'cash-for-access' scandal, Mandelson was the only minister to speak up for the fallen hero in his hour of need.

At the age of thirty, Draper had arrived. He had become a director of a newly formed public affairs consultancy, GPC, which at the beginning of 1998 had taken over his former employers, the consultants Prima Europe, in a deal from which Draper and his fellow directors had made a handsome profit. His climb up the ladder of political influence had been just as fast. Draper had deep roots in the modernising influences which took Tony Blair to power, and he was a member of one of the party's most powerful cliques, its 'north-east mafia' of MPs, local councillors and political activists. On leaving university, he was taken on as an assistant in the Newcastle upon Tyne East constituency office of the Labour MP Nick Brown, and it was there that he met Peter Mandelson, who had been selected to fight the nearby constituency of Hartlepool in the 1992 general election. A few weeks after his downfall, Draper reflected on the start of their friendship when being interviewed by John Humphrys for the BBC radio programme *On the Ropes*: 'Peter said I was wasted in Newcastle and he asked, "Why don't you come and work for me?" Peter was one of my heroes. He was one of those who saved the Labour Party from destruction.' Draper joined Mandelson's staff at Westminster as an assistant and within four years was describing himself as the MP's 'chief political adviser'. In 1996 he left to join Prima Europe, one of whose founders was Roger Liddle, co-author with Mandelson of the pre-election book *The Blair Revolution*, which gave an 'inside account of New Labour's plans for Britain'. In the preface the two authors said they owed Draper a 'special debt'; he had made a 'major contribution' to the book and they considered New Labour was fortunate that it could boast a 'whole new generation' which shared his 'organisational energy, political commitment and realistic vision'. Draper was the driving force behind *Progress*, a glossy magazine which promoted New Labour, and once Blair was elected, his access and connections provided him with the material for his first book, *Blair's Hundred Days*, which chronicled the 'breakneck pace' at which the new government began implementing its manifesto commitments.

Draper's insider status had conferred on him considerable credibility as a pundit for New Labour, and by summer 1998, on the strength of his contacts and his nose for intrigue, he was writing a weekly page of political news for the *Express* under the title 'Inside the Mind of New Labour'. Political journalists valued Draper's regular insights into 'tensions and disagreements hidden from public view'. I had been particularly struck in May 1998 by an article in the *Spectator* in which Draper revealed that Mandelson believed Rupert Murdoch could be persuaded to drop his opposition to European monetary union and might order the *Sun* to support Britain's entry to the single currency. Draper backed this assertion up with a quote from the transcript of an interview Mandelson had given to a Channel Four documentary, *Blair's Year*, in which he said that Murdoch was a pragmatist and that if the euro had been established successfully, and he saw that 'everyone's flocking to it and we're losing out by being apart from it, he would say OK, we've got to go in'. As Draper appeared to be well informed about Mandelson's thinking, I made a particular note of this remark. When the programme had been broadcast the previous month, other journalists had reached the same conclusion. Stephen Castle, political editor of the *Independent on Sunday*, said Mandelson's intervention showed that Blair believed Murdoch could be won and it was a line which the government had started spinning. After the European summit in Cardiff in mid-June, Robert Peston, political editor of the *Financial Times*, reported in the paper's assessment of the British presidency on 22 June that the Prime Minister hoped his attempts to demonstrate that the EU had become less intrusive in British affairs would make it 'more likely he could get Rupert Murdoch and his *Sun* newspaper on side for a pro-Emu campaign'. Labour's spin annoyed the *Sun*'s Eurosceptic political editor, Trevor Kavanagh, who suggested to the paper's newly appointed editor, David Yelland, that they plan a response. Their retaliation, two days later, was another of the *Sun*'s infamous front pages. 'Is THIS the most dangerous man in Britain?' screamed the headline beside a photograph of Blair. A front-page opinion column said the *Sun* had been forced to 'think the unthinkable' about Blair because he seemed 'determined to scrap the pound and take Britain into the European single currency'. Inside the paper there was another photograph of Blair, wearing a black mask.

I was on early duty that morning and in my report for the 7 a.m. news I said the paper's trenchant tone would be a disappointment to the government because 'ever since the *Sun* backed Labour in the general election, there have been confident predictions from some of Tony Blair's closest advisers, including Peter Mandelson, that Rupert Murdoch's biggest-selling newspaper would drop its opposition to British entry'. For the next news bulletin at 8 a.m. I had to freshen up my report with reaction from the shadow Chancellor, Francis Maude, who had just been interviewed on *Today*. On returning to the newsroom at 7.45 with my updated report I was told that the minister without portfolio had telephoned to complain. He had told the bulletin editor that my use of the word 'prediction' was incorrect: he had merely referred to what he 'hoped' Murdoch might do over the euro. I told the editor that I thought Mandelson's quote from Channel Four was quite clear and that he was predicting that Murdoch could eventually be won over to the euro. When I asked why I had not been called over to speak to Mandelson myself, the bulletin editor said the minister had refused to let his call be put through to me, saying that 'talking to Nick Jones would not be a pleasurable experience'.

By now there were only ten minutes to go to the 8 a.m. news and, although I was confident about my original wording, I knew there was not enough time to talk it through with the editor, and so I had no alternative but to drop Mandelson's name and amend my script to say that 'Blair's closest advisers have been doing all they can to persuade Rupert Murdoch's biggest-selling paper to drop its opposition to British entry'. I could not help smiling to myself at Mandelson's technical brilliance in carrying through his complaint. He had timed it to perfection. He had undermined the accuracy of my story minutes away from transmission and left me insufficient time to argue my case. I had read in the gossip columns that Mandelson was an avid partygoer, and Polly Toynbee had written in the *Guardian* of how she had watched him dance with 'inspired grace, lithe and mercurial, delighting all with his infectious pleasure'. I felt his complaint that morning had all the flair and flourish of the paso doble: he had dazzled my editor, cast doubt on my story and, before disappearing, had finished me off with a memorable put-down.

However, even my amended 8 a.m. report had apparently caused apoplexy in the Downing Street press office and the next complaint, from Alastair Campbell, had none of Mandelson's elegance. He said it was a 'non-story' because the *Sun* was merely restating its known opinion, and my report had been a 'typical inside the BBC beltway wank'. So agitated was Campbell by *Today*'s reporting of the *Sun*'s front page that he telephoned a complaint to the Press Association, condemning what he said was the 'BBC's excited coverage' about a newspaper opinion column which was not 'terribly newsworthy'. Chris Moncrieff, the agency's chief political writer, took the call. He told me that Campbell was furious that the *Sun*'s views were being publicised; he had spent the previous day giving his evidence to the select committee and had been caught unawares by the story. George Pascoe-Watson, the *Sun*'s deputy political editor, told me that Trevor Kavanagh had been working with David Yelland on the front page for several days. 'What happened was that after the Cardiff summit, the mood music from the Blair lot was that opinions were changing on the euro and they were saying that the *Sun*'s muted response showed they were getting away with it. That really got on Trevor's tits and that was when he started work on it with the editor.' In view of the criticism of my radio reports, I asked if Campbell had complained to the *Sun*'s political desk. 'No we don't get complaints from him.

Sometimes Alastair might call me a wanker but it's just a laugh.' And indeed, at the eleven o'clock lobby briefing that morning Campbell raised no objection to the *Sun's* front page. He said the paper had a known opinion on the single currency and Blair would not be lying awake worrying about it. Yet despite his best endeavours to play down the story, it had created a stir and was being followed up by the lunchtime bulletins. To get some fresh reaction for my television report for the *One o'Clock News* I decided to interview Derek Draper.

When I went to meet him at the reception desk he was on the phone, but he finished his conversation within a few minutes and told me he had just been getting a rundown on Campbell's lobby briefing. 'It really is annoying when Alastair says something is a non-story and isn't newsworthy. People will be talking about the way the *Sun* has attacked Blair and how the paper is picturing him in a black mask. Labour can't ignore it.' He was surprised when I told him that Campbell had complained about my reports that morning and that Mandelson had challenged my interpretation of his Channel Four interview as a 'prediction' which, I said, seemed to cast doubt on Draper's article in the *Spectator*. 'I don't give a toss what Peter is saying about my article if he's using it as his way of complaining to the BBC. He needs to grow up. The interview he gave to Channel Four was one of the rare occasions when he said something which he regretted. We all know he's on a charm offensive to win over Murdoch and he didn't want to reveal his hand.'

My encounter with Draper and the insight which he had given me into his interlocking contacts and friendships within New Labour, and the access they afforded him, was fresh in my mind twelve days later when the *Observer* published its investigation into the activities of lobbyists who were said to be 'earning thousands of pounds a month for their firms by exploiting their contacts in Whitehall and Westminster'. Gregory Palast, an investigative journalist based in New York posing as the representative of an American energy company, had asked a number of lobbyists to indicate what kind of services they could provide, making a point of contacting former assistants and advisers to Labour's shadow ministers. Of those he approached, Derek Draper was easily the most talkative, and his boasts were to be the cause of his downfall.

Palast's two-page report in the *Observer* on 5 July listed his discussions with various lobbying companies. Once Draper realised that his firm, GPC, was in competition with other lobbyists for the proffered American business, he was 'determined to display his prowess at opening the doors to power... Draper assured me that, if we wanted access to government, "I can have tea with Geoffrey Robinson. I can get into Ed Balls." But of course that would be available only to a client paying the lobbyists' fees.' Palast said he kept asking Draper to prove his insider bona fides. 'Draper rose to the challenge... "There are seventeen people who count and to say I am intimate with every one of them is the understatement of the century." ' When Palast attended GPC's annual reception at the Banqueting House, he asked Draper if there was anyone who could vouch for his influence, and it was at this point that he was introduced to Roger Liddle, who had joined the Downing Street policy unit as an adviser after leaving Prima Europe. Liddle handed Palast a card with his Downing Street and home phone numbers. 'He then made an extraordinary offer. "Whenever you are ready, just tell me what you want, who you want to meet and Derek and I will make the call for you." ' Next time Palast met Draper, he was given a copy of *Progress*. 'Draper had just sent his weekly column to be published in the *Express*. "I don't write that column without vetting it with Peter Mandelson." ' At their final meeting, 'his mood was philosophical... "I don't want to be a consultant," he said. "I just want to stuff my bank account at £250 an hour." '

On Monday, Palast's sensational disclosures were front-page news: Draper had lit the blue touch paper to so many potential stories that the newspapers were spoilt for choice. The lead story in *The Times*, *Guardian* and *Daily Mail* was the demand by the Conservatives that Roger Liddle should be sacked from the No. 10 policy unit for having offered to use his position to help a commercial client. Much of the coverage on the inside pages was devoted to dissecting the *Observer*'s suggested list of the seventeen people who Draper thought were running the country. Elsewhere that morning, events moved quickly. GPC announced that Draper had been suspended and the editor of the *Express*, Rosie Boycott, terminated his £70,000 a year contract as a columnist. She said he had been sacked because the paper was in danger of being manipulated by someone who was too closely involved with the government. 'Columnists must be independent and they must certainly not be discussing their column with a government minister.'

Downing Street's initial response to the *Observer's* story was that it contained no evidence that access or information had been traded for cash, and Campbell reinforced that line at the 11 a.m. lobby briefing. Roger Liddle had, he said, been interviewed and asked about the allegations, but he 'has not been suspended, nor will he be'. Liddle had simply handed over a business card and said he would be happy to pass on an expression of interest, but that was not improper; what the *Observer's* story reflected was the 'lobbyists' inclination to talk up their influence'. By mid-afternoon the government appeared to have got a firm grip on events. Permanent secretaries in the various Whitehall departments were told to remind all special advisers of the requirement they were under to 'conduct themselves with integrity and honesty' during contact with outside interest groups. When Campbell briefed the lobby again at 4 p.m. it was evident he intended to go on the attack against the *Observer*.

During radio and television interviews that morning Gregory Palast had not been entirely clear when asked if he had tape recorded all his conversations. Campbell acknowledged that the single most damaging claim against the government involved the alleged conversation with Liddle, so the *Observer's* editor, Will Hutton, had been asked to supply a tape of it to allow Downing Street to determine exactly what had been said. After Palast declined to tell *Newsnight* whether or not he had made a recording of his conversation with Liddle, Campbell moved in for the kill. A late-night statement was issued to the Press Association: unless the *Observer* handed over the tape, together with a transcript, by 11 a.m. next morning, the Prime Minister's office would assume that it did not exist. Campbell had seen the immediate weakness in Palast's position. He had met Liddle at GPC's annual reception and his subsequent report had not made it clear whether he had taped the conversation or was relying on his memory. Investigative reporters can find their work is undermined if they fail to be consistent when outlining the basis on which their enquiries were conducted: either they have a tape of what was said and have transcribed it, or they have a contemporaneous note of the conversation, or they have a memorised account which was written up immediately afterwards. Next morning the *Observer's* deputy editor, Jocelyn Targett, was interviewed on *Breakfast News* shortly after 7 a.m. and was forced to admit that although Palast had 'half a dozen tapes and lots of contemporaneous notes' the conversation with Liddle was 'not on tape, and we never claimed it was on tape'.

The confirmation that no tape existed was just what Campbell had been waiting to hear. His tactic of questioning the validity of Palast's reporting had achieved an instant result: Downing Street had succeeded in undermining the *Observer*'s credibility and diverting attention from the rest of Palast's allegations. Although the *Today* programme had begun the morning stating that no minister was available to be interviewed about Liddle's future, there was now a sudden change in the running order. Shortly after 8 a.m. Downing Street fielded Peter Kilfoyle, a junior minister at the Office of Public Service, who said that on the basis of Targett's answer, Liddle had 'no case to answer' and the matter was closed. Later that morning, when questioned by reporters, Tony Blair leapt to Liddle's defence and said he had not thought it right to 'dismiss someone and ruin their life and their prospects' unless there was proof of wrongdoing. But he expressed his distaste for people who were 'fluttering around the new government, trying to make all sorts of claims'.

There was to be no easy escape for Derek Draper, who was on holiday in Italy when the *Observer* published its story. In a desperate attempt to save his career he flew back to London where, standing outside the offices of his solicitors, he accused the *Observer* of 'attempted entrapment'. He demanded that the paper publish the full transcripts of Palast's tapes because he was confident they would show he was not guilty of doing 'anything unethical'. Peter Mandelson was also on the attack. He demanded a retraction of the *Observer*'s claim that he routinely vetted Draper's column in the *Express*. Mandelson had waited a day before responding and had obviously given careful thought to his tactics. By delaying his offensive until after Liddle got the all clear, he was able to concentrate his efforts on doing all he could to salvage Draper's reputation. He told *The World at One* that although Draper was a 'bit of a show-off and rather good at selling himself', that was not the same as saying that he 'breaks the rules or is a congenitally dishonest person... I know Derek. He is a bit of a showman. He gets above himself. But now he has been cut down to size and I think probably he will learn a very hard lesson from what has happened.' Mandelson spent some time in the Millbank studios doing radio and television interviews, and when *The World at One* was off air he grabbed my arm to complain about my own contribution to the programme. In my report on Draper's influence within the party, I pointed out that he had become a regular pundit on behalf of New Labour and, as I had seen after the *Sun*'s attack on Blair, he could obtain an instant rundown on Campbell's lobby briefings. Mandelson accused me of shifting my ground. '*The World at One* said Derek was someone who had been "put up" to speak for Labour, but you said he was "prepared to speak on Labour's behalf". No one else would have spotted that, but I noticed that you had changed your line.' While I was being admonished, Mandelson's adviser, Benjamin Wegg-Prosser, stood beside him, wagging his finger at me, saying repeatedly, 'You've no evidence, you've no evidence.' I stood my ground and said that Draper had spoken regularly on behalf of Labour on radio and television programmes when no minister or party spokesman was available, and I considered this reflected the importance of his position among the New Labour modernisers.

The agitated behaviour of Mandelson and Wegg-Prosser revealed their determination to do what they could on Draper's behalf, and they were obviously annoyed to have had no warning of my story. I had checked at the 4 p.m. lobby briefing the previous day whether Downing Street was prepared to confirm that Draper was given a briefing before his interview with me about the *Sun*'s front page, and Campbell, while denying that Draper had ever been briefed by the Downing Street press office, said that 'he could have been briefed' by the Labour Party. Three days later, after questions in the Commons, Blair set the record straight in a written parliamentary answer amending Campbell's categoric denial: 'Draper has had no briefing from any press officer that was not available to any other journalist calling the press office . . . Any call from Draper would be dealt with routinely by a press officer, rather than the chief press secretary.'

In a succession of interviews, Draper struggled valiantly to limit any further damage to his fellow lobbyists and his friends in the government. He acknowledged that he had been foolish and, in what appeared to be a line he had worked out in advance with Mandelson, he said he would have to pay the price for his brash and boastful behaviour. 'I hope Mandelson is still a friend of mine . . . I still support him and if he says Derek should stop showing off, he is probably right. You may say about me, "he's a bit of a tosser" but what has he done wrong?'

8 Exeunt

'A moment of madness' was the explanation given by the Secretary of State for Wales, Ron Davies, for a sequence of events which began on Clapham Common and which, by the end of the evening of 27 October 1998, had supplied the genesis for an array of tabloid stories that would rival the exploits of David Mellor, the disgraced Conservative 'Minister for Fun'. In each case a cabinet minister was said to have indulged in the kind of off-beat sexual behaviour which was guaranteed to fascinate the popular press, but which both maintained was journalistic invention. However, despite the similarities in the treatment the two men received at the hands of the newspapers, the circumstances surrounding their resignations provided a stark contrast between the incompetent but benign news management of John Major's government and the ruthless control exercised on Tony Blair's behalf.

Lurid and titillating stories about the alleged bizarre sexual tastes of the Secretary of State for National Heritage excited the tabloids throughout the summer of 1992. 'David Mellor and the actress' was the rather matter-of-fact headline in mid-July for the front-page splash in the *People* which broke the news of his affair with Antonia de Sancha. Unlike many of his ministerial colleagues Mellor was ready to stand and fight, and he struggled valiantly against his tabloid tormentors for well over two months in a desperate attempt to keep his job before finally resigning in late September. Week after week the stories kept coming and the *Sun*'s headline writers were determined not be outdone: their initial disclosure that 'She gave a great toe job' was followed seven weeks later by another front-page classic of the tabloid genre, 'Mellor made love in Chelsea strip!' In his letter of resignation, Mellor thanked the Prime Minister for having decided in

July that his 'folly in becoming embroiled in revelations of an affair' did not warrant him leaving the government but he had concluded it was 'too much to expect' his cabinet colleagues to have to put up with a constant barrage of tabloid stories.

Major's brave act of loyalty in continuing for so long to support a much-maligned minister was seen by his opponents as having illustrated a fatal weakness in his political make-up: indecisiveness. By dithering over whether Mellor was to stay or go he had subjected his government needlessly to weeks of debilitating publicity, a mistake which Tony Blair and Alastair Campbell had no intention of repeating. The swiftness of their response to the *News of the World*'s deadline for publishing details of Robin Cook's affair with Gaynor Regan showed that they would not hesitate to take incisive action the instant they heard of a sexual indiscretion which might endanger the government's reputation. Nevertheless, if he thought it was justified, Blair could be just as resolute as Major in refusing to be pushed around by the tabloids, and his willingness to go on shoring up the career of Geoffrey Robinson, his beleaguered Paymaster-General, was on a par with his predecessor's reluctance to allow the newspapers to claim Mellor's scalp.

When it came to the risky adventures of Ron Davies in October 1998 there was no question of the newspapers being first with the news: for once in an alleged sex scandal, it was Downing Street which took the initiative and surprised the media. Political journalists were caught unaware by the minister's departure and were amazed at the brutal efficiency with which it appeared to have been executed. Davies tendered his resignation once he had informed Blair of what he acknowledged was 'a serious lapse of judgement' which had occurred after he had driven from Wales and parked his car near his home in south London. 'I went for a walk on Clapham Common... I was approached by a man I had never met before who engaged me in conversation... He asked me to accompany him and two of his friends to his flat for a meal.' After being robbed of his wallet at knifepoint and having his car stolen, Davies went to the police. 'In allowing myself to be placed in this situation, with people I had never met and about whom I knew nothing, I did something very foolish.'

Downing Street could not be faulted on the speed with which it operated: after a mid-morning conversation in the Prime Minister's office about the events of the night before, letters were exchanged and news of Davies' resignation was released just after 4 p.m. Davies did one pooled interview for television and radio outlets in which he said he was guilty of a lapse of judgement: 'It is something I regret . . . I was the innocent victim of a crime.' But Davies did not explain precisely what had happened, and his tantalising reference in his resignation letter to having acted foolishly became a source of considerable conjecture in the news media. Indeed, his interview raised more questions than it answered. Why was he refusing to give a full account of what happened? Why did a minister who had been mugged think it necessary to resign? Journalists' suspicions about the unexplained reasons for the resignation were heightened when the interview was broadcast. One of the BBC's cameras was running as Davies opened the door and entered his room at the Welsh Office, and immediately behind the minister the figure of Alastair Campbell could be seen. The instant Blair's spokesman realised he had been caught on camera, he retreated behind the door so as to get out of shot. Campbell's furtive behaviour confirmed that this was no run-of-the-mill resignation but the downfall of a minister in highly embarrassing circumstances, requiring the tightest possible control. At a lobby briefing later that afternoon, Campbell told journalists that Davies denied absolutely that there had been a sexual encounter or that he had been looking for gay sex. His resignation had been accepted by Blair because it was a serious lapse of judgement for 'a cabinet minister to meet a stranger in a public park and drive off around south London'. Downing Street's haste in seeking to draw a line under the affair seemed admirable in terms of news management – the faster they acted, the better their chances of limiting the damage – but a heavy price would be paid for the failure to persuade Davies to give a convincing account of his escapade, or to offer a credible version on his behalf through Campbell and explain why it warranted a resignation.

'Cabinet Minister quits in gay sex scandal' was the *Sun*'s headline on 28 October over its account of how a 'glittering ministerial career' fell apart after a night of shame which began with the 'cabinet hardman picking up a Rastafarian at a homosexuals' hang-out' and ended when he found he had been dumped at a housing estate in Brixton which was 'a haunt for muggers, drug-pushers and hookers, known as crack alley'. The other tabloids had reached the same conclusion: 'Shame of gay sex cabinet minister' was the *Mirror*'s front-page splash. But the *Sun* was ahead of its rivals and had found space for an unexpected twist to the story. 'Mandy outed on TV' said the headline over its report of how viewers of *Newsnight* had been told that Peter Mandelson, the Secretary of State for Trade and Industry, was 'certainly gay'.

Jeremy Paxman, who was presenting the programme, was caught off guard when Matthew Parris, the openly gay political columnist on *The Times*, told him there were at least two other gay members of the cabinet. Instead of moving swiftly on to the next question, Paxman queried what he had been told and, given the opportunity, Parris had no hesitation in naming names: 'Well, Chris Smith is openly gay and I think Peter Mandelson is certainly gay.' Chris Smith, Secretary of State for Culture, Media and Sport, revealed he was gay shortly after getting elected for Islington South and Finsbury in 1983 and for some years he was the only MP to have made it public. Some newspapers had mentioned that Mandelson was gay but he had never responded to the reports and *Newsnight*'s reference was one of the most explicit. The *Sun*'s rapid response to a late-breaking story included an instant editorial which said the paper knew that 'Mandelson has struggled with this issue for many years...The British people will not turn on Mandelson because he is gay. And they will sympathise with him for the way in which he was "exposed". We say to Mandelson: tell the truth.'

By inviting Parris to volunteer information about the sexuality of cabinet ministers, Paxman had come right up against the BBC's guideline that the private lives of individuals should not be discussed unless broader public issues had been raised, and his conduct produced a swift response. Programme editors were issued explicit instructions in a memo sent out by Anne Sloman, the BBC's chief political adviser: 'Please will all programmes note that under no circumstances whatsoever should the allegation about the private life of Peter Mandelson be repeated or referred to in any broadcast.' This edict, however, came too late to prevent Mandelson's 'outing' on *Newsnight* giving further impetus to the Davies story and providing an additional stimulus to those newspapers which had put a great deal of effort into investigating the mysterious circumstances surrounding Ron Davies' visit to Clapham Common.

The political fallout from the Welsh Secretary's sudden departure had thrown up another significant problem. Although Davies had resigned from the cabinet, he told Blair that he still intended to seek election to the new Welsh assembly, in the expectation of becoming its first secretary; but this posed an awkward dilemma for the Labour Party. If Davies felt he was unfit to serve in Blair's administration, why was he still considered suitable to lead a new authority in Wales? Political correspondents spent forty-five minutes at the 11 a.m. lobby briefing on 28 October going over the previous day's unanswered questions and the inconsistencies in Davies' position, but learned nothing more: there were, Campbell insisted, 'no salient facts' in Downing Street's possession which were not available to the news media. He repeated the denials which Davies had given to Blair of there having been any involvement in gay sex or drugs; there was nothing to suggest that the events on Clapham Common formed part of a wider pattern of behaviour. Campbell implied that the Prime Minister's staff were as mystified as the journalists as to what might have happened. 'You think there are elements to the story that have not been fully explained. Maybe we feel the same way too.'

Next day's newspapers took Campbell to task and suggested that Davies' admission of having done something 'foolish' was simply a device to avoid further accusations of sleaze. Colin Brown, the *Independent*'s chief political correspondent, said Campbell's answers 'bore a striking resemblance to the selective use of words' deployed by President Clinton to avert damage over the Monica Lewinsky affair. Jonathan Freedland, writing in the *Guardian*, had been struck by the way Campbell had lurked over Davies' shoulder as he arrived for his BBC interview. 'The face of the executioner was just visible . . . It provides visible proof of what Westminster watchers all suspected: that a "resignation" this swift and clinical could only have been the handiwork of the master. For Campbell had demonstrated his penchant for instant, surgical troubleshooting in the earliest days of the Blair government, when he delivered the famous airport ultimatum to Robin Cook.' Trevor Kavanagh, the *Sun*'s political editor, sympathised with the Prime Minister and his press secretary. Blair was said to be angry that Davies had repeatedly dodged answering questions and refused to come clean. 'Blair still has no idea why the Welsh Secretary picked up three strangers. And Downing Street admit they may never get to the bottom of it.' Davies and his family had been spirited away to a secret address so that he could 'think through' his future. After having had two days to reflect, he announced that he would step down from the job of leading his party into the Welsh assembly elections in 1999. His decision to relinquish Labour's lead role in the principality did nothing to quell press speculation. There were so many fresh lines of enquiry that it was front-page news again for the third morning running. Six suspects had been arrested in Brixton and more details were emerging about the events that preceded the mugging. Under the headline 'Davies told lies to police', the *Daily Mail* claimed that he had been forced to quit after changing his story when 'confronted by sceptical officers who warned him it was a serious offence to mislead the police'.

Once a political sex scandal has developed into a media free-for-all, extricating the Prime Minister from the story is no easy task. On the morning after Davies' departure, the Minister for the Cabinet Office, Dr Jack Cunningham, tried to distance the government from any future association with the Welsh Secretary's escapade, telling *Today* that piecing together what had happened was a matter for Davies and the police. 'I am sure there will be more damaging stories and allegations but that will focus on Ron himself and what brought him into this situation . . . All the Prime Minister knows is what I have told you . . . The business of government goes on.' Dr Cunningham's hands-off approach seemed to be the appropriate follow-through in the immediate aftermath of a tightly controlled resignation, but the story was proving to be so embarrassing to the government that by the end of week drastic action had to be taken. Much of the press criticism had focused on the lack of a convincing explanation for his sudden departure from the cabinet and, in a fresh attempt to limit speculation, Davies agreed to answer questions put to him by BBC Wales and HTV. In his first interview he had shown little remorse for his conduct: although admitting to a lapse of judgement, he had implied he was innocent of any wrongdoing and, to begin with, his friends were insisting that he still hoped to become first secretary in Wales. The impression that he might have been forced to resign under duress gained further credence in the light of his failure to apologise publicly to his family, colleagues or supporters – an omission that loomed large in the context of a government that had all but made contrition into an art form. Blair made his first apology just a month after becoming Prime Minister, when he expressed regret for the way Britain had failed the Irish people 150 years earlier during the potato famine which claimed a million lives, and deployed the tactic of saying 'sorry' with great effect when taking the blame for Downing Street's initial evasiveness over Bernie Ecclestone's £1 million donation. Other ministers, too, had become adroit at using a display of contrition to limit damaging publicity and assuage disappointment at unpopular announcements. Frank Dobson, the Secretary of State for Health, told *Today* in February 1998 that he was 'embarrassed' about an increase in hospital waiting lists for which he was 'partly responsible'. Two months later he apologised again, telling listeners to *The World at One* that he was 'genuinely sorry' that the nurses' pay award could not be met in full and would have to be staged. If Ron Davies were to stand any chance of convincing the media that his denials of gay sex and drug-taking were genuine, he would have to give a fuller account of what had transpired and show regret for the damage which his behaviour had caused to Labour's prospects in Wales. Although Campbell was no longer lurking in the background or directing affairs in Cardiff, there was a visible reminder of the advice which he had given: newspaper photographs taken just before the interviews revealed that Davies had written the word 'sorry' with a red ballpoint pen on the back of his hand to make sure he did not forget the message which he knew he had to convey.

Glyn Mathias, political editor for BBC Wales, said Davies emerged from three days in hiding looking tired and red-eyed. 'He kept breaking down as we interviewed him but he said to us, "I know you boys have a job to do, so do it," and it showed he was expecting some tough questions.' Mathias asked him four times if he was gay but the former minister kept repeating the same answer: 'I am not going into that... I am not going to get involved in a discussion about my own private life... I believe everyone has a right to privacy... I am a libertarian.' Davies acknowledged that his behaviour in going off with strangers was bizarre. 'I realise I should have extricated myself from that... It was a moment of madness for which I have subsequently paid a heavy price. It has caused embarrassment to the government, to my parliamentary colleagues, to my family and to my constituents and I am deeply, deeply sorry for it.'

Davies failed to convince the *Sun* of his sincerity: 'You fake' was the bold front-page headline over an enlarged photograph of the back of his hand: the accompanying article said the reminder to plead 'I'm sorry' had exposed his regrets as 'a sham'. The act of contrition carried even less weight with the Sunday newspapers, whose investigations revealed what the *News of the World* said was a 'secret double life' of regular visits to 'gay haunts'. The *Express* and *Sunday Telegraph* both led on speculation that Blair feared the former Welsh Secretary was about to commit suicide. Their reports were based on Campbell's briefing to the Sunday lobby, at which he accused the newspapers of putting Davies under huge stress: 'You just want the agony to continue. You lot wouldn't care if the poor guy topped himself, because that would make a good story.' Davies himself called the allegations in the tabloids about his private life 'lurid, unpleasant lies and fantasies masquerading as stories' and, in an emotional resignation statement to the Commons the following Monday afternoon, condemned media intrusion into his personal affairs as an 'arbitrary abuse of power'. In what the *Mirror* said next morning was a reference to his 'traumatic childhood at the hands of a brutal father', Davies told the House that it was not the first time in his life that he had been 'badly beaten and hurt'. He had learned 'a very hard lesson at a very early age' that one cannot allow powerful people to bully the weak. 'We are what we are. We are all different – the product of both our genes and our experiences.'

Out of all that weekend's coverage, it was the *Observer*'s account of events which switched the focus back to Downing Street by challenging the accuracy of Campbell's briefings on what the Prime Minister had been told about the incident. A report from the police in Brixton, it said, was on the desk of the Home Secretary, Jack Straw, first thing on the morning after the incident at Clapham, and it was Blair who summoned Davies for an urgent meeting. This was a sequence of events at variance with guidance given to journalists on the afternoon of the minister's resignation, when Campbell gave the impression that it was Davies who had taken the initiative and that it was 'to his credit' that he had gone to Blair to explain what had happened. Furthermore, at the lengthy briefing on the second day of the story, journalists had been assured that there were 'no salient facts' known to the Prime Minister, that were not also available to the news media.

In the light of the *Observer's* disclosures, lobby journalists renewed their questioning, subjecting what Colin Brown, the *Independent's* chief political correspondent, said was 'one of the toughest grillings' which the Downing Street press secretary had faced. Campbell admitted that his guidance the previous week had been incomplete: the Home Office had informed No. 10 that Davies had been in an incident on Clapham Common involving a black male and that Blair was 'aware that was what Ron was coming to see him about'. The *Independent* took the view that it was Downing Street's 'economy with words', made evident by Campbell's subsequent disclosures, that had 'allowed the affair to keep running' and revived questions about a cover-up. Campbell sought to justify his position by emphasising that the investigation in Brixton had always been a matter for the police: 'I was answering questions based on what Ron Davies had told the Prime Minister... It is my job to brief as we see it.' Nevertheless the Prime Minister's spokesman had been forced to correct briefings which he had given the week before, and *The Times* wondered whether his failure to reveal information which should have been made public was part of Downing Street's attempt to reduce the Welsh Secretary's 'transgressions to the minimum needed to justify a resignation'. Next day No. 10 issued further guidance: when Campbell briefed journalists the week before he was 'acting in good faith' and was not aware of the information which Scotland Yard had passed to Blair's chief of staff, Jonathan Powell. In its blow-by-blow account of the government's handling of the resignation, the *Sunday Times* said a cock-up rather than a conspiracy seemed to be to blame for the discrepancies in the press secretary's guidance: Powell had not briefed him soon enough about the police investigation. But Campbell's credibility had been at stake, and as he grappled with questions about misleading the lobby, he 'ignored repeated pager messages summoning him to Tony Blair's side' for an engagement at Westminster Hall. 'New Labour had tumbled into one of the oldest traps in politics: the cover-up. Despite Campbell's denials it had been found out trying to disguise what it knew about the antics of Ron Davies.'

While the continuing fallout from the resignation of one minister was being explored inside the Sunday papers, their front pages had news of sensational disclosures about another member of the cabinet, the agriculture minister Nick Brown. 'Minister confesses gay fling to Blair', was the *News of the World*'s headline over its account of how Brown had been forced to make a statement about his sexuality after the paper had obtained information about his 'lover's kiss'n'tell threat' to reveal details of their two-year affair. Brown's former partner was said to have made a series of 'lurid and fanciful allegations about gay sex encounters' which the paper admitted it had not been able to 'substantiate in any way' so had not published. However, after Brown was approached about the allegations, the Downing Street press office supplied a statement to the *News of the World* on his behalf at five-thirty on the Saturday evening before publication, and it was this that provided the basis for the story. In his statement, the minister confirmed that there had been a relationship but said it had ended well before the general election, and he denied that he had ever paid for sex. Brown said he had always wanted to keep his sexuality private, and he was sorry and deeply embarrassed that his friends and family would find out about it through the *News of the World*. 'I ask them for their understanding, and assure them, as I have assured the Prime Minister, that there is nothing in my past or present to give them any doubt in my ability to serve them and the government.'

Although Downing Street had again been forced to respond to a Sunday newspaper investigation, No. 10 moved swiftly to blunt the impact of the *News of the World*'s story by saying that Brown was safe in his job. Paul Lashmar, who investigated the government's handling of the story for the *Independent*, said the *News of the World*'s editor Phil Hall rang Brown at the Ministry of Agriculture late on the Friday afternoon and told him of the allegations being made by his former lover. Brown contacted No. 10 and, after a series of calls between the press office and the paper, two statements – one on behalf of Brown, one on behalf of the government – were supplied to the *News of the World* and then issued to the media generally. 'Blair backs newly "outed" gay minister' was the headline in the *Sunday Times*, which said the Prime Minister had been given a full account of the relationship and was satisfied it was a private matter which had no bearing on the minister's work.

The decision to issue statements simultaneously on behalf of Blair and Brown, in good time for the rest of the Sunday papers, put the *News of the World* on the defensive. Downing Street's rapid response gave the *Observer* sufficient time to prepare a leading article complimenting the government on the way it had handled the 'so-called outing' of Brown, a gay man who had made no secret of his sexuality. 'Tony Blair has this weekend performed one of the first truly enlightened acts since he came to power... The *News of the World* has performed one of the more disreputable tricks of its time... After weeks of disturbing hypocrisy about the sexuality of politicians, a line has finally been drawn... The *Observer* supports Blair wholeheartedly in his instinctive support last night of Brown... and Brown deserves unflinching support from his party, the government and wider society.' Downing Street's prompt backing for the Minister of Agriculture was also praised the following morning by the *Daily Telegraph*, which remarked that the No. 10 press office had not repeated the mistake it made with Ron Davies of leaving questions about his sexuality unanswered.

Blair's support for Brown was endorsed enthusiastically by other members of the cabinet. Alun Michael, the new Secretary of State for Wales, praised the dignified way in which his colleague had dealt with the allegations. When asked for their reactions, MPs from across the House expressed dismay at continuing press intrusion; there was no attempt to pass judgement on Brown's private life. As had been so noticeable during the traumatic aftermath of Ron Davies' resignation, parliamentarians remained steadfast in their determination to avoid making political capital out of the personal distress of politicians and their families. That restraint was maintained even when it emerged that there was insufficient evidence to support court proceedings against those said to have been involved in mugging Davies. A case against the man accused of the robbery was abandoned and the Crown Prosecution Service announced that the five other suspects arrested in Brixton would not be prosecuted. Although the tabloids interpreted this as substantiating the claims about the weakness of Davies' story, there was no attempt by opposition parties to reopen the incident.

Three weeks before the Welsh Secretary's resignation, Tony Blair had urged newspapers to be less intrusive. In his address to the 1998 party conference in Blackpool he promised to do more to support policies which strengthened the family but, no doubt conscious of John Major's ill-fated 'back to basics' campaign, said he hoped his speech would not be used as a justification for another round of newspaper stories about broken marriages and failed relationships: 'I challenge the media: don't use it as an excuse to dredge through the lives of every public figure.' Now, in the middle of a spate of stories around political sex scandals, the tabloids protested their innocence: the trigger for them, they insisted, was Ron Davies himself, who had resigned well before journalists had any inkling of what had happened. However, the reporting of his Clapham Common escapade had resulted, within the space of two weeks, in the 'outing' of two more cabinet ministers, and although the coverage of the revelations about Nick Brown was far less homophobic than Downing Street might have feared, this had all proved too much for the *Sun*. 'Tell us the truth Tony... Are we being run by a gay Mafia?' was the front-page headline over a report which said the news that Nick Brown was the fourth gay member of the cabinet had 'set alarm bells ringing'. Trevor Kavanagh, the paper's political editor, demanded to know how many more cabinet ministers had 'skeletons in their closets'. He said that if one in every ten adults was homosexual, four actively gay ministers in a cabinet twenty-one strong was double the national average – and there might be 'more ministers yet to come out'. This story was another reflection of the erratic course which the paper had been pursuing under the editorship of David Yelland: ten days earlier, after Matthew Parris had 'outed' Peter Mandelson on *Newsnight*, the *Sun* insisted that it did not 'matter in the slightest' if a minister was homosexual because the 'old fashioned era of gay bashing is over'. Other newspaper editors were taken aback by the sudden reversal of tone, which seemed to indicate that Yelland had lost his way.

Most of the papers had been highly supportive of Brown, and the only problem facing Alastair Campbell at that morning's eleven o'clock lobby briefing was how to steer a course around the *Sun*'s outburst and an interview on *Today* in which the Deputy Prime Minister, John Prescott, had called on the Press Complaints Commission to investigate the conduct of the *News of the World* which, he said, appeared to be acting as 'judge, jury and executioner'. Campbell played down Prescott's complaint, insisting that the government still favoured self-regulation by the press. He thought Brown had been treated with 'sympathy and understanding' and that if the coverage was looked at in the round it was a 'reflection of what is now a greater public understanding of the difference between private lives and public office'.

'Blair backs the *Sun* over gays' was Yelland's response next morning in a front-page report which claimed that Blair had backed the way the paper had 'played fair with outed' Nick Brown. However, in reality the *Sun* was using Campbell's briefing to beat a hasty retreat from the fiasco of its scare story about a 'gay Mafia': in an editorial the paper declared that it was 'not anti-gay'. By the following morning Yelland had made a full surrender and promised that in future the *Sun* would not reveal the sexuality of any gays, whether men or women, unless 'it can be defended on the grounds of overwhelming public interest... because we recognise that public attitudes are changing'. In order to demonstrate his own sincerity, and as a gesture of support for Peter Mandelson, Yelland sacked Matthew Parris from his weekly column in the *Sun* and gave readers a personal pledge as editor: 'The *Sun* is no longer in the business of destroying closet gays' lives by exposing them as homosexuals.' When interviewed by Donald Macintyre in the *Independent*, Yelland denied he had performed a U-turn. He stood by his paper's claim that there was a 'gay Mafia', but he acknowledged that the days when people discriminated against gays 'openly or even privately' were passing.

In the same interview, Yelland said that in the five months he had been editor he had proved that the *Sun* was not in an incestuous relationship with the Labour government because it 'shits all over Tony Blair' and Campbell had 'gone nuts' with the paper twice that week. Yet however convincing Yelland might have thought he sounded when he tried to put some clear water between the *Sun* and the government, the Prime Minister's press secretary and the rest of the Labour Party's publicity team still regarded the paper's response as a yardstick by which to judge tabloid reaction, and it appeared that no request which it made could be lightly ignored. At the Labour conference the previous month, the *Sun's* coverage was sycophantic. Its front-page headline the day after the Prime Minister's speech endorsed Blair's determination to press on with his 'juggernaut of reforms' in the boldest terms – 'This Tony's not for turning' – and on an inside page there was evidence of the exclusive access which Campbell was ready to provide to a loyal paper. The *Sun's* showbusiness editor, Dominic Mohan, had been granted a photo-opportunity at which Blair praised Mohan's daily 'Bizarre' column of showbiz news: 'Tony shook my hand and said: "It's nice to meet you because I read Bizarre and I think it's wonderful . . . Bizarre is fun to read and I like to keep up with all the showbiz news."' Such a blatant prime ministerial plug for the paper and so keen a profession of interest in its 'showbiz news' bordered on the unbelievable bearing in mind the repeated assertion of the Downing Street press office that the Prime Minister had a take-it-or-leave-it attitude when it came to reading the newspapers.

The *Sun*'s conference coverage had been equally flattering about Peter Mandelson, whose speech was given a rave review for having delegates 'rolling in the aisles' as he used a 'one-man laughter show' to win over critics who hated his 'shadowy influence as Labour's Prince of Darkness'. In his interview with the *Independent*, Yelland said it was 'bollocks' to suggest that the *Sun* had been seeking to ingratiate itself with Mandelson so as to influence the decisions which he was taking as Secretary of State for Trade and Industry. However, Mandelson had been in the job only six weeks when, in September 1998, Rupert Murdoch's satellite television company British Sky Broadcasting announced a £623 million takeover bid for Manchester United Football Club. After taking advice from the Office of Fair Trading, Mandelson ordered that the bid should be referred to the Monopolies and Mergers Commission, which provoked a bitter a response from Murdoch at the annual meeting of British Sky Broadcasting. He accused the government of showing 'excessive caution' because of the way his newspapers had supported Labour at the election. After telling journalists that he did not blame Mandelson personally, he said it was ridiculous for a government to be 'influenced by a few paranoid hacks in Fleet Street' – at which point he was pulled away by Tim Allan, the company's director of corporate relations and formerly Campbell's deputy in Downing Street.

Yelland's attempt to deny that the *Sun* had been toadying to Mandelson in the weeks before the announcement of the monopolies investigation bore little relation to reality. Few ministers had attracted the kind of hero-worship which had been dished out so unquestioningly by the country's biggest-selling newspaper. 'For Pete's sake get this man in,' was the *Sun*'s advice to Blair in the week before the July 1998 cabinet reshuffle. The following day he was given the full makeover, with the headline 'Who loves ya, Mandy' emblazoned over a page of pictures illustrating the 'remarkable list of Mandy's Mates' who ranged from 'royalty to Hollywood stars'. The day after his appointment to the cabinet the *Sun* said it was delighted that a 'Blairite star' like Mandelson had been made trade supremo, a job which he richly deserved and would shine in. The only note of caution had been sounded over his support for European monetary union, and even there it was not until three months later that the paper took a critical tone. In a speech to the annual conference of the Confederation of British Industry in November 1998, Mandelson signalled his support for the single currency in the clearest possible terms: 'We've made it clear we will join when it is in Britain's interests.' Mandelson was noticeably more definite than ministers had sounded previously in substituting the word 'when' for 'if', and this attracted the condemnation of the *Sun*'s Eurosceptic political editor, Trevor Kavanagh. 'Outed' was the one-word headline over Kavanagh's report that Mandelson and the Chancellor, Gordon Brown, had both 'sensationally come out of the closet and admitted they are a couple of raving Euro fanatics'. By this point, judging from the strong undercurrent of hostility being displayed towards him by many other newspapers, the cooling-off in the *Sun*'s adulation of Mandelson was somewhat overdue.

The new Secretary of State for Trade and Industry's first big speech had been to the TUC conference in September 1998, and it came at an awkward moment for the trade union movement. Mandelson had ordered that discussions should be reopened with the employers over the legislation proposed in the *Fairness at Work* white paper, and his department was also considering whether to privatise the Post Office. He did his best to put delegates at their ease: 'You will always get from me – honesty, straight talking and candour. No grandstanding, no playing to the gallery – no more spin, honest.' Three weeks later, at the end of the Labour Party conference, he said that he was at last feeling comfortable with himself, having finally emerged from his shadowy role as a fixer and media manipulator which he readily acknowledged had made him a focus of hatred for the previous fourteen years. In an interview with Tom Baldwin of the *Sunday Telegraph*, Mandelson described the pleasure he felt at having won promotion to the cabinet and on taking charge of his own department. 'If I think about myself now, the first thing I feel is sheer happiness... As I walked around the conference, I sensed people were no longer embarrassed to look me in the eye... and I recognise that as a cabinet minister I'm going to have to become more grey and platitudinal in what I say.' And yet, before the month was out, disclosures about his private life had delivered another setback to his ambition to be treated at last as a 'proper politician'. Once Matthew Parris had told *Newsnight* that Mandelson was 'certainly gay', there was no holding back by the newspapers. Some journalists had been waiting for years to settle old scores with Labour's pre-eminent spin doctor: now, at last, they had the excuse they had been waiting for and a ready-made opportunity to intrude into his sexual life. The controversy provoked by his 'outing' dominated the Sunday papers that weekend and the *Express* led the field with an exclusive photograph of a 'Brazilian student who is Mandelson's close friend'.

Punch, the magazine owned by the Harrods proprietor Mohamed Al Fayed, devoted much of its next edition to a highly colourful account of what was said to have taken place in July when, as minister without portfolio, Mandelson had paid an official visit to Rio de Janeiro: 'In London, Peter Mandelson treads carefully as a sober-suited minister of the Crown. But, in Rio, he trips the light fantastic, letting his hair down with chums such as Fabulous Fabrizio.' A few newspapers made guarded references to *Punch's* allegations, but the story only took off after William Hague used his reply to the Queen's Speech to take a pot shot at 'Lord Mandelson of Rio' and to predict that the Secretary of State would end up as one of 'Tony's cronies' in the House of Lords. Martin Dowle, a former BBC political correspondent who was the director of the British Council in Rio and Mandelson's host, denied they had toured gay haunts. He said the Secretary of State would have needed to be 'superhuman to go out nightclubbing' in view of the heavy schedule for his visit, and they had returned home by 10.30 p.m.

Another area of Mandelson's private life which was being investigated by journalists was his purchase six months before the 1997 general election of a £475,000 house in Notting Hill. Newspaper diaries had taken a great interest in the ability of a backbench MP, on a salary of £43,000, to buy an elegant four-storey property in such a fashionable area of London. *Punch* took a close look at Mandelson's finances in its February edition and concluded that as his mortgage was only £150,000 on a house worth £500,000, it looked as if 'a pal who did not like to see him slumming it' had stumped up the other £350,000. The mystery surrounding what *Punch* described as his transformation into a 'well-off man-about-town' was one of the lines of enquiry which was pursued throughout the summer and autumn of 1998 by the *Mirror's* political columnist Paul Routledge, who was writing an unauthorised biography of the Secretary of State.

Routledge was in competition with another author, the *Independent* columnist Donald Macintyre, who was seen as being more sympathetic towards Mandelson than most other political journalists and who had received some cooperation from him. Both books were due to be published early in 1999, but Routledge's was attracting the more interest. He hoped it would prove as controversial as his earlier biography of Gordon Brown, which the previous winter had exposed the Chancellor's continuing sense of grievance over the way Tony Blair, with Mandelson's help, had won the Labour leadership election in 1994. Routledge knew that he was regarded as a troublemaker by both Mandelson and Alastair Campbell, and he believed that it was as a result of their intervention in May 1998 that he lost the chance of becoming political editor of the *Express*, a job which he said was offered to him by the paper's new editor, Rosie Boycott, but then withdrawn.

A close friend and confidant of Routledge was the Chancellor's press officer, Charlie Whelan, whose cooperation had proved so invaluable when he wrote his semi-authorised biography of the Chancellor. Unlike Campbell and the other special advisers and party press officers, Whelan enjoyed drinking with political journalists and regularly lunched with Routledge in the press gallery dining room. The pair were well known for their badinage: when on the lookout for a journalist to buy him lunch, Whelan would joke about needing a 'nosebag', at which point Routledge would promise him another 'tbl', which in their jargon was a two-bottle lunch. As they fraternised so openly, most political correspondents assumed that Routledge's biography would reflect the latest twists and turns in Whelan's longstanding feud with Mandelson and investigate the unanswered questions about the Secretary of State's sudden accumulation of wealth. Speculation about the book's likely contents, and the damage which

Routledge might be able to inflict on Mandelson, intensified towards the end of the year when the *Sunday Times* announced that it planned to serialise the new biography the following January.

It is at this point that the story turns into a whodunit, because the drama which unfolded in the four days before Christmas ended with the resignation of Mandelson and the departure a few hours later of the Paymaster-General, Geoffrey Robinson, unmasked as his secret benefactor. Piecing together the precise chain of events is no easy task, because the journalists involved have been determined to protect their contacts. The most sensational disclosure which Routledge intended to make in his book, *Mandy: The Unauthorised Biography*, was that Robinson had provided Mandelson with a loan of £373,000 to help him with the purchase of the house in Notting Hill. Whelan was thought to be the most likely source of this information. He had spent a lot of time with the Paymaster-General, both at the Treasury and at his penthouse flat in Park Lane. In helping the minister to fend off questions from journalists investigating his former business life, Whelan must have become fairly well acquainted with Robinson's financial affairs.

After news of Routledge's imminent disclosure was picked up by Mandelson's special adviser, Benjamin Wegg-Prosser, the countdown began to a crisis which would shake New Labour to its very foundations. Once Mandelson knew for certain on Thursday, 17 December that his secret was on the point of being made public, he informed his permanent secretary, Michael Scholar, and then warned Alastair Campbell, who notified the Prime Minister. Blair was preparing to make a statement to the House of Commons about the launch the night before of air strikes against Iraq by the United States and Britain. His immediate concern was to discover whether there had been a possible conflict of interest and he asked the Cabinet Secretary, Sir Richard Wilson, to check with Scholar to make sure that Mandelson had taken steps to distance himself from the inquiry which the Department of Trade and Industry was conducting into Robinson's business interests and his former links with the late newspaper proprietor, Robert Maxwell. Scholar told Sir Richard that although he had previously been unaware of the Paymaster-General's loan, Mandelson had taken steps the previous September, when the department began its inquiry into Robinson's affairs, to ensure that both he and his ministerial colleagues were entirely divorced from the investigation. Once assured that Mandelson had insulated himself from the inquiry, and that there was consequently no conflict of interest, Blair took no further action and throughout the following weekend was immersed in the continuing air strikes against Iraq and the task of briefing world leaders on the reasons why Britain was supporting President Clinton's attempt to destroy Saddam Hussein's chemical and biological weapons.

Mandelson's secret finally became public knowledge four days later, on the evening of Monday, 21 December, as the *Guardian* prepared to publish the results of a lengthy investigation carried out by its reporter David Hencke – who was said to have been tipped off about Robinson's loan two months earlier by a source entirely independent of Charlie Whelan. Once other journalists learned what the *Guardian* intended to publish next morning, the story took off. Mandelson was alerted at five o'clock that afternoon. He had evidently contemplated his response in the event of the information leaking out and thought through a strong defensive strategy, because even before the story had appeared in next day's newspapers he launched himself into the task of trying to prove that despite his acceptance of Robinson's £373,000 loan there had been no conflict of interest. He gave his first interview to *Newsnight.* When tackled by the programme's presenter, Gordon Brewer, he delivered what gave every appearance of being some well-rehearsed answers: 'Geoffrey is a very wealthy man who is very generous... He is a friend of mine of nearly twenty years' standing and he made this offer before the election to help me purchase my house... Geoffrey asked for confidentiality and I respected that... The outstanding amount is £332,000 and I pay interest at the base rate of the Midland Bank... I hope to repay the remainder shortly.' There was no need, he insisted, for him to have informed his permanent secretary about the loan in September, because he had asked to be insulated from the inquiry into Robinson's affairs and had not seen any papers relating to it. He had not told Blair either, because it was a personal matter. 'My job now is to make a clean breast of what has happened... With the benefit of hindsight, I rather regret this and it would have been better if all the facts had been out, but I have satisfied my permanent secretary and the Prime Minister that there has been no conflict of interest and no infringement of the ministerial code... Whatever mud is thrown at me by the *Guardian* or anyone else I shall resist it... There is no conflict of interest so the matter of resignation does not arise.'

Mandelson's pre-emptive strike was backed up by a statement from the Downing Street press office confirming that Blair was confident the Secretary of State had been 'properly insulated' from the Robinson inquiry; but their combined efforts did little to lessen the impact of the coverage in next day's newspapers. The *Guardian* went hard on the way Mandelson had kept the loan a secret from Blair for more than two years and then concealed it from his civil servants on becoming a minister. Sharing the by-line on the story with David Hencke was another *Guardian* reporter: Seumas Milne, who had taken great delight the previous January in disclosing the contents of Paul Routledge's biography of Gordon Brown in advance of its serialisation. Milne said Whelan was 'widely believed' to have leaked details of Robinson's loan to Routledge, although not to the *Guardian*. Most of the coverage concentrated on the background to the loan, and only two papers offered an explicit opinion on the minister's conduct. The *Express* said Mandelson had made a 'gross error of political judgement' which Blair could not overlook, while the *Sun* took a stronger line, saying that it was no way for a minister to behave: 'This affair stinks, stinks, stinks. And we say that even though we have been supportive of Mandelson.'

Undeterred by the hostility of the press, Mandelson went on the offensive again first thing that morning. He told *Today* there had been no wrongdoing: there was no political motivation behind the loan and no reason why he should have considered it inappropriate to accept Robinson's money. As a politician he had signed up to the likelihood of having his actions interpreted unsympathetically, and he was well aware that newspapers liked sensational stories. 'That does not mean there is anything sinister about this or a conflict of interest ... Peter Mandelson and Geoffrey Robinson happen to be two fairly publicity-friendly, controversial, fairly exotic personalities who have come together. I think the reason why journalists are so agitated is because they smell a darn good story.' As I listened to his interview I could hardly believe what I was hearing: here was one of the foremost media tacticians of his generation admitting that he had thrown journalists something meaty to get their teeth into, while blithely acknowledging that despite all his past experience in crisis management he had failed to take any evasive action during his eighteen months as a minister to minimise the potential for adverse publicity. In his years as director of Labour's publicity department, Mandelson had been at the forefront of a regime which was ruthless in weeding out politicians who could not withstand sustained scrutiny by the news media. To get selected to stand in prominent parliamentary by-elections, candidates had to pass what the party's press officers termed the '*Sun* test': they had to be sure that there was nothing in their previous political, business or personal life which might emerge during the campaign and damage Labour's prospects. If Mandelson had been forced to face a selection panel he would inevitably have been asked about his financial affairs. Labour's computerised database, Excalibur, would have identified plenty of newspaper cuttings about his lavish lifestyle, including no doubt the February story from *Punch* which was almost correct in its calculations concerning the purchase of the Notting Hill house.

I felt that once Mandelson started applying to himself the tests which he had helped institute within the party, he would see that his position was untenable. He had been caught out concealing a massive loan from a Treasury minister who had already been forced to apologise to MPs for failing to make a full declaration of his shareholdings and directorships and whose affairs were being scrutinised by government inspectors. Mandelson's claim that he had not broken the strengthened ministerial code which Blair had introduced on taking office seemed at variance with reality. One of the key requirements was the importance of ministers understanding that it was the impression which their conduct created which mattered as much as the facts. Ministers were told to avoid accepting 'any gift or hospitality which might, or might reasonably appear to, compromise their judgement or place them under an improper obligation' and to avoid 'any danger of an actual or apparent conflict of interest' between their ministerial position and their private financial affairs. They were required to work within 'the letter and spirit of the code'.

As Mandelson pursued his campaign of self-justification, going from one radio and television studio to the next, he seemed oblivious to another harsh lesson of media presentation. If his tactic of seeking to defend himself were to fail, his eventual downfall would look all the worse in the light of his high-minded protestations of innocence. This was a high-risk strategy for Downing Street, too, and yet the line from the press office could not have been more definite: Blair had 'full confidence' in his Secretary of State who was doing an 'important job well'. None the less, as the day progressed, the outlook became bleaker as the questioning moved on to other potentially damaging ramifications. In an interview with ITN's newscaster, Dermot Murnaghan, Mandelson was asked whether he had informed the Britannia building society about Robinson's loan when he obtained his £150,000 mortgage – applicants being required to say whether they intended to borrow any other money to assist in the purchase of their property. He said that he could not recall whether or not he had mentioned it, and in any event that he did not think he was required to reveal 'a personal arrangement'. Here were loose ends that could only too easily unravel. Another line of questioning from journalists concerned the minister's failure to declare the loan in the register of MPs' interests. After being repeatedly pressed on this point he released a copy of a letter he had written seeking the advice of Elizabeth Filkin, the new Parliamentary Commissioner for Standards, in which he told her he did not think the loan needed to be registered as it was 'not a gift or gained through my being an MP'.

By late afternoon Mandelson realised he was making little headway with his twin-track approach of expressing regret for the lack of disclosure while at the same time insisting there was no conflict of interest. At ten o'clock that evening he spoke on the phone to Tony Blair, who was staying with his family at Chequers, and, according to Downing Street, informed the Prime Minister that he felt he had no alternative but to resign. Although Blair was said to have reached the same conclusion he suggested they both sleep on it, anxious no doubt to avoid taking any precipitate action. By delaying a decision for those few hours they would be able to see whether Mandelson's strenuous efforts to clear his name had had any effect on the newspaper coverage the next morning. In the event they were greeted with a damning set of headlines which heralded the start of New Labour's blackest day. Downing Street said that when Blair and Mandelson spoke again at 10 a.m., the beleaguered minister insisted that his mind was made up and they both agreed he would have to leave the government immediately.

Any lingering thought in Mandelson's mind that he might be able to cling to office must have been dashed when he saw page after page devoted to examining the damage he had inflicted on the sleaze-free government which Blair had promised. The impact of the way the story had been reported must have had a devastating effect on both men. The size of the loan and the secrecy surrounding it had taken journalists' breath away, while Mandelson's lack of judgement in allowing himself to remain so dependent for so long on a fellow minister seemed totally at odds with the reputation which he had cultivated for himself as New Labour's master of control. The sheer surprise of the whole episode helped to make the story a political sensation. None of John Major's disgraced ministers had been savaged quite so comprehensively or so viciously on what after all was still only the third day of the story. The *Sun*'s front page mocked the promise Blair had given in July after the lobbyists' cash-for-access scandal:'"We are on the side of ordinary people against privilege. We must be purer than pure"...So how the hell can Mandy stay?'Trevor Kavanagh said the Secretary of State's whirlwind tour of radio and television studios had raised more questions than he had answered. 'Master of Deception' was the headline over the *Daily Mail*'s account of the 'Mandelson mortgage maze', which accused Mandelson of having misled the paper two years earlier by suggesting that the money for the house had 'come from legacies through his mother'. Under the headline 'Peter Panic' the *Mirror* claimed that Mandelson intended to use 'family resources' to pay off the loan within weeks, but the paper's columnist Paul Routledge said nothing told the public more about New Labour than the 'sleazy saga' of his secret loan. The *Express* said it was 'literally incredible that a man supposedly so savvy and politically astute could fail to appreciate how contemptible his behaviour would appear'. The *Daily Telegraph* seemed almost lost for words when ridiculing Mandelson's assertion that the loan was 'an entirely personal, non-political confidential matter' between two friends.'It is a measure of the mix of ambition, greed, talent, flamboyance, charm, vanity, social climbing, insecurity, shallowness, risk-taking, corner-cutting and sheer comic lack of self-awareness that make up Peter Mandelson that only he could take seriously the version of events he described.'What particularly puzzled *The Times* was the timing: it was in October 1996, when Labour politicians were 'making hay with Tory sleaze', that the party's prime spokesman gave way to his 'vaunting social ambitions' and embarked on his 'dubious deal' to buy an extravagant house in Notting Hill. David Hencke, the *Guardian* reporter who broke the story, had investigated the 'spectacularly brief' inquiry which the Prime Minister conducted when he was told of the loan, and concluded that it was 'remarkably cursory given the fine words and high standards promised by Tony Blair'.

Even before Mandelson spoke to Blair at ten that morning it was obvious that his resignation was only hours away. Dr Jack Cunningham, Minister for the Cabinet Office, told *Today* that his colleague had made a misjudgement in not informing his permanent secretary of the arrangement. 'Peter Mandelson recognises this, that he should have made this clear... In retrospect we'd say yes, perhaps this could have been handled much better.' The announcement that Mandelson was leaving the government was released just before the lunchtime news bulletins, and an hour later political journalists crowded into the Downing Street press office to obtain copies of the resignation letters. Mandelson's opening line underlined the drama of his departure: 'Dear Tony, I can scarcely believe I am writing this letter to you. As well as being one of my closest friends you are a close colleague whose leadership and political qualities I value beyond all others... As I said publicly yesterday, I do not believe that I have done anything wrong or improper. But I should not, with all candour, have entered into the arrangement. I should, having done so, have told you and other colleagues whose advice I value... I am sorry about this situation. But we came to power promising to uphold the highest possible standards in public life. We have not just to do so, but we must be seen to do so.' In thanking Mandelson for his contribution to the government, Blair was short and to the point: 'It is no exaggeration to say that without your support and advice we would never have built New Labour. It was typical of you, when we spoke last night, that your thought was for the reputation of the Labour Party and the government and that you believed that since there had been a misjudgement on your part, then, as you said to me "we can't be like the last lot" and that what we are trying to achieve for the country is more important than any individual. But I also want you to know that you have my profound thanks for all you have done and my belief that, in the future, you will achieve much, much more with us.' For once Alastair Campbell had lost his bounce as he sat down to take journalists' questions on the exchange of letters. He said Mandelson had found it 'a pretty wretched experience' going round the studios trying to defend himself. 'He is very angry with himself... He wished he had never taken out such a huge loan and he wished he had told the Prime Minister and others about it... It was the right course of action to go, but the Prime Minister is saddened that one of the most talented politicians in the government, and in our generation, has had to resign.'

Before leaving his department, Mandelson gave interviews to the BBC and ITN. He acknowledged immediately that he should have been more open about having accepted such a large loan from a friend so as to 'protect myself against an appearance' of a conflict of interest. 'I should have foreseen how in government, when people learned of this, how it might appear... I didn't think it through... A little alarm bell should have gone off in my head. I cannot explain why it didn't... It was a mistake and I have paid a very high price for it.'

Geoffrey Robinson's departure an hour later had nothing like the same impact because it had been predicted for some weeks that once MPs had left Westminster for the Christmas and New Year holiday the Paymaster-General would resign quietly so as to save the government further embarrassment over the continued disclosures about his complex financial transactions. He told Blair in his resignation letter that his intention in making the loan to Mandelson was to 'help a long-standing friend, with no request for anything in return' and he had not misused his position as an MP or minister despite being subjected to 'a persistent but unfair' set of allegations about his business affairs. 'There comes a time when, after more than twelve months of a highly charged political campaign, the point has been reached when I feel that it is no longer right that you or your government should be affected by or have to contend with these attacks.'

The hurried resignation of two senior ministers created a vacuum at the strategic heart of New Labour. At one fell swoop Blair had lost not only his party's longest-serving strategist and election supremo, but also Labour's richest and most successful businessman who, as an unpaid Treasury minister, had helped devise and oversee the introduction of the windfall tax on the privatised utilities. For political journalists there was an eerie feel to the afternoon. The rapid exit of two key figures in the New Labour hierarchy under a cloud of suspicion meant a dearth of the glowing tributes which usually follow in the wake of high-profile cabinet departures. John Prescott and Jack Cunningham undertook the task of containment, touring the studios to stress that it was still business as usual for the government. They could only hope that the remaining loose ends, such as the confusion surrounding the information which Mandelson had given to the Britannia building society, would be tied up as quickly as possible. One of the few party activists ready to give interviews in Mandelson's support was the former lobbyist Derek Draper, who had become a phone-in host with Talk Radio after losing his job as a director of GPC. Draper was busily reinventing himself as a serious commentator and he was keen to shake off his disastrous wide-boy image. At his hour of need the previous July, when his world fell in during the 'cash-for-access' affair, Mandelson was the only minister prepared to speak up on his behalf, and he was anxious to demonstrate his loyalty in return. Draper thought resignation was 'wholly disproportionate to the mistake' and he felt the news media were underestimating the number of friends who would stand by the former Secretary of State as he rebuilt his career. Labour's former chief spokesperson, David Hill, who had worked alongside Mandelson as the party's director of communications, thought it was a tragedy that he had been forced to resign. 'People will say about Mandelson, love him or hate him, that his advice to Blair and his contribution to the party were invaluable. He deserves his reputation as a star of New Labour.'

For all the plaudits on his past achievements, Mandelson's departure in such inauspicious circumstances had damaged not only his integrity as a party frontman and spokesman but also his future authority as a campaign chief – and, in some eyes, the authority of the New Labour government itself. Of next morning's newspapers, it was only the Christmas Eve edition of the *Sun* which contrived to give a seasonal feel to the story. Under the one-word front-page headline 'Stuffed' it printed a large photograph of a roast turkey out of which popped a picture of Peter Mandelson's head, his face grimacing with pain. The columnists were at one in concluding that he had had no alternative but to resign. The *Daily Telegraph*'s Boris Johnson said the danger for Blair, now that 'Mandy has gone, is that the lipstick, the varnish, the gloss will start to come away ... and behind the gloss? What do we see? Just a load of politicos on the make.' In his column in the *Mirror*, Paul Routledge said 'Mandygate' had thrown into question the future of New Labour as a political force. Matthew Parris agreed: New Labour's 'city of dreams has been more comprehensively wrecked in two nights of media bombing than anything Tony Blair could organise for Baghdad'. But his fellow columnist on *The Times*, Peter Riddell, believed that in his five months as a cabinet minister Mandelson had become 'one of the most effective advocates and implementers of the Blairite agenda', while the *Independent*'s Donald Macintyre complimented Mandelson on his decisiveness in deciding not to hang about once he realised the 'show was over'. As resignations went, he said, it was a class act: one of his 'most valuable skills has always been to read where the story is going'. And Hugo Young, writing in the *Guardian*, lamented his departure, though not without a note of criticism: 'He is an able, uncorrupt, if careless politician, with a breadth of vision few of his colleagues could get anywhere near. This episode showed the worst side of him, his dissembling and evasiveness in the face of straight questions from newspapers that were probing for what turned out to be an indisputably public aspect of his private situation.'

Despite the note of gloomy finality conveyed by the Christmas Eve editions of the newspapers, Mandelson's special adviser, Benjamin Wegg-Prosser, was doing all he could to put a brave face on the situation, and he continued valiantly to brief the news media. After picking up what the Press Association said was the 'grim-faced ex-minister' from the now notorious house in Notting Hill and driving him to an undisclosed destination, he gave journalists an outline of his boss's future plans. Wegg-Prosser was twenty-four, and sometimes when conversing with him I found it difficult to understand how so young and inexperienced an adviser had come to be entrusted with the task of briefing the media on behalf of a cabinet minister. Certainly no one could question his loyalty or dedication: when on late night duty I spoke to him quite frequently on the phone, and sometimes he became quite agitated when he insisted that I had got the wrong end of a particular story or when trying to explain why newspaper reports about Mandelson were incorrect or misleading and should not be repeated by the BBC. Usually there seemed no point in challenging what he was saying, because he was obviously doing his master's bidding and carrying out faithfully the instructions which he had been given. He had evidently taken a crash course at New Labour's school for spin doctors, and late on the afternoon of Christmas Eve I had the somewhat surreal experience of listening to him still spinning away on his patron's behalf.

He told me that Mandelson intended waiting until the New Year before deciding what to do. 'Peter doesn't want another backroom job or to go back to being a spin doctor. He wants to rebuild his career. Of course he'll have a lower profile to begin with, but you can report that his friends are suggesting that he might decide to stand as a candidate for Mayor of London. It is an option he will consider and don't forget the connection. His grandfather, Herbert Morrison, was leader of London County Council, so it would be following family tradition.' Wegg-Prosser's confirmation that Mandelson had no intention of returning to his previous job of behind-the-scenes propagandist was a recognition of reality as well as a statement of preference, for his power as a spin doctor had effectively been smashed. Few journalists would be prepared in the immediate future to take what he said at face value or to trust his off-the-record guidance, and so great was the damage to his reputation that he had lost his most powerful weapon of all: his ability to intimidate reporters on the strength of his access to Blair and his connections with newspaper proprietors and broadcasting executives.

Some of the Boxing Day newspapers carried a photograph of Mandelson looking rather forlorn as he arrived at his mother's home on Christmas morning carrying his presents, a bottle of wine and a tin of sweets. By now some of the columnists had taken pity on him. Matthew Parris was full of remorse in *The Times* for what he acknowledged was his own stupidity in making the remark on *Newsnight* about Mandelson's homosexuality which had given journalists a stick with which to beat him; he recognised that he had made a grave mistake in forgetting that there were many journalists and broadcasters to whom Mandelson's menacing manner had given offence. 'There was an army waiting to report any slingshot but their own against him.'

Mandelson's vulnerability once he had been 'outed' on *Newsnight* had made a deep impression on the *New Statesman*'s political editor,

Steve Richards. He interviewed the minister two weeks before his resignation and was struck by the fear he expressed about where the media were likely to attack him next. 'When I said I was pleased that he had stepped up the case for the single currency, he replied: "Yes, but every time I do there's an attack on Gay Mandelson in the *Sun*. There's a correlation between the two, you know."' Andrew Marr, writing in the *Observer*, believed there was a simple explanation for the vindictive mood of the *Sun*, which had been 'courted obsequiously' by Mandelson and New Labour. 'If you woo your natural enemies and snub your natural friends then, when things go wrong, your enemies will revert to type and your natural supporters won't be there for you.' The author Robert Harris took the blame for having given Mandelson the idea of buying a house in Notting Hill. Mandelson was a regular guest at Harris's home and godfather to his daughter, and at one stage the two men had been house-hunting together in west London. In his column in the *Sunday Times*, Harris said Mandelson had helped draw up the tough new code of conduct for ministers and had then fallen victim to the 'insane' requirement that 'not only must there *be* no conflict of interest in public life, there must *appear* to be no conflict... Nobody goes to jail for *appearing* to commit a burglary.' Harris said he was not surprised that the Blair government had 'crumpled even more quickly than its predecessors' when the tabloids were allowed to act as judge, jury and executioner and it was 'a hanging offence merely to *appear* suspect'.

Benjamin Wegg-Prosser's cheery assessment of the likelihood of Mandelson's returning to public office was reflected in a succession of speculative stories over the Christmas and New Year holiday. Two strongly canvassed options were that he might become a figurehead for an all-party group promoting British entry into the European single currency, or alternatively help organise Labour's campaign for the 1999 elections to the European Parliament. Another option which was floated after it was revealed that Mandelson had spent the night after his resignation at Chequers was that Blair might ask him to continue as chairman of a new Anglo-German working party which had been set up to look at economic and welfare policies. Mandelson was also reported to be anxious to help Oxfam and to encourage the take-up of voluntary work in third world countries.

The positive spin which was being put around on behalf of the principal casualty of the affair was in sharp contrast to the menacing tone being adopted towards Charlie Whelan. After their success in securing the scalps of Mandelson and Robinson, the newspapers had moved on to their next target and, judging by much of the post-Christmas coverage, the Chancellor's press secretary could have been forgiven for thinking he had taken on the starring role of villain in a Boxing Day pantomime. Most political correspondents seemed to be convinced that it would only be a matter of days before Tony Blair got his way and ordered Gordon Brown to sack his special adviser. Whelan had taken the precaution of disappearing from the scene once the *Guardian* broke the story and remained out of contact throughout the festivities, spending most of the holiday in the Scottish Highlands. The absence of the prime suspect only served to heighten interest in his likely fate, and a wide variety of unnamed sources predicted that Alastair Campbell and Mandelson's friends would not rest until he was fired. As Whelan was regarded as being the original instigator of much of the feuding between the respective supporters of Brown and Blair, his removal was regarded by some newspapers as a foregone conclusion. When asked on the day of Mandelson's resignation about Whelan's likely fate, Campbell, was careful to avoid saying anything which might be written up as Blair attacking Brown but it was obvious that he had finally lost all patience with the Chancellor's press secretary. He told the lobby that he had no intention of getting drawn into speculation as to whether Whelan was to blame for leaking details of the loan:'The Prime Minister is not a conspiracy theorist… and my view is that it's a waste of time worrying about that sort of thing.'

In his only substantive interview over the Christmas period, Mandelson told the *Observer* that he had no intention of seeking revenge.'I don't care about Whelan. I will refuse to let him become a wedge between myself and the Chancellor. I don't want any inquiries, tribunals or post-mortems into what happened.' Mandelson's appeal for restraint did nothing to reduce the clamour for the dismissal of Brown's aide. Kevin Maguire, the *Mirror*'s political editor, claimed Campbell and Whelan had become 'deadly rivals' and predicted that it was the Chancellor's adviser who would lose the first 'big political fight' of 1999. The *Sun* said Whelan was doomed because it had been told by a senior No. 10 official that the government would not be 'held to ransom by one little oik'. Joe Murphy, political editor of the *Mail on Sunday*, even drew up a list of what he said was a 'lynch mob' of Downing Street officials and cabinet ministers who were demanding that Whelan be sacked. Most stories quoted remarks attributed to the Deputy Prime Minister, John Prescott, who was overheard at ITN's headquarters saying that Whelan was behind the resignations and that as he was the 'cancer in the heart of it all', they had got to get rid of the 'bastard at last'. On 1 January, however, there was an about-turn when some newspapers claimed that Prescott had relented and was recommending that Brown should be allowed to retain Whelan, given that there was no conclusive evidence that he had leaked details of the loan.

The story was already on the point of turning into a Whitehall farce when Paul Routledge rewrote the script and suggested in the *Mirror*, which had taken over serialisation rights to his biography, that it was Mandelson who had leaked the story in the first place, miscalculating the degree of public outrage it would provoke. Routledge claimed that the Secretary of State had committed 'political suicide' after a sneak thief looked through proofs of the book at the *Mirror*'s office in the press gallery and then warned him that his secret was about to be exposed. The suggestion there was a sneak thief at work caused quite a stir among the political correspondents. Wegg-Prosser told the *Guardian* that he got his tip-off from a 'media friend' who had looked through the book's proofs for twenty minutes, but he refused to name his source. Routledge castigated the way the story had been reported by the 'tame public school revolutionaries' of the *Guardian*. 'Once it became clear that Mandy's minions were co-operating with the *Guardian* on a damage-limitation exercise,' he said, 'I abandoned any attempt to keep the lid on the scandal.' Alan Rusbridger, the *Guardian*'s editor, issued a forthright denial of this suggestion. His paper had been working on the story 'quite independently for several weeks', and Mandelson 'confirmed it when we approached him shortly before publication, but he was not our source'.

Routledge did his best to protect Whelan by insisting that he was not responsible for telling him about the arrangement between Robinson and Mandelson – 'I had known about the loan for nearly a year, from a quite different source, whose name I shall never reveal' – but speculation about the timing of Whelan's dismissal continued throughout the New Year weekend, and by the morning of his return to work on Monday 4 January the papers were hopelessly confused as to what might happen. Both *The Times* and the *Daily Telegraph* thought that he was likely to keep his job. Their optimistic assessment was based on an interview given by the Leader of the House, Margaret Beckett, who told Radio 5 Live that she was not in the business of demanding anyone's head on a platter. 'Charlie is an excellent communicator, as is shown by his success in getting across his message.' But, under the headline 'Whelan ready to quit', the *Guardian*'s political correspondent, Lucy Ward, said the Chancellor's spin doctor had told friends he was prepared to go voluntarily once he received an alternative job offer.

On reporting for work, Whelan went straight to No. 10 to inform Campbell that he had decided to resign; he then issued a statement to the Press Association repeating his denial of having leaked information about Mandelson's loan. 'I do however take the view that the job of press secretary becomes extremely difficult if the spokesman, and not the department he serves, becomes the story and the subject of excessive attention. It is absurd that, on the day the euro starts trading, in the week the monetary policy committee is meeting and when the Chancellor is working on a number of important initiatives for the New Year, that there is such attention focused on me. Therefore, as soon as an appropriate opportunity becomes available, I will move but, in the meantime, I will continue to do my job at the Treasury to the best of my ability.'

Campbell did all he could to draw a line under the story as quickly as possible by reminding the lobby that Downing Street had consistently said there was no evidence that Whelan was responsible for the leak. 'Peter Mandelson resigned because of what he did, not because of who divulged the information.' He paid tribute to Whelan's contribution during the five years he had worked for Brown: 'I think Charlie played a very significant role both in opposition and in government... Charlie has gone... We move on'; and he joined Whelan in deploring the media's preoccupation with spin doctors. 'Press officers simply are not as important as the media makes out... There is an obsession about them which goes way beyond their real importance.' However, when it came to questions about choosing Whelan's successor, Campbell had no alternative but to change his tune and to admit that the appointment of a new press secretary for the Chancellor was sufficiently important to justify his involvement. 'Gordon, I have no doubt, will organise his arrangements so that they suit him. I have got no doubt that Gordon will want to be sure that we are all happy with the arrangements we get.'

Campbell had not gone so far as to suggest that he and Blair would have a veto over Brown's selection of Whelan's successor, but the inference was clear: the opportunism and adventurism of opposition were behind them and there was to be no place in the future for another buccaneering free spirit. Downing Street required total control over the message which was being put out in the government's name and that meant an end to the freelance activities which had been conducted on the Chancellor's behalf. Whelan's great failing, indeed, was his inability to make the transition from opposition to government. His headline-grabbing antics were much admired when John Major's faltering administration was Labour's only enemy, but as press secretary to the Chancellor he had become the second most important spokesman for the government, required to think strategically about the long-term presentation of the Chancellor's economic policies and not just about the next day's headlines. In the event, Whelan had allowed himself to become a leading player in the ongoing saga of the Blair–Brown feud when the greatest service he could have given would have been to play down the hurt feelings which Brown harboured about having stood aside for Blair in the 1994 leadership contest. Whelan was also perceived as something of a threat to the New Labour project itself. His most useful contacts tended to be concentrated among the very journalists despised most of all by Blair, Campbell and Mandelson on account of their allegiance to the left wing of the party or their close links with the trade unions. His continuing association with his former employer, the Amalgamated Engineering and Electrical Union, was itself a bone of contention. I well remember the look of disdain on Campbell's face when he confirmed that Brown's absence from Treasury questions in mid-March 1997 was attributable to his wish to attend the funeral of Jimmy Airlie, the AEEU's Scottish executive member – a decision that took him away from Westminster six weeks before the general election, depriving him of a key opportunity to attack the Conservative Chancellor, Kenneth Clarke. Airlie was a former Clydeside shipyard fitter who became one of the leaders of the historic work–in at Upper Clyde Shipbuilders and was one of Whelan's heroes.

Whelan's announcement of his imminent resignation represented the final step in the break–up of the formidable campaign team which took over the party's media operation when Blair won the Labour leadership and helped secure the party's sensational landslide victory of May 1997. There were four key players: Mandelson was in charge of campaign headquarters at Millbank Tower; Campbell was press secretary to the party leader; David Hill was the party's chief spokesperson; and Whelan dealt with the media on the Chancellor's behalf. The first breach in the team came when Hill left the party's staff in May 1998 to become a director of Sir Tim Bell's public relations firm, Bell Pottinger Good Relations. Mandelson's resignation, after a mere 150 days as a Secretary of State, had dealt another blow to the formidable election–fighting force which Labour had created. With Whelan now also on the way out, Campbell was the only one of the foursome still holding high office. His position as the Prime Minister's official spokesman had become all–powerful and at last he could reign supreme. He had in fact been consolidating his control throughout the second half of 1998. Mandelson's promotion to cabinet rank in July had already helped clear the decks; now Whelan's removal had eliminated the sole challenge to his authority and the last vestiges of the separate fiefdoms which had been established when Labour were in opposition. Andrew Grice, the *Independent's* political editor, said the furore over the extent of Whelan's claimed involvement in Mandelson's downfall had been the final straw for Campbell, who had told Blair he could no longer work with the Chancellor's press secretary. Brown had spoken to Blair on the telephone during the Prime Minister's holiday in the Seychelles and they had agreed that Whelan would have to quit so that the government could 'draw a line under the Mandelson affair'.

The *Guardian* said it was unrealistic to hope that the 'end of Whelanism' would herald a return to the 'golden age of government information officers whose sole purpose in life was to create a well and neutrally informed citizenry'. Nevertheless, the 'triumph of spin' had been an unwelcome development in British political life and the paper hoped that the Prime Minister's press secretary would give serious thought as to how the government could best relate to the news media. 'The demise of Charlie Whelan should make Alastair Campbell thoughtful rather than triumphalist . . . He should be laying down basic rules to do with honesty, attribution and straight-dealing. No more rogue operations: no more cosy relationships with favoured newspapers or "helpful" correspondents. Charlie Whelan must not have died in vain.' Most of the comment columns read like obituaries, but words of praise were few and far between. The *Mirror* was one of the exceptions: Paul Routledge said Whelan had combined 'a grasp of New Labour's economic policy with a firm parade of the bad lad tendency', and the paper's political editor, Kevin Maguire, considered that Whitehall had been robbed of its 'most colourful backroom fixer' who knew so much that he could 'rock No. 10 if he lifted the lid on New Labour'. Peter Oborne, writing in the *Express*, said he was sure political journalists would look back in ten years' time and wonder how Whelan had ever been allowed to operate in the way he did. 'The contrast between those dreary Treasury officials and hard-drinking, foul-mouthed, irrepressible Charlie could not have been greater.' Weighing in from the opposite corner were the *Daily Mail*'s two regular bruisers, Bruce Anderson and Sir Bernard Ingham, who revelled in what the paper said was another 'episode in that recent Whitehall farce, *Spin Doctors Behaving Badly*'. Anderson castigated Whelan's gall in blaming excessive media attention for his demise when he had spent five years 'not only stirring up media attention but glorying in it'. Sir Bernard said he hoped Whelan's 'crashing fall' marked the 'beginning of the end of the era of the spin doctor'.

Frank Dobson, the Secretary of State for Health, was one of the few ministers prepared to go out on a limb: in a Radio 5 Live interview, he poked fun at Whelan's self-indulgence in having allowed himself to become more important than the message. 'There is an old saying that you can be a successful poisoner or a famous poisoner but you can't be both, and I think the same applies to spin doctors.' Derek Draper told *The World at One* that he thought Whelan's demise highlighted inherent dangers for the Labour Party in allowing ministers to have their own spin doctors. 'New Labour has put in place an infrastructure of which the sole purpose is to spin, and as there are dozens of hacks going out to lunch with them you finish up with an endless diatribe which makes the government look as if it is always feuding

... and in the era of New Labour spin, the wound never heals.' Ken Livingstone reached the same conclusion in the *Independent* in what he hoped would become the Charlie Whelan annual memorial column. He said a 'climate of back-stabbing between powerful barons' in the government had escalated because of the outpourings of the spin doctors. In my view, Draper and Livingstone were correct in their analysis: the circumstances surrounding the three resignations showed that the government was no better than its predecessors when attempting to use the news media to achieve effective crisis management.

Rivalry between ministerial advisers had increasingly come to be regarded as the root of the problem. In the immediate aftermath of Mandelson's resignation, Jack Cunningham was taken to task on *Today* for his failure as cabinet 'enforcer' to discipline Charlie Whelan and the other assistants whose briefings were damaging the reputations of various ministers. Dr Cunningham admitted that the press had been 'awash' with stories which troubled the government. 'Quite clearly we need to put behind us some of the activities of people who may think they can conduct their own agenda on their own account, whether it conflicts with the government's aims and objectives or not ... Unauthorised, anonymous briefings have caused trouble for the government, are causing trouble, and have to stop.' However, Dr Cunningham acknowledged that he was powerless to act. He had been charged with the task of sorting out policy disputes within the government and only the Prime Minister could decide whether a special adviser should be sacked. Accordingly, the New Year brought repeated calls for Blair to order a shake-up on his return from South Africa, where he had gone on an official visit at the end of his holiday in the Seychelles. John Prescott was the first minister to put the blame fairly and squarely on aides who had been 'talking behind their hands' to journalists: their activities, he said, had not served Labour well in the year and a half since the general election. The former minister Frank Field had joined the clamour for Whelan's dismissal, complaining that the whole system of unattributable briefings was breaking down because of the 'excesses and obscenities' of the Whitehall spin doctors who dissembled once they were challenged and denied ever having spoken to journalists. But Field's protestations, like the pained hand-wringing of Prescott and Cunningham, had completely missed the point: the system they were all bemoaning was entirely of the Labour government's own making. Although Blair had proved that he could be far more expeditious than John Major in sorting out scandals or sacking errant ministers, his administration had ended up attracting just as much bad publicity as the Conservatives. Any advantage gained through the Prime Minister's decisiveness was more than outweighed by the endemic feuding and backstabbing among the special advisers.

The circumstances surrounding the enforced resignations of Mandelson and Robinson had been just as unseemly as the furore over Formula One's exemption from the tobacco advertising ban or the activities of the lobbyists caught up in the cash-for-access affair. In all three instances it was politically appointed special advisers rather than well-established civil service press officers who had been in the front line dealing with the news media. Some of the questions about the business affairs of Bernie Ecclestone and Derek Draper were quite properly the province of the Labour Party rather than the government. However, at moments of real crisis, when there is the risk of senior colleagues being forced to resign, most Prime Ministers have tended to rely on the expertise of trusted civil servants to fend off enquiries from journalists and to help their administrations get through a difficult few days. Whitehall's mandarins have become well versed in the art of throwing a protective cloak around an endangered minister. But when trouble crowded in for Messrs Mandelson and Robinson, the first point of contact for political reporters was not a departmental head of public relations or a Whitehall information officer but Wegg-Prosser or Whelan.

Blair's cabinet colleagues had failed to grasp the significance of the shift in responsibility which had accompanied the influx of special advisers. In previous years, if a political career had been at stake, no Secretary of State or minister of the Paymaster-General's rank would have entrusted their media relations to an aide as young and inexperienced as Wegg-Prosser or as excitable and unreliable as Whelan. Labour's trainee spin doctors had found it all too easy in opposition to 'grab the agenda' when the Conservatives were on the run and when there were plenty of political journalists anxious to do their bidding. Once in government, facing the full force of the news media's hostility, ministers needed to draw on wiser counsels; and at times of turbulence experienced civil service press officers had a far stronger track record than party workers in shielding their masters from aggressive questioning. The characteristics about which Alastair Campbell had been so contemptuous, such as a reluctance on the part of civil servants to give an instant response or their preference for adopting a cautious approach when talking to journalists, were exactly the kind of defensive mechanisms which needed to be deployed on such occasions. Having handed over so much authority to their special advisers, ministers could hardly complain if their information staff beat a hasty retreat once the going got nasty. Press officers in the Treasury had made plain their distaste at getting dragged into the task of briefing journalists over Robinson's intricate financial affairs; and in the final twenty-four hours before their Secretary of State resigned, information staff at the Department of Trade and Industry showed no hesitation in passing on to Wegg-Prosser journalists' questions about whether Mandelson had informed the Britannia building society about the details of the Paymaster-General's loan.

Labour's growing dependence on politically appointed special advisers paid for by the taxpayer continued to cause irritation among Conservative and Liberal Democrat MPs, who made repeated attempts to obtain more details about the range of duties they were performing. At Question Time in November 1998 a spirited defence of their work was mounted by the Parliamentary Secretary at the Cabinet Office, Peter Kilfoyle. He said that through their use of special advisers, ministers could drive Labour's agenda forward from the centre in a way that avoided 'compromising the political impartiality of civil servants'. Kilfoyle insisted that the government had been 'open and above board' in allowing the advisers to show a degree of party political commitment which would not be permissible for a civil servant. 'We believe that by distinguishing clearly and openly the role of special advisers, it avoids any creeping politicisation.' In a further move towards formalising their status, the Cabinet Office announced that as from December 1998 the salaries of the advisers would be regularised in a 'clear and coherent framework' in line with civil service pay rates and would extend in three bands from £26,000 to £76,000 a year. The restructuring included pay increases of up to 3.5 per cent, well above the Chancellor's 2.5 per cent target for the public sector. Alastair Campbell's salary of £91,000 was considerably higher than the average as he was one of several aides whose remuneration was linked to a more senior civil service grade. The total pay bill for the seventy special advisers was put at £3.6 million, twice the amount under John Major's government.

The high-profile positions of the special advisers and the moves towards formalising their status indicated that this was no temporary phenomenon. Although Peter Kilfoyle had denied that the work of advisers was politicising the civil service, the tasks they were performing were clearly political in character and the prominence they were being accorded did represent a shift of power within the government. The largest concentration of advisers was in Downing Street, where of the nineteen allocated to the Prime Minister six were engaged in press relations work. The presence of so many political appointees in No. 10 was regarded by Tony Blair's opponents as yet another step towards a presidential style of government. The seventy advisers whose appointments he approved were, however, only a fraction of the number of political appointees signed up by a new President of the United States. In September 1996 there were 8,000 posts within the US federal government which were non-competitive appointments involving advocacy of the policies and programmes of President Clinton's administration. Nearly 300 of these posts were in the President's executive office, but most of them were civil service leadership and support positions spread throughout the administration. It is an illustration of the safeguards required by the United States House of Representatives that after each presidential election, the Committee on Government Reform and Oversight publishes a list of these 'policy and supporting positions' in what is commonly known as the 'Plum Book'.

In his evidence to the House of Commons Select Committee on Public Administration in June 1998, Alastair Campbell had assured Conservative and Liberal Democrat MPs that there was no need for parliament to police the rules governing the work of the special advisers in the Downing Street press office. He said there was no danger of the taxpayer funding Labour Party propaganda because he had no intention of being proactive when it came to party political activity. 'I do not brief on issues related to the Parliamentary Labour Party ... If anything newsworthy were to occur at a meeting of the

PLP, there is a party press officer on hand . . . I do not brief on issues to do with the national executive and anything to do with the national executive I will refer to a party spokesman.' He accepted there might be 'grey areas' but his instinct was to 'err on the side of caution'. I had smiled to myself when I heard Campbell give these undertakings to the Select Committee because I knew that if he was under pressure, or if he felt that the Prime Minister's interests were being threatened, he would have no compunction whatever about giving journalists the leadership's line on party issues.

The first real test of his resolve came on the eve of the 1998 Labour conference in Blackpool, when it was announced that four members of the Grassroots Alliance, including the left-winger Liz Davies, had won seats on the party's restructured national executive committee. The result was a snub to the leadership and a setback for Tony Blair, because Ms Davies had been deselected as Labour's candidate in Leeds North East after it was alleged she had breached party discipline and brought the party into disrepute. Campbell's principal task in Blackpool was to help prepare Blair's speech, and when he appeared before the select committee he justified the presence of special advisers at Labour conferences on the grounds that their role was to brief journalists on new policy initiatives by the government. However, after it was confirmed that Ms Davies had won a seat on the executive, Campbell sent his deputy, Lance Price, to brief journalists on Blair's response. Price denied that her election represented a 'groundswell of opinion' against the leadership: although Ms Davies 'would not get past a selection committee as a Labour candidate', she was entitled to stand for the national executive. Price was one of the six special advisers in No. 10 responsible for media relations, and when he saw me taking a full note of what he was saying he paused and looked down at my notebook. 'You do know', he said, 'that I should not be briefing you like this about the national executive.'

At a Downing Street lobby briefing six weeks later, Campbell again showed no hesitation in dealing with what was strictly a party issue and happily volunteered his opinion on the merits of Ken Livingstone, the leading left-wing candidate in the contest for Mayor of London. Discussions about the selection procedure were being held by the London Labour Party and Blair had made no secret of his determination to stop Livingstone securing the Labour nomination.

A copy of the note taken in No. 10 of the briefing given by Campbell was faxed immediately to the headquarters of the London party so that it could be used to strengthen the hand of those campaigning to introduce a selection procedure which would open up the contest to other candidates and was likely to result in Livingstone's elimination. Throughout the Downing Street note of the briefing Campbell is referred to as 'PMOS' (Prime Minister's official spokesman). The note stated that the Prime Minister welcomed the new selection procedure because it would 'ensure that suitable people represented the party' after Labour had suffered for years in opposition from 'a lack of discipline and effective professional organisation and communication'. It continued: 'The PMOS said that the Prime Minister had always made clear that one of the reasons he was in favour of elected mayors was that he saw it as an opportunity for people who were not from conventional, political backgrounds to stand. This was not a system designed to exclude Ken Livingstone. There were all sorts of politicians who would kick against the grain from time to time and would vote against the government from time to time.'

Campbell's decision to supply the London Labour Party with the text of his lobby briefing on the Mayor of London, so that it could be used in the campaign against Livingstone, was not an isolated instance of such activity, and I considered it formed part of what had to be seen as the systematic politicisation of the Downing Street press office. In October 1998 I discovered that a short summary of the 11 a.m. lobby briefing had begun appearing each day at the bottom of the confidential *Daily Brief* which was prepared at Millbank Tower and faxed direct to the offices of Labour MPs. Under the headline 'News from today's lobby briefing' it gave a rundown on the line Campbell was taking each morning. As might have been expected from a party which prided itself on speedy communications, the *Daily Brief* arrived within half an hour of the lobby briefing having finished, so that any Labour MPs being interviewed that lunchtime on radio or television would be up to speed on what No. 10 was saying. When he gave his evidence to the select committee, Campbell said the purpose of preparing Downing Street's daily summary of his briefings was to ensure that 'every government department' had an account of what had been said and that his staff could check quotes against subsequent news reports. At no point did he tell the Conservative and Liberal Democrat MPs on the committee that the summary was also being used for Labour Party propaganda. In his evidence, the Cabinet Secretary, Sir Richard Wilson, told the committee that he saw the lobby note every day; but again, he made no mention of the fact that Downing Street intended to send a copy to Millbank Tower so that an edited version could be faxed to Labour MPs.

Campbell's refusal to allow the select committee an opportunity to listen to tape recordings of his briefings was subsequently pursued by the Conservative MP David Ruffley; at his request it was reconsidered by Robin Mountfield, the Permanent Secretary for the Office of Public Service, who later provided additional written evidence. Mountfield said the lobby briefings were recorded 'purely for operational reasons' in order to provide the basis for 'immediate and authoritative summaries' of what Campbell had said, and that their release to MPs would contravene the arrangements which had been made. Again, Mountfield made no reference to Millbank Tower's use of the lobby note for party political purposes. The task of editing down the summary of Campbell's briefings so as to provide short extracts for Labour's *Daily Brief* inevitably entailed passing a political judgement on the information which Downing Street had supplied and, by its very nature, the selection process was a partisan act. I felt that if the guidance being given by the Prime Minister's press secretary was being used within the hour for Labour Party propaganda, this strengthened my argument for having the briefings recorded for use by radio and television; for if the lobby system could be politicised in this way, there was an even greater need for public accountability. The safeguard provided by televised briefings at the White House in Washington is that the American news services have their own recordings of what the President's press secretaries have said and if a story suddenly changes, or there are suggestions subsequently of a cover-up, radio and television stations can replay the original answers and draw attention to any alterations or discrepancies in the official guidance. White House briefings given during the lengthy proceedings involving Monica Lewinsky and President Clinton have shown how even apparently innocuous answers can have profound significance months later. As pressure mounted for the President's impeachment, responses given by the White House press secretary, Mike McCurry, formed part of the montage of material which was used by radio and television programmes to illustrate Clinton's evasions.

McCurry resigned in October 1998 in protest at the way he felt he had been used unfairly to perpetuate a deception about Clinton's sexual relations with Lewinsky. In an interview with Kirsty Wark on *Newsnight*, he described the difficulty he faced knowing that he might be caught out by the White House press corps for giving untruthful answers. 'I had to go out every day and wriggle out of the maze of questions thrown at me, yet Clinton knew it was a deception. I don't think he sent anyone out to lie but he allowed a deception to go on, knowing the truth...We spent most of the year assuming his denial was something so direct you could rely on him. His wife believed it and I believed him when he said he had not had sexual relations with Monica Lewinsky. I had no idea that a tortured definition of sex was lurking behind that denial.' McCurry said that finally, before his resignation took effect, he asked to be left 'out of the loop' so that there was no danger he could be accused of perpetuating a story which was unreliable.

When *Special Correspondent* examined the way the White House press corps had reported the Lewinsky affair, McCurry acknowledged the damage which had been done to the credibility of presidential briefings. 'The press corps criticised me for not having basic information. No one could say we lied, but the White House didn't give enough information in response to legitimate questions.' Despite the drawbacks identified by the journalists in Washington, televised briefings had proved their value as a check on the President: McCurry, as White House press secretary, was not prepared to lie on Clinton's behalf, nor would he continue a deception, knowing that his words were audible and visible to the entire country rather than only to the members of an exclusive club of journalists.

The argument used by political journalists at Westminster against televising the Downing Street lobby briefings is that the bulk of the information is mundane and that the presence of television cameras would inhibit the press secretary. I consider that misses the point. Journalists rarely know how stories will develop, and if a briefing has been recorded it might well prove to be a valuable source of material in the light of subsequent developments. During British general election campaigns every single news conference given by the major parties is televised automatically, if necessary on a pooled basis, because an answer which might appear irrelevant in the morning could have enormous significance later in the day or perhaps at some other point in the run-up to polling. I consider the same argument applies to lobby briefings at No. 10: an answer given one morning might only become relevant the following week. The Labour Party's selection of items from Alastair Campbell's briefings for the *Daily Brief* in October and November 1998 illustrates my point. The Downing Street briefing given on 28 October, the day after the resignation of Ron Davies, merited a five-line report. It included Campbell's assurance to the lobby that the Prime Minister's decision to accept the Welsh Secretary's resignation was based 'wholly on the facts set out in his letter' and that there were 'no salient facts known to the Prime Minister or his officials that have not been set out in public'. When Campbell admitted on 5 November that his previous briefing was incomplete and that the Prime Minister had been notified in advance by the Home Office of the incident on Clapham Common, the *Daily Brief* made no mention of what had been said at No. 10, nor did it seek to correct the information given the week before. Campbell insisted throughout the Davies affair that he had acted in good faith, but I thought the discrepancy between the two briefings provided an example of an occasion when radio and television stations might have wished to replay his earlier answer to illustrate the way the story had changed. A week later the *Daily Brief* reported Campbell's verdict that the news media's coverage of the 'outing' of Nick Brown had been 'broadly fair', although that did not mean that the Prime Minister accepted the '*Sun*'s view that there is a gay mafia running the country'.

Complaints by political correspondents about the accuracy of Campbell's briefings over the Ron Davies affair prompted some tough questions in December 1998 when the Minister for the Cabinet Office, Dr Jack Cunningham, appeared before the Select Committee on Public Administration. David Ruffley and Andrew Tyrie, the two Conservative MPs who had questioned Campbell the previous June, were anxious to discover more about Dr Cunningham's role as the minister responsible for coordinating policy and about the part he was playing in the meetings held each morning to plan government publicity. He admitted that he was an infrequent attender at the daily meeting and preferred having a 'one-to-one' with Campbell. When asked by Tyrie whether he thought it was conceivable that the Prime Minister's official spokesman was responsible for any of the denigration of cabinet ministers which was being attributed to anonymous sources, Dr Cunningham said he knew of no evidence to suggest this. After refusing repeatedly to expand on his original answer, and after the question had been put to him for a fifth time, he finally agreed with Tyrie that it was 'inconceivable' that Campbell had used his briefings to denigrate ministers in the government. Having heard Dr Cunningham explain the difficulties he was experiencing when trying to take effective action to stamp out anonymous quotes, Ruffley said that if the Minister for the Cabinet Office was serious about laying claim to being the government's 'enforcer' he was proving as 'potent as a politically neutered Tom'. Dr Cunningham's reluctance to venture an opinion on the reliability of the Downing Street press secretary reflected Campbell's power within the government, which I considered provided another justification for televising the lobby briefings.

Campbell's own principal reason for refusing to allow his guidance to be broadcast on radio or television was that it would personalise his role and build up a government official into a public figure in his own right, a development which would challenge ministerial accountability and undermine the need for ministers to be the public face of the government. However, although he has tried to persuade journalists to preserve his anonymity as the Prime Minister's official spokesman, he has been named almost routinely by some newspapers. A survey by *The Times* showed that Campbell was mentioned by name in a total of 2,241 newspaper stories in 1998, which was more than was achieved by nine members of the cabinet. Therefore he had already become an identifiable personality; and although he could not be questioned in public or held to account for what he had said, he was making regular pronouncements on the government's behalf. Campbell further argued that if his briefings were televised, political correspondents would attempt to set the agenda on the news media's behalf by throwing questions at him on a range of controversial issues unrelated to the political or parliamentary business of the day. While this might be a valid factor from the government's standpoint, journalists could argue that in an age of instant communications the

11 a.m. and 4 p.m. briefings represented two windows of opportunity when the Prime Minister's official spokesman could quite properly be asked to comment on the day's events.

Another factor that had to be considered was Campbell's readiness to take advantage of the briefings to make highly contentious points of his own. After the second night of air strikes against Iraq in December 1998, he told the lobby that reports from Baghdad by British television journalists should have included clearer 'health warnings' about the information being given out by the Iraqi regime. Although several broadcasters at the briefing pointed out that their colleagues in Baghdad were making it clear in every report they transmitted that they were working under Iraqi restrictions and had extremely limited access, Campbell persisted with his criticism and urged British television reporters to be more cautious. 'The truth is the Iraqis have a track record of using and abusing the Western media ... and the truth is you cannot believe a word they say. There should be more health warnings.' I felt it would have been far more appropriate for these concerns to have been expressed in a public forum which would have allowed radio and television journalists an opportunity to test the views which were being put forward on the Prime Minister's behalf.

Of all the arguments in favour of televised lobby briefings, perhaps the most compelling was a growing feeling among many MPs that Campbell's unique status as a politicised civil servant necessitated at least some degree of accountability. In January 1999 the government published its formal response to the inquiry by the Select Committee on Public Administration and said that it would keep the 'on-the-record' system of lobby briefings under review. Ministers noted that the committee had found 'no clear evidence' that Campbell was giving some correspondents special treatment and reiterated the principle that government information should be provided to journalists 'even handedly'. Nevertheless, the departure of Peter Mandelson and the removal of Charlie Whelan had strengthened Campbell's control over the Whitehall publicity machine and had enhanced his position as the pivotal figure in the government's relationship with the news media. Unlike any previous Downing Street press secretary, Campbell was allowed to sit in at meetings of the cabinet and was therefore fully conversant with ministerial discussions. His unprecedented access and powerful role in No. 10 had not gone unnoticed among the upper echelons of the government's information service. On her retirement in January 1999, Romola Christopherson, the long-serving director of information at the Department of Health, said she considered Campbell had effectively become the unelected deputy prime minister. In an article for the *Sunday Times* on 10 January, she said Campbell had emerged as the 'monarch of all he surveys'. His grip on his kingdom was absolute. 'He is ever-present at Blair's elbow and in his ear, and you can bet that the Prime Minister turns to him on policy as much as presentation. He is more at the centre of the "big picture" than anyone else in the cabinet ... He knows who really did say what but also – perhaps even more important – they all know he knows.'

Ms Christopherson considered that Campbell was probably 'clever enough' not to get stuck in the mud of unpopular decisions. Charlie Whelan was not so confident about Campbell's chances of withstanding the intense media pressure which went with his increasingly isolated position at the pinnacle of the government's publicity machine. In an interview for the *Sunday Telegraph* on 17 January, he revealed that Campbell had warned him four months before his own downfall about the danger of allowing himself to be treated as the news story. 'It seems that he has been proved right and in many ways I fear that journalists will now go after Alastair. He is already very high profile and without me to take the blame for everything, he may find himself becoming the lightning conductor.'

Whelan had succeeded in turning his own ignominious departure to his advantage, as had Mandelson's special adviser, Benjamin Wegg-Prosser. They both secured jobs in the news media: Wegg-Prosser became personal assistant to David Yelland, editor of the *Sun*; Whelan was signed up as a football columnist by the *Observer* and as a presenter for Radio 5 Live. The combination of his love of soccer and his inside knowledge as a former government spin doctor ensured that Whelan was instantly in demand as a commentator after Blair unexpectedly gave his support to calls for the Football Association to dismiss the England coach, Glenn Hoddle, who had provoked a storm of criticism at the end of January for suggesting that disabled people were suffering for sins committed in previous lives. Blair condemned Hoddle's remarks as 'very offensive' when he was interviewed on *This*

Morning by Richard Madeley and Judy Finnegan. After his sacking by the FA, Hoddle told the *Mirror* he was 'sad and disappointed' by Blair's intervention. Campbell insisted that Downing Street's transcript of the interview showed that Blair had not called for Hoddle to be sacked, but in response to Richard Madeley's question, 'So he should go then?', he was clearly heard replying: 'Yes.'

The Prime Minister's very appearance on ITV's daytime chat show that Monday morning generated considerable press comment, because the previous day the *Observer* had revealed that Campbell planned to adopt a new media strategy, bypassing the national newspapers because of what he perceived as their obsession with 'trivia, travel expenses, comment and soap opera'. A spate of stories about expensive ministerial flights, including the use of Concorde at taxpayers' expense, had infuriated No. 10, and Campbell was determined to retaliate. Claiming that policy announcements were being repeatedly 'dumbed down' by the national press, he said he intended to work more closely with provincial newspapers, women's magazines and ethnic publications. Needless to say, columnists on the nationals had a field day contrasting Campbell's strictures about the 'trivia' of political reporting with Blair's willingness to chat away to Richard and Judy about his family's New Year holiday in the Seychelles and the future of the England soccer coach.

Campbell's new media strategy attracted further publicity when he turned his attention to the broadcasters and demanded that ministers should be allowed to appear on television and radio 'live and unedited'. He set out the case for letting politicians communicate directly with the public in a speech to the Fabian Society on 9 February, in which he urged broadcasting organisations to adopt a different agenda from newspapers because the print media's centre of gravity had moved 'downmarket' and their 'herd instinct' was stronger. Campbell, who wasted no time in demonstrating his determination to break free from what he considered to be the trivialised agenda of Westminster's political correspondents, was supported in his initiative by Steve Pope, a journalist from *New Nation*, one of Britain's leading black newspapers, who had been invited to accompany Blair on his visit to South Africa. In writing about his experiences, Pope said he understood why Campbell so disliked the 'scummy' journalists of the national press and television: 'A bigger bunch of middle-class, public school, ego-tripping, arrogant, smug, patronising, cynical, nasty, self-important merchant bankers you'd be hard pressed to find.'

Another of Campbell's initiatives was directed at winning positive coverage for Britain in the overseas press. After forty foreign journalists attended a Downing Street seminar on the success of the New Deal programme in getting unemployed youngsters into work, Campbell contrasted their enthusiasm with the lack of interest being shown by political correspondents at Westminster. According to a report in the *Observer* on 14 February, Campbell told the foreign press corps that after spending ninety minutes at No. 10 listening to their questions, he wished he could 'hide a camera here for my lobby briefings at eleven o'clock or for my Sunday briefings, which are a collectors' item'. I reread the quote several times just to make sure I had not misunderstood the significance of his remarks: Campbell had gone one small step towards acknowledging one of my arguments in favour of televised lobby briefings. If the cameras were present the conduct of political journalists would be opened up to public scrutiny, and viewers and listeners would be able to judge the validity and relevance of their questions.

Campbell is not the first Downing Street press secretary to try to put the lobby correspondents in their place. Harold Wilson's press secretary, Joe Haines, stopped giving lobby briefings altogether in 1975 after concluding they were an 'institutionalised conspiracy'. Campbell has indicated that he would like to abandon the afternoon briefings, which he finds time-consuming and unproductive. None the less, they do give journalists an opportunity to hold the government to account and occasionally, however hard he tries, his guard slips and the spin can be revealed for what it is.

Downing Street's refusal to countenance criticism was frequently taken to inordinate lengths, as illustrated in February 1999 by the ruthless rubbishing of a hard-hitting report by the Select Committee on Foreign Affairs which had investigated the failure of the Foreign Office to block a British arms shipment to Sierra Leone in breach of a United Nations weapons embargo. The government's rebuttal procedures swung into action well before copies of the report were released under embargo at 8 a.m., two hours before publication. After I had discussed the likely scope of the report on *Today* at 6.30 a.m., the

Foreign Office's deputy head of news, John Williams, rang to say that Robin Cook rejected the findings and intended to stand by his officials. Blair told the *Jimmy Young Programme* later that morning that the criticism was 'disproportionate and unfair'. Next day, when challenged by William Hague at question time, Blair insisted that he had indicated all along that the government would 'respond carefully' to the report. When I enquired at the 4 p.m. lobby briefing precisely when Blair had given this undertaking, Campbell said he did not know but he was sure it had been delivered. When I pointed out that the transcript of the *Jimmy Young Programme* contained no such assurance, he laughed and brushed aside my question: 'I'm sure the Prime Minister said it somewhere ... Well, all right then, he said it to me.' If Campbell's cavalier response could have been broadcast, it would have confirmed MPs' worst suspicions of a concerted attempt to denigrate the committee's report.

The task of winning over British public opinion in favour of joining the European single currency might yet provide a highly appropriate launch pad for another review of the lobby system. In the weeks preceding the euro's introduction in January 1999, the government began adopting a far more assertive stance in the face of Eurosceptic scare stories in newspapers like the *Sun*. As the Prime Minister's attempts to appease Rupert Murdoch's newspapers have got him nowhere, it is at least arguable that he should adopt a bolder approach and do more to open up the political process to television and radio. Moreover, the resignations of Peter Mandelson and Charlie Whelan have provided an opportunity to break the mould. Central to their work as spin doctors was their close, manipulative relationship with newspapers. If Blair wants to get a blast of fresh air into the murky world of political journalism, where better to start than by allowing cameras into lobby briefings so that the public can see what was being said on the government's behalf? Campbell's forthright delivery when answering journalists' questions, coupled with the rapidity of his repartee and the clarity with which he can express himself, makes him an ideal public spokesman. If the pressure for televised briefings were to increase and cameras were to be allowed into the Downing Street briefing room, I can think of no one better suited to the task of becoming the first No. 10 press secretary to appear on screen.

Index